BARE YOUR SOUL

The Thinking Girl's Guide to Enlightenment

Edited by Angela Watrous

SEAL PRESS

Contents

*"I expected her to shave her head, or experiment with drugs,
or start dating an ex-con. I thought maybe she'd become a vegan.
Instead, she started going to church."*

*"I'd long since realized that in some circles it was assumed that
I wasn't religious—presumably because true queer liberal types
could never be involved with an organized religion, never get
sucked into something so passé as faith."*

*"A few hours later, as I in-line skated home over the Brooklyn Bridge to
Manhattan, I realized I had just been called to the Islamic faith."*

*"I'm bound to both Judaism and Islam by the laws of
religious lineage—through my mother I am Jewish;
through my father I am Muslim."*

*"I didn't believe in God. In truth, I thought of him as a little
like Ronald Reagan, if he existed at all."*

*"I became more than myself, my awareness expanded to sense the gestalt of
ravers, humanity, bonded to the universal flux of life."*

Acknowledgments

Bare Your Soul would never have happened without the persistence and enthusiasm of my editor, Leslie Miller. I thank her for knowing even before me that this project and I were destined for each other. Thanks, too, to Faith Conlon, Christina Henry de Tessan, Jessica Hoffmann and all the folks at Seal Press and Avalon for lending their unique talents and support to this book.

Immeasurable gratitude to Eleanor Martineau, whose unwavering support in all of my personal and professional endeavors is a never-ending source of wonder and joy in my life. Thanks to Carole Honeychurch, my sometimes coauthor and eternal friend, for her faith in me and her ability to tell it like it is, just when I need to hear it. To Melissa Levine, whose own path toward enlightenment is a constant source of inspiration and companionship. To Rachel Michaelsen, for teaching me how to access the recesses of my mind and spirit. And to my dad, Harry Watrous, who has always trusted me to make my own decisions, and has supported me in all of them.

This book would not have been possible without each and every one of the contributors. Individually, they've crafted the most personal of narratives and shared the beauty and depth of their spirits. Collectively, they tell a much greater story, whose intersections and overlaps continue to surprise and inspire me. I thank them all for their dedication to the process.

**For my grandma, Bessie Irene Watrous,
who shared with me the beauty of her faith.**

Introduction

In today's urban-chic, pop-culture-inundated world, how do we integrate our search for enlightenment with our myriad of social identities? Is it possible to separate our personal spiritual endeavors from the glut of yoga tapes, herbal fads and advice from Oprah? And why do we even feel the need to think about this faith stuff, anyway?

These are just a few of the questions that underlie each of the essays in *Bare Your Soul*—a new guide to faith that is for soul-searchers, skeptics, reformists and neo-traditionalists alike. Inside, young women who were born into the third generation of feminism lay their minds and their souls bare. Their stories are startling and honest, a refreshing departure from the soft-focus look at spirituality that is driven so many of us away. While these essays may indeed inspire, they are more intended to provoke thought and further inquiry. This is not a book about blind faith, though it is a book about deeply held beliefs, matters that have been carefully considered by the mind and felt in the heart.

When I started this project, the first thing I did was poll the women around me about their feelings on the topic of faith. From the get-go, I was surprised to discover how very little I knew about the internal spiritual leanings of women in my generation. Even among my close friends, I had rarely discussed these matters—

though I'd heard so much about everything else in their lives. I knew about their career goals, their family histories, their physical and emotional health, even the intimate details of their sex lives. Yet spirituality was uncharted territory, and right away I could tell that it was a thorny one to navigate. I started to wonder: Is spirituality one of our generation's few remaining taboos?

Never talk religion or politics. This was the common understanding among those of our parents' and grandparents' generations—because both topics are deeply personal and highly subjective, and disagreement is bound to occur. All around the world, and throughout history, people have warred over even the slightest perceived differences in religious belief, causing later generations to decide that silence was the safest tactic. Considering the impact of the current frenzy of fundamentalist conflict on our world today, it wouldn't be imprudent to wonder if we, too, should continue to avoid such a loaded topic in mixed company, keeping our discussions isolated to work or movies or our latest fling.

Except that we can't do things the way our parents did, because we have a different set of choices, conflicts and truths. Whether our families raised us within a specific belief system or warned us against all things religious or spiritual, as adults we've been left with questions, longings and discrepancies we have to reconcile for ourselves. And it isn't easy, especially since real reflections of how young women are negotiating these issues are largely absent from popular culture: While we're encouraged to read Bridget Jones's diary and certain guides for hunting and fishing, we're left without a handbook for deeper questions—conflicts that the perfect mate, the hottest nightspot or even the most up-to-date feminist theory doesn't resolve. *Bare Your Soul* attempts to create a snapshot of spirituality in the third wave—how we're reworking tradition, what we've co-opted or borrowed and what still pisses us off.

No longer an automatic part of family lineage, faith, or the rejection of such, is a personal and complicated choice. And while we are benefiting from the freedom that has been bestowed upon us, the burden of making those choices is real. In this anthology, women of all backgrounds and traditions, living all sorts of beliefs and practices, share how investigating questions of spirituality affects their lives and their identities. Their stories reveal the multiplicities, divergences and commonalities of our experiences, allowing us to emerge from isolation and share in each other's journeys.

The social and political progress we've made as women over the past thirty years has had a profound impact on our relationship with our bodies, our minds and, yes, even our spirits. And this progress—much of which was hard-won when we were toddlers struggling to form our first words—has afforded our generation with more options about spiritual interpretation than ever before.

Unlike our feminist foremothers, for example, we're no longer required to reject religious establishments in order to be strong and independent. We're discovering that we can be radically political and spiritual. In "Sex and Catholic Girls," Caurie Miner Putnam talks about the revelation that transformed her into a staunchly pro-choice Catholic. In Diane Biray's essay, "A Flash of Lightning," she discusses the connection between her Buddhist practice and the social activism that has taken her all around the world. And Sonya Huber, author of, "Just Another Anarchist Antichrist Godless-Commie Catholic," finds that the only way for her to meld her earthly and spiritual pursuits is to go back to the church of her childhood and try to effect social change from the inside.

The liberation of our bodies—how we use them, where we take them—has had a direct impact on our spiritual paths. No longer expected to settle down immediately and start a family, many of us have taken advantage of our greater freedom to embark on spiritual pilgrimages. In "The Million Step Program," Stephanie Groll journeys to Spain and walks five hundred miles in hope of taking one step toward personal growth. Pramila Jayapal, in "Pilgrimage," chronicles her return to India, where she seeks to reconcile her lack of devotion to Hinduism with her desire to feel like a "true" Hindu Indian. And, closer to home, Griselda Suárez has her own "Pilgrimage on Mission Street," finding her goddess, Tonantzin, on the early morning streets of San Francisco.

Many of the traditional roles we've been expected to play as women are ones that we still desire—as long as they're on our own terms. In Juleigh Howard-Hobson's essay "Raising a Family the Good Old-Fashioned Way," she navigates the role of modern mom with the help of ancient goddess spirituality. Liesl Schwabe, in "The Altar and the Playhouse: Householder Buddhism," finds that her Buddhist studies have only just begun when she leaves India and returns to Brooklyn to start a new phase of her life with her partner and their son. And in "A Call to Service," Trudi M. H. Frazel discovers that it's her spiritual path, not mere societal pressure or gender expectations, that draws her to the practice of selfless service.

It is in difficult times that our spiritual beliefs are most challenged. The question of whether they will be illuminated, strengthened or shattered is one that we can only speculate on before the moment presents itself. In "A Yogini in New York," Deborah Crooks finds herself at a yoga retreat in New York during the fateful events of September 11, challenging her to continue her practice of mindful breathing in the midst of the soot and her grief. In Claire Hochachka's essay "The Road toward Islam: A Traveler's Tale," she finally answers the call to Islam that she'd felt for years, two months after watching the World Trade Center collapse. And, in a more personal threat of tragedy, L. A. Miller finds the strength of her atheism challenged when her father falls suddenly ill, in "The Last Conversation."

Perhaps one of the reasons spiritual writings by younger women seem so refreshing is that, unlike so many of our older counterparts, we can't pretend to have it all worked out. For various reasons, each of us is struggling to reconcile what we believe with what we live. In "Practicing Faith," Maliha Masood grapples with the discrepancy between the strength of her Islamic faith and the reality of her less-than-stringent religious practice. In Twilight Greenaway's essay, "My Sister's Keeper," she finds that her younger sister's venturing into organized religion forces her to rethink both her assumptions about religion and the meaning of her own life. And, finally, in "On Ki," Eleanor Martineau touches on the more elusive spiritual ideas that inform her life, never pretending to fully comprehend any of them.

We make meaning out of our lives in infinite ways, and countless religious and spiritual practices express that process. It would be impossible to represent each of those practices in a single anthology. Instead, *Bare Your Soul* brings together a diverse (though certainly not exhaustive) group of essays that each illuminate a unique truth, while speaking to each other in a way that gives the collection greater resonance. The points of connection transcend the boundaries of specific faith, illustrating the places where each of us struggle and succeed.

Investigating and revealing our spiritual beliefs can leave us feeling profoundly exposed. During the process of revising their essays for publication and oftentimes coming to deeper realizations in the process, many of the contributors experienced anxiety about expressing ideas that weren't yet solidified. Going public with some of our most intimate beliefs while they're still taking shape is challenging. But writing is an involved and ongoing process, as is spirituality. It's hard to say that either is ever really final. All we can do is put a period at the end, try to encapsulate our feelings and beliefs in that one distinct moment, and know that while this particular piece may be finished, there is always more to say and more to learn.

ANGELA WATROUS
Oakland, California

My Sister's Keeper
Twilight Greenaway

My sister was strangely secretive about the whole thing. In fact, I don't think I heard about it from her at all. I guess I must have known that things would change for her in college. But I expected her to shave her head, or experiment with drugs, or start dating an ex-con. I thought maybe she'd become a vegan.

Instead, she started going to church.

I know, I know. To some this would seem the better option. But to me, the older sibling, the one born when our parents were following Swami Sachidananda and using the word "consciousness" a lot, it was a little traumatic.

As kids, Mara and I were so close it was sometimes suffocating. I was Beezus, she was Ramona. We're three years apart, but we shared a bedroom, had all the same clothes, watched the same TV shows. After school, before our ballet class, we would spend hours at a time in the public library, doing homework, avoiding homework, reading the racy parts of the fashion magazines. In high school I moved into my own room and started wearing only dark colors and carrying my journal everywhere. My need for autonomy was overwhelming. I hated being part of a duo, hated that her name was always attached to mine, that we were so often referred to as "the girls." I harassed her relentlessly, accused her of imitating everything I did. One night, at dinner, in a cold, adolescent frenzy, after Mara had

1

chimed in about something with an innocent "me too," I slammed my fist down on the table and said, "Get your own life!"

Soon enough, she did. She became part of the student body government, went to prom with an older boyfriend and had a social circle all her own. Within a few years I left home for college, and we became virtual strangers. Soon, we saw each other only a few times a year, and rarely spoke on the phone. While she assimilated nicely into small-town culture, I practiced what I thought was bohemian living at a small liberal arts college half a continent away.

Mara has always been drawn to tradition. And while both of my parents rejected their religious roots, she seemed to gravitate toward the slivers of Christianity (on my dad's side) and Judaism (on my mom's) that remained in our family. Our parents were not uninterested in spirituality, but they never enforced or advocated any kind of regular ritual or practice. I was too caught up in reconciling all the other ways my family was different to notice an absence of organized religion, but Mara might have seen the general lack of ritual or sense of heritage as central to our unorthodoxy. Now, I wonder if this didn't make her long for religion from an early age.

On the rare occasion when our grandparents brought my sister and me along to temple for a Jewish holiday, I would sit patiently and wait for the food or the dancing. I liked lighting the Hanukkah candles, but I never could remember the prayer you're supposed to say while you light them. Mara had memorized this prayer by the time she was ten, as I'm sure she had done with the Lord's Prayer from the Bible—one of my dad's favorite things to recite when he put us to sleep at night. While I didn't recognize it at the time, she was always collecting bits and pieces of religion and tradition and committing them to memory as we were growing up.

Dad had kept a Bible around, a lingering trace of his Episcopalian upbringing, and I'd often picked it up as a child, read bits, studied the images. But I'd felt about it the way I felt about most old literature: respectful, somewhat awestruck, but in an abstract way.

One winter break I picked up a Bible, thinking that it might have arrived in a box left over after my grandma had died. It had beautiful leather binding and I remember thinking it looked like something I would have bought in a vintage bookstore. I opened it to find Mara's name in it. While this didn't exactly surprise me at the time, I don't remember taking it seriously. I knew she'd been going to church. But I don't think I cared, or knew how to care about what this meant.

Then again, I wasn't paying very close attention to anything my family was doing at the time. While Mara was, unbeknownst to me, setting out to have her deepest questions answered, I was going through my own set of changes. There was that whole business of getting on with life after college. There was the attempt to navigate my first "adult" relationship, a new city and all kinds of notions about a career path that would sweep me off my feet, fulfill me personally and allow me to pay my off my loans.

Then one day, my uncle called from across the country. My sister had sent him a fundraising letter for a spring break trip she was taking with her church group to help build houses in a poor neighborhood somewhere in the middle of the country. He was sending her money, he said. But he was a little concerned. Did I know much about this group? he asked. And it was then that he used the words.

Born again.

When he did, I nearly dropped the phone.

My mind flooded with extreme images: I flashed on the missionary friend I'd made in high school who was always so much fun until she informed me that my blood was on her hands if I didn't agree to accept Jesus Christ into my life. I imagined the homophobic people I'd seen on television calling gay marriage "a crime against humanity," and anti-choice fanatics marching with signs showing bloody fetus parts. I couldn't realistically imagine Mara doing any of those things, but I also didn't have a real sense of how she would respond to issues like gay marriage or abortion. It dawned on me just how out of touch with her life I'd become.

So I did what any opinionated big sister who feels she has lost all understanding would do: I called my mom and yelled. Not at her, exactly. But I needed answers. And she did have some. They were not the ones I wanted to hear, but they were surprisingly real. In fact, my mother's presence of mind about the whole thing almost caught me more off-guard than the very fact that my sister was a born-again Christian.

From what I could ascertain, Mara had been involved with a group at a Christian student center called The Inn since she'd gotten to school, and yes, technically, they were more or less "born again." Not that I even knew exactly what that meant. But, my mother said it was "not something I should worry too much about."

"Mother!" I yelled into the phone. "She's born-again!"

It might have been that my mom had been witnessing the progression of Mara's new faith for a while by that point. She had also been doing some "spiritual searching" of her own in the years since we'd left home. After a brief bout with *A Course in Miracles*, she started going to a Jewish temple after years of rejecting her roots. At that point I still assumed these were all just coping mechanisms, phases she would outgrow like the fad diets she was always trying as Mara and I were growing up. It wasn't until years later that I realized that it was more than that. And maybe that's also why I'd had a hard time taking Mara's decisions seriously—no one close to me had ever been committed to placing religion or spirituality at the center of their life before. My mom never said it directly, but I could tell that she trusted Mara and wanted to support her. Looking back, I'm glad that she felt so confident. But at the time it didn't make me feel any better. My sister had always acted as a sort of mirror for me. Her participation in a religion that I had never been drawn to understand or appreciate caused a little bit of an identity crisis for me. We had been paired off so much when we were younger that learning about such a stark difference between us forced me to realize how few expectations I had of our relationship, or, for that matter, of myself in it. I saw that what had been a very passive, "tolerant" approach, was really more of a cop-out.

In college I had a sizable faction of friends and classmates who were actively studying and practicing Buddhism. And I admired them for dedicating themselves like this. I felt utterly mystified by their ability to meditate and practice; their bravery and perseverance; their bold desires to participate in concrete actions that would bring them closer to some absolute reality, to themselves. Some spent time in monasteries, others simply started incorporating meditation seriously into their lives—either way, I saw my friends as taking very individual journeys. For this reason, I didn't make the connection between my Buddhist friends' path and my sister's spiritual process.

I had gotten to a point where I knew I wanted to go through my life as awake as possible. But my sense of how this should happen was all very abstract. I had all kinds of ideas and conflicts about art and politics, and it felt important to work for social justice. I knew that there was a great deal of my own abstract kind of spirituality behind this drive, but everyone I had admired up until that point appeared to have rejected the structure inherent in most forms of organized religion. Especially Christianity.

There was a very vocal missionary group in my home town, and I saw a lot of my grade-school friends change their lives drastically to be part of it. Many even went on missions to other parts of the world and came back to tell me that I would not really know how to live until I knew God. Almost all of the Christian images I'd seen in movies and on television showed rigid, politically conservative people. When I got to school, "Christian" was often used to imply "judgmental" and "fanatic," and I didn't stop to think very much about it. Even as I saw myself as tolerant and progressive, I had unconsciously bought into a lot of anti-religious hype.

Up until that point, I had always believed that people involved in group religion were victims of some kind of low-grade mind control. I couldn't see much beyond the Christian Church's potential to oppress and dominate. In retrospect I realize these were extreme perceptions, but at the time that was how I saw things, so I was really worried about my sister. I assumed that her decision to join a church group was a symptom of her inability to make decisions on her own.

When Mara and I finally started to talk and write to one another, I realized that it was nowhere near that simple. In fact, she had been asserting her right to make decisions. Christianity must have been refreshingly different from what we had known as children. And choosing to participate, for her, was a strong and personal decision.

She did admit to craving a sense of belonging. Not that there's anything wrong with belonging, but at the time I still believed it was something the truly strong, truly kick-ass people in the world didn't need to directly pursue. I think that's the main reason Buddhism seemed more acceptable to me, because I saw it as something you did on your own terms, something based on hard work and a process that didn't require a sense of faith in what you couldn't see. Christianity, on the other hand, was not only something that involved being a member of a congregation, but it required faith from the get-go: a belief in one God, one way, one answer.

But Mara hadn't found an answer, per se. On the contrary,

she was starting to do a lot of important questioning. As she disengaged herself from this particular church group, she was still reading books and talking about her experiences with Christianity, but she started to locate a lot of her own spiritual questioning.

Eventually she did admit to feeling manipulated by the group, and I believed her. After the fact, she would laugh and refer to friends who "had been sucked in, just like me." I knew it helped her to have a sense of humor about it. But that also didn't mean that her faith meant any less to her, or that her reason for seeking out church hadn't been true and real.

And she didn't stop going to church altogether, nor did she cut off all her ties with the friends she had made within the group. In fact, some whom she'd met in her first few years of college had similar experiences and felt disillusioned and manipulated.

When we talked about it she was able to say, "I felt really alone," and she admitted that the church community had filled a tangible need for something soothing, something that promised love and connection and a special place just for her. I could relate. But I felt at a loss for words. Not because I was embarrassed for her or ashamed of how weak she had been, but because I was amazed at the strength it took to recognize that, not to mention what it must have taken to tell me about it.

Suddenly I wasn't irate, I was a little envious. What, I asked myself then, had I done in the last years to deal with my own sense of isolation, loss, existential grief? In Mara's desire to find a larger meaning in life, she had gone right to the source—while

I had spent years groping my way through . . . what? Psychotherapy? Journal-keeping? Codependent relationships? A liberal arts education? Poetry? Colored Christmas lights? An enormous collection of thrift-store sweaters?

My own path had been a lot more piecemeal. At times, even scattered. While I would do most of it over again, it had taken a lot of hard emotional work to get through my early twenties. When I really try to pin down my own sense of spirituality, I realize that it is not something I want to separate out from the way I live my day-to-day life, nor from my work as a writer.

I spent a lot of my young life vehemently rejecting community and the kind of support that is only possible when you are part of a group. And it wasn't always so good for me. I started wondering about what Mara might have to teach me in this department.

I had spent a lot of time separating from things, as a way of becoming myself, making sense of my life, while she had joined a group. It was around this time that we started talking on the phone more and visiting one another, and she came to live with me for the summer before her last year at school. It became clear that we were both moving towards balancing these defining decisions. I knew I needed community and support. She was taking more time to question things on her own. This helped us get close again, after too many years of what had seemed like a mild-mannered acquaintance at best.

While I knew that my own process of healing had been something I'd needed to do on my own, I still felt some guilt for not playing a larger role in her life. But when I put this and my anxiety about the Christianity thing aside for a while, and got to know her, I understood that we had never stopped having things in common.

In the years since we'd been close Mara had become an artist. And just like when we were kids, we found ourselves gravitating to the exact same things, liking a lot of the same music, borrowing each other's clothes again. Only this time, I reveled in our similarities. We had each earned them in our own way.

Most importantly, Mara hadn't forgotten the tolerance our parents had taught us, nor had she adopted the right-wing politics that I'd always assumed was the universal Christian agenda. I was a little embarrassed for even thinking she might have. Of course, her being Christian was still an important difference. It implied that there are things that she believes that I may never even understand.

I think that Mara became a practicing Christian partly because she felt disconnected from people. I also felt a sense of disconnect, and it hurt me, but not in a way I could recognize or focus on at the time. Feeling close to Mara has reminded me that when I am paying attention to my family, it helps me pay attention to myself. I feel more connected, more whole. And this, to me, is a big part of what spirituality means. Connectedness. Wholeness.

Does this mean that I, too, am becoming a more "religious" person than I have been? Well, the questions my sister's faith brought up haven't gone away. I do believe that there is something to all of this. That there is a force of some kind behind the way the sunlight moves and the way your knee throbs when you hit it against the leg of a table. But I'm not sure that this force doesn't come from us, from our connections to one another, and the work we do daily in relation to one another.

Spending time with Mara has reminded me that we can be spiritual and sharp, compassionate and awake, connected and critical-minded all at once. But she and I still have a lot to talk about. I still feel a deep sadness about the years she and I spent so distant from one another. Still, it's nice to know that she and I are arriving at a lot of the same places these days. It gives me hope that we'll be able to connect even more deeply about our shared past as time goes on.

For now, I'm just enjoying learning from her, letting her serve as that mirror that reflects the things I do and don't want to see in myself. And I do wonder what it would feel like to surrender to the idea that there is "an answer," even if only for a while. I know that's not the only thing organized religion is about for most people, but I have a sense that, in the beginning of her search, Mara must have felt that way, like there was a clear set of directions to follow in order to be rewarded, to live a good life, to feel protected. But I also know that there's a fair amount of anxiety involved too. What if you don't do the right thing, what if you don't get to heaven?

I have a strong hunch that everyone in an early stage of belief might feel this combination of anxiety and relief—no matter what kind of belief it is. I also have a hunch that it always gets more complex, and that it always leads inward. I suspect as much because I've witnessed it in myself. For all I contend about the differences between Mara's life and my own, I also know that writing has been, for me, a kind of spiritual path. It is an ever-evolving set of choices that brings me closer to people while allowing me the personal space and the independent integrity I may always need.

Sometimes I try to imagine my sister in a religious setting for the first time. I try to picture what she must have looked like. She may have bowed her head forward with the kind of familiar concentration we both share, or brought her long hands up towards her chest in prayer. Either way, I imagine it might have felt like she was planting herself, like a seed, in a warm, accepting place. I can imagine this feeling because I have had it myself. Many times, in fact.

It happened for the first time when I was thirteen. I was standing in the stacks of a huge university library, reading at a frenzied pace. I stopped and looked around, loving the way the old books looked, the way they smelled, the way they seemed as if they had been abandoned there, left for me to find by chance. I could see someone my age walking through the same library years later and finding a book with my name on it. In my mind, that girl would feel the same excitement, the same glow in her chest, as she read *my* words. That day I began to believe there was a path for me, that it would be evident and that I would follow it. Of course, as soon as I started to investigate that path more deeply, I felt all the universal anxiety and fear. But for that moment it was pure, white light. Something like faith.

Coming Clean
Angela Watrous

When I was nine years old, I was baptized at Halcyon Southern Baptist Church.

I wore a white choir robe over a pair of cotton granny briefs. The pastor and I waited behind the polyester curtain that shielded the baptismal pool when it wasn't being used to cleanse mortal sins. He helped me into the chest-deep water as the congregation sang the invitation. *"Come home, come home. Ye who are weary, come home. Softly and tenderly, Jesus is calling, calling 'Oh, sinner, come home'."*

I was a serious kid who soaked up everything that went on around me and I already felt pretty burdened and weary, so it was not lightly that I was taking this spiritual step. The idea of the constant companionship of a loving God felt appealing, and wholly possible. As I prepared to commit myself to a spiritual life, I tried to sit still in the warm bath water and focus on the significance of the moment. But my baby fat made me buoyant, and my body kept sliding up toward the surface.

Suddenly the singing stopped, the curtain opened and we were exposed to wooden pews filled with the church family I'd known all my life. Brother Harold, the same pastor who'd married my already-divorced parents in that very church, held my hand and addressed the congregation.

As he spoke, I looked out at my family, sitting in the front pew of the bare white church. It was strange to see them there, both because my grandma and I always sat in the back row with her church-lady friends, and because I'd never seen my dad in church before. While years earlier my dad had helped lay the foundation for the building we were sitting in, as well as for my faith, church was no longer a part of his religion, for reasons he kept to himself. But he'd made an exception for this day, and his eyes filled with tears as he smiled at me. My aunt, the family photographer and a dedicated Sunday school teacher, snapped a picture before sitting down next to her husband.

"By the hand of the Father, the Son and the Holy Ghost, I baptize thee." Brother Harold cradled my head with one hand and covered my mouth and nose with the other, gently pushing me back into the water. I clung to him as he held me under and I floated, anchorless. And then he pulled me back up, a whooshing of water and air and "amen's" all around me.

What had brought me to that moment was not so much a chain of discernible events as it was a sudden and swift realization. While I had been attending church twice a week for over five years, it had always been a place to play with other kids and show off my advanced skills in memorization more than anything else. Sure, I'd mastered my verses and I could recite all of the books of the Bible in order, but that had mainly been for the adult approval and the penny-ante prizes.

Then at church one Wednesday night, our teacher explained to us that when you felt that God was asking you to acknowledge your love for him, it was time to go forward during the invitation after the sermon and ask to be baptized. As she spoke,

I felt a swirling inside of me. It's not that I hadn't believed before that moment, but rather that it had never really hit me that believing or not believing was something I had to choose. As she spoke, I prayed silently, telling God that I did believe in him, and I could feel a warmth pouring into my heart. It felt sort of like a water balloon, swelling to capacity, except that I didn't need to make a knot to hold the love in, and it didn't feel like it would ever break. With that fullness came relief, that God wasn't just some amorphous figure floating in the clouds, that I could feel a divine presence inside my own body.

Once the awareness was there, it billowed up inside of me. I mentioned it to no one, but the next Sunday, during the invitation, it seemed like the pastor was talking directly to me. My breath stuck in my throat; I felt a physical force pulling me toward the front. It took me weeks to finally go forward, to walk up to the front of the church all the way from the back row. But once it was actually happening, and the decision-making process was over, it felt like there'd never been any decision to make in the first place.

The first time I realized I was a lesbian, it happened exactly the same way: an immersion in community, a sudden awareness and, finally, an undeniable pull to make a choice that had already been long decided somewhere deep inside of me.

During my first year at an all-women's college, I assumed that anyone not kissing another woman in front of me was straight. I'd been theoretically queer-positive as a teenager, at least in comparison to the majority of my classmates, who threw around

15

gay slurs for kicks. But college life brought with it a much broader measuring stick, and it was pretty overwhelming to walk to class every day on a path that had "Dyke Power" scrawled across it in large red letters. Overwhelming because I could *feel* that power reverberating throughout the small wooded campus, and I didn't know what to make of it, or how it related to me.

So I slipped into the most religiously conservative mindset that I'd ever had. Suddenly I found myself believing that in order to love God, I had to disapprove of lesbians. One evening on the way back from dinner, my straight friend Melissa saw me watching a couple walking ahead of us. She must have perceived my concern (no doubt my brow was furrowed), because she said, "Don't worry. Soon you'll just think they're cute." They were holding hands, swinging their arms and laughing together, stopping every five or ten steps to embrace and kiss and smile into each other's eyes, and their affection for each other was sweet. I could feel their happiness, and it felt pure and good. But my suddenly stern God was watching, so I mumbled my obligatory, "I'll never think *that's* cute."

Melissa didn't really respond to my comment. She shrugged it off, forgot all about it in fact, because, a year older than me, she'd already gone through her own version of my experience during her freshman year. My process of shutting down before opening up, of reacting to an incredibly urgent and powerful atmosphere with some trepidation, wasn't alarming or surprising to her. And she was kind enough to give me the space to go through it in my own time.

By my second year of college, I'd acclimated—just as Melissa had so wisely predicted. I'd become politically enlightened, and more importantly I'd formed close friendships with several queer women. But while my judgment had dwindled significantly, there was still a part of me that wondered if I was supposed to be trying to hold onto it. Did God really expect my moral disapproval? Why had I started believing that in the first place? It all seemed really fuzzy and muddled, and there was no one I knew who was both liberal and Christian that I could talk to about my questions.

Then one night, sitting around the dinner table with a group of close friends, drinking tea and talking for hours, I realized that I felt more at home than I'd ever felt in my life. None of our differences—sexual orientation, class background, academic major, religious beliefs—kept us from connecting with one another deeply that evening, or so many other times like it. As we sat there together, in that simple moment, I was overcome with humility and gratitude that God had brought me there, to spend that time in my life with these women. And I realized suddenly and clearly that there was no way God could possibly love anyone at that table any less than I did—regardless of whom they slept with.

It was this relationship with my friends—none of whom identified as Christian themselves—that brought me back in touch with my brand of Christianity. Instead of the intolerant God that I'd felt policed by since I'd arrived at college, I felt reconnected with the love-one-another God of my childhood. This was a God I could worship without losing respect for myself or anyone else. And it was good to have him back.

Not too long after this renewed commitment to my spiritual path, though, I was forced to give up going to church altogether. One Sunday morning my boyfriend and I dragged ourselves out of my twin-sized dorm bed, flipped the required sign on the bathroom door to warn the other women that there was a "man in the bathroom," and stepped into the shower, taking turns with the water and the shampoo. After rinsing ourselves awake, we headed over to the white church with the steeple where I'd been going for years.

We found our seats in the back row of the church, saying our good mornings to the more dedicated early risers who'd already been to Sunday school. During the hymns, the organist and pianist dueled it out and I lifted my voice, singing the songs of my whole lifetime of Sunday mornings. During the prayers, I bowed my head and felt the hum of a hundred people all focusing on bringing our attention to God, to something infinitely greater than ourselves. And in those moments, all of my growing frustrations with the church seemed unimportant. Sure, I still felt exasperated with the promises of celibacy elicited from the gawky teenagers in the church. And it was becoming increasingly difficult to refrain from raising my hand and asking questions during the sermons, especially as the vaguely political messages increased in frequency. But I'd gone to church all my life, and religious worship had always been my main street to spiritual connection.

Then our pastor launched into the most politicized election-year sermon that I'd ever heard, and as he spoke I could feel my already-loose religious hinge pins coming undone. Apparently, the real "problem with America" was all of those queers and welfare moms, draining the system with their nonconformity and depravity and poverty (which were synonyms in this sermon).

My muscles gripped at rage, completely shutting down the connection to God and to the people around me that I'd felt so strongly only minutes before. As the pastor's voice got louder and more excited, my mind ran through my lack of options. I didn't have the guts to get up and walk out, I didn't feel entitled to say anything and I didn't have the biblical knowledge to back up anything I might have said to oppose the preacher anyway.

Instead, when the service was finally over, I funneled out the doors with the rest of the congregation, hugging the pastor goodbye as usual, his damp cheek pressed against mine. I couldn't say a word, but once outside, my boyfriend and I looked at each other in disbelief, and I said, "I will *never* set foot inside there again." The severing between myself and church was immediate, and it has never been mended. I decided to put my spirituality on the back burner for a while, to sleep in on Sunday mornings and just see where the current took me.

The following semester, I developed an increasingly undeniable attraction to a woman in one of my classes. No doubt partially due to my less-than-queer-positive religious background, I'd never consciously considered the possibility of being with women before. But whenever she'd slip into the classroom out of the heavy November rain, pulling off her knit cap and running her ringed fingers over her hair, I had to admit that I felt something. A longing. A desire.

At first, I did a little bargaining with myself. It would be okay to own up to my attraction if it was just for her, an aberration of sorts. But for me that would have been like believing in Jesus and not in God. It was impossible to separate something that, while distinct, is also so inherently connected. The awareness was there, and eventually, despite my initial inclination to contain it, my desire to be with women spilled over into every cell of my body. There was an external choice to be made, but somewhere inside me I had always believed.

The funny thing about religion, particularly Christianity, is that somehow it's okay in certain circles to make sweeping generalizations about its followers. Case in point: In an educated, liberal crowd, the people who aren't total freaks know that saying blatantly racist, sexist and homophobic things isn't socially acceptable. But I can't tell you how many times I've been in a conversation where people say offensive things about Christians. Especially within the queer community, where so many people feel outraged or hurt by the actions and policies of the church and its followers.

Not long after I'd recognized my bisexuality, I was at a literary event talking to Patience, a lesbian who was in one of my writing classes. We were sipping champagne and eating water crackers with brie, and for once no one was wearing sweats. Then, in the middle of a perfectly nice political conversation, Patience said, with a bitter edge in her voice that I would come to hear often, "Well, we can blame that on those fucking Christian assholes, now can't we?"

This wasn't the first time I was confronted with my "one of them" status face to face. So I thought maybe I could help her see that not all Christians were the same by flinging myself over the magnificent gap between her and the Republican Party. I'd tried this route before, with varying results, and speaking up had always felt like the way to keep my integrity intact. Still, my heart was pounding when I said, "Well, I'm a Christian, and I didn't have anything to do with that. Not all Christians are conservative Republicans."

Patience and her companion both stared at me as if I'd just admitted to killing small children for kicks. She mumbled something like, "No, of course not," before managing to detach herself from the conversation and move as far away from me as possible. I cringed in humiliation as I moved on in the mingling process, for the first time wondering if I should have just kept my mouth shut.

Why the sudden regret? After all, I'd been confronted with anti-Christian vibes on plenty of previous occasions, and I'd long since realized that in some circles it was assumed that I wasn't religious—presumably because true queer liberal types could never be involved with an organized religion, never get sucked into something so passé as faith.

It was unsettling to oppose Patience because what she was saying was largely true. The religious right was gaining ground, and I felt a similar contempt toward the whole "family values" posse. It hadn't escaped my attention that these political crusades against queers, women, the poor and people of color were being perpetrated in the name of Christianity. After all, I myself had already stopped going to church because of the hate-speak that I'd been subjected to there. But because I still identified as Christian, there was, up until that moment, a very clear distinction in my mind between Christianity as a faith and those conservative political factions.

But suddenly that distinction felt blurry. I felt like I had to pick a side: liberal lesbians or Republican Christians. If I didn't choose for myself, I worried that my alliance would be assigned by default. What if my admission of being Christian caused Patience and others like her to lump me in with Newt Gingrich, Pat Robertson, Jerry Falwell and the like? What if they assigned that my being Christian meant that I ran with the God Hates Fags crowd and harassed women at anti-choice rallies? At that tender moment in my sexual identity, being a part of the queer community was too important to me to take that chance. So while I was public about being queer, I found myself responding to comments like Patience's less and less.

As the years went by, it got to the point where when I heard the word "Christian," I felt an almost instant judgment and disapproval. I was fed up with the anti-queer agenda that seemed so prevalent in all the major Christian denominations, and I'd given up on defending them, even to myself. It wasn't hard to take the next step, to buy into the idea that Christians were dangerous at worst, foolish at best—even though my own Christian faith was still intact. Unwittingly, I'd come to see *myself* as the dreaded other.

Part of me worried that being a Christian meant that deep down I must be the evangelical, self-righteous Christian I least wanted to be. No matter that I've always been pro-choice, that Democrats are far too conservative for my taste or that I don't even believe that the biblical evidence for condemning queers is convincing. A small, dark part of myself had landed on the belief that I was the ultimate Jesus freak, the Bible thumper, the born-again lunatic who should be avoided at all costs.

And, to some extent, I am all of those things. I don't believe mine is the only valid spiritual path, but I do see it as one way, and Christianity is at least part of my way. I have a deep and constant spiritual connection to an unseen something or someone that I identify as Jesus, even though saying that name in public still feels like a social gaffe. When alone, I sometimes find myself singing gospel hymns in the shower. And while I haven't cracked (or thumped) my Bible in years, I can still recite lengthy verses off the top of my head. Not that I'll be using *that* trick at parties.

Despite the fact that I've been keeping my spiritual inclinations hush hush, I've always maintained the trappings of a bona fide spiritual practice. I pray on a regular basis—to give thanks, to receive comfort, to ask for support and sometimes just to check in and say "hi" (my God doesn't require any formalities). And if questioned directly, I never deny my faith, largely because this feels like snubbing a loyal friend behind his back.

But practicing a religion without acknowledging it to others— or being able to accept it as a personal asset instead of a fatal flaw—is tricky. In the past, I assumed that things could be kept separate, which seemed like it left me with a better chance of not alienating others or myself. But I've started to realize that I'm not a Styrofoam plate, neatly compartmentalized, each dish separate but equal. Approaching my life that way makes me feel fragmented and inauthentic, and it isn't really working for me anymore.

There's a part of me, hovering on the surface, that wishes I could just drop this whole God thing, that I could live my life with a less externally conflicting set of beliefs and affiliations. But when I go deeper into myself, what I'm left with is that same feeling I had when I was nine—the awareness of a presence, of a loving and tender God. The existence of something constant, unwavering and deeply compassionate. Someone who gets my jokes. And, most importantly, someone whose love has the power to heal my own weary heart and give me the strength to continue to open myself to others when the opportunity arises.

When I'm in touch with that presence, I have no reservations. Biblical interpretations that differ from mine and believers who spread messages of judgment and hate are still troubling, but they are ultimately inconsequential to my personal relationship with God. And far from being separate, my politics, my queer identity and my intimate relationships all stem directly from my connection to the divine. It's my external life, the othering of my various public identities, that has always made them seem separate. But inside myself the overlaps and connections are becoming more integrated every day. If God really is love, then my love is God. My love of women is God.

Not long ago, I found myself sitting on the couch of the woman I was courting. The lights were low, there was strummy-strummy music playing and we were having one of those unfurling conversations. Past loves. Family stuff. The usual personal information you don't necessarily broadcast, but that all of your close friends know about in detail. In the past, religion would never have been on the menu. And in this instance, I knew that she was a self-defined skeptic about all things spiritual. So when the topic came up, my first inclination was to shrug it off and change the subject. It just seemed so much easier than risking alienating her.

But as I looked at her, I knew it was time to come clean. If I was going to open myself to the possibility of loving her, I couldn't keep the source of my love hidden. I needed to have a little faith in her ability to see me for all of who I am, because if I didn't start somewhere I would never get to that place of integrated authenticity that's been so elusive thus far. So I told her the story of my religion, the whole complicated truth, and as we spoke, the words rinsed over me in a cool, cleansing stream.

The Road Toward Islam:
A Traveler's Tale

Claire Hochachka

New York City, November 2001

I was sleeping nestled against my friend Simon in his quiet
Brooklyn apartment when suddenly a sound wound its way into
my slumber—a note dancing on the periphery of my consciousness. First one, then many. Simon breathed heavily beside me.

"Simon! Simon! Do you hear that?" I whispered to him,
shaking his shoulder. "Can you hear it?"

Simon roused himself and turned sleepily to me. "Hear
what?" he mumbled.

"What time is it?" I asked him urgently. *What time is it?*

Simon rolled over to grope for the clock on the bedside table.
"It's 5:30 A.M.," he said, looking at me, groggy but concerned.

Prayer time for Muslims. I knew this from the time I'd spent
in the Middle East. I also knew there were no mosques anywhere near Simon's apartment, and that even if there were, no
mosques in New York call the prayer over loudspeakers like they
do in the Middle East.

"What the hell's going on?" Simon asked, annoyance
dawning.

"Simon," I said, turning to him with a smile. "I just heard the
call to prayer."

It was the first day of the Muslim holy month of Ramadan. A

few hours later, as I in-line skated home over the Brooklyn Bridge to Manhattan, I realized I had just been called to the Islamic faith.

Islam means "surrender to God," or dedicating and entrusting one's entire life—with all its ups and downs—to a divine power. A Muslim is a person who lives in submission to that power. The definitions are clear and simple. The practice is more complicated, especially for a young, blond, Western woman. Especially now.

Two months prior, on the morning of September 11, I was skating to work after my daily yoga practice when I saw the first plane fly overhead. I ripped my MP3 player from my ears in time to hear the terrible *boom* as the plane hit the north tower of the World Trade Center. The building went up in flames before my eyes. An hour and a half later, I stood on the West Side Highway, not ten blocks from the remaining south tower, watching, not breathing, as the tower crumbled to the ground in a fantastic mushroom cloud. In shock, I skated away from the dust, and didn't stop until I reached my apartment in the East Village. As I opened the door, a book lying on my bed caught my eye: *Remembering God: Reflections on Islam* by Charles Le Gai Eaton. I felt physically sick. Countless numbers of people had just perished at the hands of terrorists acting in the name of Islam. Logically, I knew that Islam had nothing to do with the catastrophe I'd just witnessed, but right then I couldn't bear the sight of the book. I buried it behind the others in my bookcase.

Now, as the Middle East is exploding once again into blood-letting between Jews and Arabs, as American forces are still at war in Afghanistan, as President Bush is talking about routing out terrorism and God-blessing America and as Ariel Sharon is calling Yasser Arafat "the enemy of the entire free world," the gulf between the Muslim world and the West seems wider than ever. Now would not seem like an ideal time for an American to embrace Islam. But the most intimate matters of the spirit rarely coincide neatly with global politics, and my journey toward Islam began well before September 11. In fact, I've been moving back and forth across this gulf for the last ten years, and can trace the beginnings of this complex journey to my stay with family friends in Dhaka, Bangladesh, when I was nineteen.

Bangladesh, 1991

The night before I left, my father sat me down. "These people are Muslims, and Muslims are very conservative," he said. "Show your respect for them by behaving conservatively also—this means no shorts and no short-sleeved shirts." I listened closely, at once fascinated and appalled. At nineteen, conservative was the last thing I aspired to be. But I did behave myself, and even enjoyed wearing the traditional *salwar kameez*, a flowing dress over baggy pants. After being there a couple of weeks, I was amazed to find that I was totally comfortable with their Islamic way of life.

One day, a street-corner bookseller sold me a small, ancient hardbound book called *Raja Yoga*. I devoured this tiny book, re-reading it over and over again in my little room in the back of the big house. One sentence in particular jumped off the page and reverberated within me: "The door only opens to one who knocks with sincerity." Although I didn't understand the full meaning of this line—what door? what knocking?—I knew it was significant.

I'd often emerge from my room to find the family praying together in rows. Although collective prayer, five times a day, seemed to translate into a general ambiance of love and peacefulness in the household, prioritizing prayer was strange to me. I'd never prayed in my life—not even in church. When my parents would take me to church every couple of weeks, my mother and I would giggle in the rear pews as I made eyes at the pastor's good-looking, rugby-playing son. Halfway through the service, my father would slip out the back door to walk the dog, whistling as he went. Prayer was not a priority in my family.

Aziz's oldest son gave me a set of shiny black onyx prayer beads that I carried with me everywhere, sliding the cool stones through my fingers. The family was amused by my attachment to these beads traditionally used for counting the ninety-nine names of Allah. They couldn't figure out what I was doing with them. At the time, I simply liked the feel of the stones. This same boy also gave me impromptu lessons on Islamic theology. With silky black hair and eyes animated with excitement, he would spend hours drawing me diagrams of the universe and telling me secrets about angels and *jinn*, energetic beings that exist on a plane parallel to that of humans. I had planned to stay in Bangladesh for a week, but I ended up staying almost two months.

Egypt, 1995

Four years later, when I finished university, I was eager to explore the Middle East. After my taste of Islam in Bangladesh, I wanted to go to the source of this mysterious religion and worldview. The Western media represented Arab Muslims as militant, Koran-wielding men, and veiled, oppressed women. How real were these images? At this point, all I could see of my spiritual path was its intellectual and physical components, like twin tips of an iceberg. Intellectually, I was interested in exploring the concepts that motivated and inspired people of other cultures and religions. To do this, I needed to travel. Despite some family resistance, I set off for Egypt.

Egypt captivated me with its deserts, the teeming city of Cairo and the call to prayer. Five times a day, the voice of the *muezzin* warbled across the rooftops of the city, echoing in the alleyways below. I would stand on my tiny precarious balcony, in the middle of the city, listening. The beauty of the call to prayer always brought tears to my eyes. My sister came to visit and one day, after watching my reaction, looked at me strangely and said, "I'd agree that the call to prayer is beautiful, but why are *you* so emotional about it?" I had no answer for her. I didn't know.

I've always steered well clear of the word "God." It evokes images in my mind of a stern tyrant lording over the people of the earth. Although my grandfather was a Russian Orthodox priest—a little tyrannical himself—I'd always found Christianity exceedingly dull. My childhood aversion to religion grew into vocal atheism during university—aided, in part, by my women's studies courses. I thought religion offered pat answers to complex questions.

All I could say to my sister was that I loved the rhythm of life conducted by the call of the muezzin, synchronized with the movement of the sun. Also, the chanting of the Koran flip-flopped my heart. It was an instinctive reaction.

But while my heart may have been drawn to Islam, my mind was struggling. There were a couple of intellectual obstacles blocking my understanding of the religion, and the issue closest to my heart was the role of women.

My friends back home and I, all of us confirmed feminists, had often debated about whether Muslim women were oppressed. I had done some research and, perhaps playing devil's advocate, always offered the argument that the early women of Islam—the wives of the Prophet Muhammad—were incredibly powerful and independent women. Khadija, the Prophet's first wife, was a businesswoman some fifteen years older than Muhammad. He was actually working for her when she proposed marriage. Muhammad's youngest wife, Aisha, was an outspoken woman who rode bravely into battle to fight. To this day, she is one of the most popularly consulted sources on the life and traditions of the Prophet. The Prophet Muhammad himself used to say that paradise is found at the feet of the mother.

But this was all third-hand theory. Until I actually lived in Egypt, and traveled to Syria, Jordan and Lebanon, I knew nothing about the lives of contemporary Muslim women. Part of me believed that if Muslim women were indeed oppressed, as the Western media taught me, Islam was to blame.

Syria, 1997

One afternoon, in a small conservative town in central Syria, I was sitting in a park, enjoying a green respite from the desert. A river danced through the town, its banks were verdant with foliage and vibrant with people taking pleasure in the fresh air. I caught sight of three women swathed in black *burquas* passing out pamphlets. They were wearing gloves and thick black stockings. I couldn't even see their eyes unless they looked at me straight on. I sat there idly watching as they made their rounds. A little girl wove her way unsteadily around their legs, grasping frantically for a fold of black fabric whenever she lost her balance, which was often. As the women drew nearer to me, the baby toddled in my direction. When she lost her balance this time, it was my skirt she grabbed. After righting herself, the baby stared at me in shock, her tiny hand still clutching my skirt. Then she began to wail. In a flurry of fabric, her mother materialized and snatched her up. But before the woman could retreat, I greeted her warmly: *"Salaam aleikum."*

The woman stopped in her tracks, turning to regard me with serious eyes through the narrow slit in her veil. *"Aleikum as salaam,"* she responded in a quiet voice. Her gaze darted between me, her daughter and the park at large. By this time, the two other women had joined us and the shorter one bounced right up next to me.

"Where are you from?" she asked me curiously, peering into

my face. Her young eyes held laughter. We began to talk and when the women invited me to their house, I didn't hesitate. As we walked through the narrow twisting streets into the heart of the small town, I held one of the baby's hands and her mother held the other. The buildings, made of stone and whitewashed cement, crowded the cobbled streets. Finally we reached a simple arched door set into a thick stone wall. I heard male voices beyond the door, and the women rang a bell to announce our arrival. The door opened directly onto a spacious courtyard surrounded on three sides by the house. Jasmine crept up the walls and potted plants adorned each corner. An exuberant fountain splashed water into the air.

The women quickly ushered me into a room off the courtyard, and off came three black burquas, layer by layer. Rihab, the mother of the baby, wore a stylish olive-green suit, armfuls of gold bracelets and sculpted eyebrows accentuating large dark eyes. She disappeared into a bathroom and returned with black hair falling in neat waves past her shoulders. The shorter woman was Rihab's sister-in-law, and the third woman, her mother-in-law. The older woman was wearing a simple white shift that fell in a single line from her shoulder to her ankles. As soon as she lost the black burqua, she donned a white headscarf, but not before I caught a glimpse of a jovial mass of salt-and-pepper curls. She grabbed my hand and led me to the couch where she sat next to me. Her eyes sparkled in a happy round face. Other women began filtering into the room bearing trays laden with tea, dates and biscuits. Rihab sat daintily on a couch opposite me, carefully breastfeeding her baby girl.

33

"So you live in America," she said to me in crystal-clear English with a hint of a British accent. "I live there too."

I looked at her, surprised. She seemed totally un-Western.

"Where?"

"In Boston. I'm studying Islamic theology at BU. I'm only back in Syria for the summer."

"Do you like living in America?" I asked her with some pride, thinking to myself, *Who wouldn't?*

"No," she said shortly. "I much prefer Syria."

"Why?" I asked in surprise. Her mother-in-law fed me a grape.

"I find it unwelcoming, unfriendly. People are only concerned with their work. Plus, I don't think American women are held in high regard: their men don't seem to support them, they have to go out and make their own living. And look at how the media presents ideas of beauty. Women are expected to look like Barbie."

Before I could answer, Rihab's sister-in-law bounced back into the room wearing jeans. She spoke rapidly to her mother and motioned toward the courtyard. Rihab reluctantly pried her baby from her breast and rose. "Come," she said to me.

In the courtyard, about ten female members of the large family were seated on the ground in front of a white sheet spread out and strewn with colorful pillows. As Rihab, her baby and I sat down near the white sheet, another woman came around with tiny cups of fragrant coffee. Thanking her, I took one and savored the cardamom-laced drink. All the girls and women chatted and laughed with one another. They spoke in Arabic, and, sitting among them, I drifted happily in and out of comprehension. In Egypt, I had learned to communicate quite well in the local dialect, but the Syrian dialect was different and I could only catch about half of it. The women were curious and welcoming toward me. Within minutes, I felt like part of the family. Children wandered around and a couple of babies napped in their mothers' laps. After a few minutes, Rihab's mother-in-law entered the courtyard carrying a flat round drum.

"What's going on?" I asked Rihab, sensing the excitement of the group. It was infectious.

"My mother-in-law is a *sheika*," she said.

"A what?" I asked, confused. I knew that a sheik was a spiritual leader of a community, but I'd never heard of a *sheika*.

"She leads us in prayers, here at home and at the mosque on Fridays. You know, she's a religious leader."

Our conversation was cut short by the sheika's voice: "In the name of God . . . " Then she began to recite the Koran. Soon, she began to sing and beat the drum. All the women joined in, at times clapping, at times trilling in a high pitch. This went on long into the night, and by the time I was ready to leave, I felt high. The sheika was an inspiration to me and she shed light on the strength and sanctity of women's space in Islam. As they kissed me goodbye, I agreed to return and spend time with them the next day.

Egypt, 1997

Despite experiences like the one I'd had in Syria, after two years in the Middle East I was tired. I was tired of standing out in a crowd due to my blond hair, even though I dressed like a frump and hadn't worn a short-sleeved shirt in two years, much less a short skirt or sexy dress. My shoulders slumped in an unconscious attempt to hide my breasts from the eyes of men on the street. The pollution stung my eyes, the noise gave me headaches, the desert sun lined my face. I wasn't fit because running in the street—and certainly in-line skating—would draw too much attention. By the time I left, I was convinced that I was too eccentric by Egyptian standards, too individual, too much a Western woman at heart to fit into an Islamic community—any Islamic community. Maybe I didn't like life in Egypt for the same reasons Rihab didn't like life in America. I longed for the familiarity of home.

Jerusalem, 1999

The Sufi saint Jaláludin Rumi says in a poem, "Drumsound rises on the air, its throb, my heart. A voice inside the beat says, 'I know you're tired, but come, this is the way.'"

Two years after my return from Egypt, I was itching to go back to the Middle East. Obviously, my Islamic journey wasn't over. Again, my decision drew raised eyebrows from my family and friends, but again, I was being pulled by an invisible cord. This time I chose Jerusalem.

I entered the Old City through the Damascus Gate at night. The air was rich with the scents of thyme, cardamom and roasting coffee—the fragrance of the Arab Quarter. At the small hotel, I met Jihad, a young Muslim working the front desk. We went up to the third floor and Jihad threw open huge windows to reveal the glinting golden Haram el-Sherif (Dome of the

Rock). We were so close to it that we could see the details of the mosaic that fringes the walls. This distinctive landmark is considered by Muslims to be the third holiest site in Islam.

Jihad and I stood there for hours gazing out at the city, which was glowing a soft white in the darkness. "Why am I so drawn to Muslim countries when I don't even subscribe to Islam?" I eventually said, more to myself than to him. This question had been perplexing me since my time in Bangladesh.

The rituals of Christianity didn't resonate with me. I wasn't drawn to Judaism. I found Buddhism too dispassionate, too detached. My yoga practice had evolved to the point that I was getting up at 5 A.M. daily, and my life had opened up in myriad ways. But I had no inclination to learn Sanskrit, the next progressive step, and I found it difficult to wrap my mind around the idea of worshipping the formless within the form of one or more of the host of Hindu deities. Islam alone remained compelling— but also mysterious and inaccessible. It glittered on the other side of the Judeo-Christian wall that had framed my reality. I had tried over the years to read the Koran—I'd bought my first one at about age eighteen—but it sat gathering dust on my shelf for ten years. The book simply eluded me. I'd open it every now and again, read a few sentences, then close it again. The language was heavy, and the message even heavier.

Jihad was silent, staring out into the velvet night. Just when I thought he'd forgotten the question, he found the answer. "Because your heart is Muslim," he said, as if it was the most obvious thing in the world. I laughed lightly. For some reason, I was flattered. I momentarily entertained the idea, but then my mental resistances to Islam piled up in my head and the moment disappeared into the dark night.

Suddenly a noise broke the sleeping stillness. The haunting, melodic voice of the muezzin rose over the city, beginning the dawn call to prayer. The sound filled the air and left no room for anything else. If God had a voice, I thought to myself, this is what it would sound like.

Early the next morning I wound my way through the narrow streets to the Dome of the Rock. The rough cream-colored stone had been worn down by hundreds of years of footsteps. How many of those footfalls were planted with spiritual intention, with the pure anticipation of the pilgrim? Jews, Christians, Muslims had all walked these streets for one reason: to worship God. Their divine desire was ground into the stone.

Soon I stood before the golden sweep of the Dome of the Rock. At the non-Muslim entrance, I passed by two sets of Palestinian guards who checked my bags and begrudgingly waved me in. Inside, creamy flagstones unfurled in all directions. The sky to the east was rosy. Geraniums threw red blossoms from where they grew out of cracks in the stone and cast ragged shadows on the ground. I stood there breathing, listening to the birds chattering in the olive trees overhead. If some places can vibrate with divine energy, then this was one such place. It shimmered. My thoughts were crystal clear, I felt like I was performing a moving meditation.

Finally, I slipped off my shoes and entered the grand Al-Aqsa Mosque. Persian rugs in deep maroon and dusty rose covered the floor. Glass lanterns swung overhead. A few men prayed at the front of the mosque. They stood. They bowed. Each man's head was covered with a red-and-white headscarf. A small girl played around the feet of her father.

The Dome of the Rock was full of women facing Mecca. One woman called the prayers in a beautiful melodic voice. I watched the women go up and down and say "peace be upon you" to the angels on each shoulder. When they were finished, they sat quietly on their prayer rugs.

Out of the corner of my eye I caught sight of one woman berating another for being slightly out of alignment. The berated woman wore a humiliated expression as she hurriedly adjusted her prayer mat. As I was watching this spectacle, some kind of attendant with a megaphone accosted me roughly and told me to move away from the women praying. I didn't want to move, I was enjoying the female space inside the mosque, but he herded me away like an animal. Later, I heard him shouting through his megaphone to a couple of other foreigners, "Welcome, forbidden. Forbidden, welcome." He had a terrible, grating nasal voice. I would have laughed but I was too angry. The beauty and serenity I'd experienced moments before vanished. I was left with a bitter taste in my mouth. I'd just witnessed two ugly scenes in a place of worship. Is this how members of a spiritual community behaved? If so, I was glad I wasn't a member.

New York City, 2000

Back home, I pondered the question of community and how it related to the essence of a religion. Any ugliness I had witnessed in the mosque in Jerusalem was not Islam, but what human beings did as they faltered through the practice. You can't hold a religion responsible for the actions of its followers. In my mind, I defended the essence of Islam. I separated religion from the actions of the people who practice it. For me, especially after the trials of September 11, the two will always remain separate. After Jerusalem, I began to realize that culture and spirituality are very different. Spirituality cuts across culture, and Islam is a perfect example.

Geographically, the Islamic world spreads from Morocco across North Africa, through the Arab Gulf and South Asia, to Malaysia and Indonesia. Muslims live in almost every country and culture on earth, including the United States. In each region, Islam is expressed through the filter of local culture. The numbers also tell the story. One fifth of the world's population is Muslim—one person in five—and 80 percent live outside the Middle East.

People tend to confuse a religion with the culture in which it is practiced. Female genital mutilation is not an Islamic practice, nor is the practice of wearing a burqua, which Afghani women were forced to do under the Taliban. These are local cultural traditions that have been interpreted as Muslim precepts. On the flipside, I am a quintessentially Western woman. I thrive on the intellectual and physical freedoms my culture affords me. To practice Islam, I don't have to don a burqua and lose my active lifestyle. Once I separated culture and community from spiritual essence and personal practice, suddenly Islam looked different: ultimately personal, specifically tailored soul by soul. Then one day, the door opened: I read the Koran.

New York City, November 2001

When I arrived home from Simon's that dawn, I pulled my book on Islam out from the back of my bookcase and started to study again. I had to face it: the call was proving stronger than all my intellectual, cultural and political hesitations put together. To my amusement, Jihad's words rang out in my memory: *Your heart is Muslim.* This was the beginning of my surrender.

That dawn, on the first day of Ramadan, I began my first real fast, one of the five pillars of Islam. I had fasted in Egypt the two years I was there, but only for cultural solidarity and social reasons. Cairo is one of the most festive cities in which to celebrate Ramadan. People are up all night, singing, visiting, laughing. But in New York, no one else I knew was fasting, and it wasn't easy. My day began at 5:00 A.M., with two hours of yoga on an empty stomach. This was followed by seven hours of work. By the time the sun was low in the sky, I was very empty and often delirious. But I soon discovered that the fruit of the fast lies in this very emptiness. Beyond hunger, I was able to focus on the spiritual aspects of the fast—meditation and prayer.

Muslims have an elaborate prayer structure that involves a series of prostrations choreographed to recitations of the Koran in Arabic. The goal is to pray five times a day but maintain the fragrance of prayer in everything you do.

With no community and little support, I was forced to turn to the Internet. I had to fight the feeling that I was doing something profane: learning prayers off the Internet seemed all wrong, like getting sexual pleasure from a porn site rather than with a human lover. But I had no choice, and found that it was actually incredibly easy. I immediately located an Islamic site that had the specific Arabic recitations for each of the five daily prayers, as well as special postings for Ramadan. So, facing east, with the computer behind me, I prostrated to the voice of an electronic muezzin. Islam in the twenty-first century.

I felt like I had finally accessed something that had been attracting and evading me all at the same time for so long. But not all of my friends were as excited as I was. Many of them seemed uncomfortable at the thought that I might be flirting with Islam, especially so soon after September 11, when many Americans—consciously or unconsciously—saw Islam as the enemy. A few days after September 11, a Pakistani Muslim friend of mine had commented, "When the terrorists hijacked those airplanes, they also hijacked Islam." I knew deep down that he was right. Essential Islam is based, like other religions, on principles of peace. The word "Islam" is based on the Arabic root word "peace." What the terrorists did on September 11 was not Islam, but people throughout history have used religion for their own dark ends.

Despite the violence people are inflicting in the name of Islam, and my complete disagreement with those actions, for me the essence remains protected in the prayers and the Koran. But I couldn't expect all my friends to separate the purity of the faith from the actions of some of its radical followers, and it dawned on me that some of my best friends might never understand this aspect of my life. If September 11 had never happened, I might have been able to be freer about expressing my practice. As it was, I decided to keep my practice hidden except around people who would either understand or offer their support even without understanding.

Living in North America grants me the freedom to find my spiritual way through this material world. My friends and family, witnesses to my spiritual wanderings, are products of the same free-thinking, liberal, privileged society that created me. They may not get why I'm attracted to Islam, but if they love me, they'll try to understand. And maybe one day they will.

A couple of months after hearing the call to prayer, I skated happily through the East Village, feeling freer than I'd ever felt. I didn't consciously seek this out—I didn't cover my head and go find a mosque—and I know it won't be an easy path. But I see now that Islam is the door I have been knocking on my entire life.

The Culture of Faith

Shoshana Hebshi

My birth could be perceived as a miracle—or, at least, a rare planets-were-aligned thing. "A product of love between two warring peoples," I'd casually tell people who asked about my ethnicity after noticing my black, curly hair and olive skin. But the love stopped there, after the product. My parents got a messy divorce when I was five. I know somewhere deep in their hearts they still love each other, but their differences, like those that have separated Arabs and Jews for centuries, cause too much strain.

Their opposition to each other and each other's roots is a battle inside me, in my blood. I'm bound to both Judaism and Islam by the laws of religious lineage—through my mother I am Jewish; through my father I am Muslim. By choice my parents are atheists, and, by choice, so am I. I can call on either religion if the need arises, such as during a Passover Seder or upon entering the holy city of Mecca, but I have mostly rejected the faith-oriented parts of these religions, which entwine culture with belief in *their* God.

I am an Arab and a Jew. I've experienced a mystical sensation upon entering a synagogue or mosque; I feel connected to the people there, to a history, to a sense of spirituality, but not to a God. I follow along, going through the motions of worship I know and copying those I do not. But all the while, I'm observing as though I were an outsider. When the rabbi, dressed in a Shabbat black cloak, chants the prayers in Hebrew, I appreciate it as music—ancient melodies filled with history, struggle and faith. Although I have only experienced Islamic worship since my early twenties, I feel similarly connected the moment an ancient Arabic chant begins. I don't understand the language, but the passion expressed in a few simple words, repeated again and again, fill me with an understanding of and love for my family's heritage.

The rifts surrounding my religious practice began long before I was born. My parents agreed when they began having children that they would raise them Jewish. And they did. As children, my sister, brother and I attended synagogue, learned Hebrew, became bar and bat mitzvahs and followed the laws of the Torah. Judaism's laws, commanded by God, are observed religiously, but also carry over into the larger culture. A prayer is said before practically every activity. Growing up in a Jewish household meant I was a Jew.

My parents divorced ten years after they married, in part because my father no longer had the same support for Israel's right to exist as a Jewish state (my mom said), but also because of his infidelity (my sister said). The Palestinians, in his mind, had a right to exist in that land. I grew up hearing my mom and her side of the family say the Arab world wants to crush Israel. They were, in effect, attacking half of me. When my dad and his friends said that the Palestinians had been pushed out of their rightful land and discriminated against by the Zionists and Israelis who have no right to exist there, they attacked my other half. I never knew what or whom to believe. But I did know I was Jewish and that I didn't want to participate in their arguments because I could not take a side.

My mom doesn't believe in God, and she gets uncomfortable at the mention of the word "sprirituality," but she still considers herself a Jew culturally and is very concerned with upholding Jewish tradition. She's always cooking for family dinners and Passover Seders, making sure her children are honest, upstanding citizens who vote, pay their taxes and are well-educated and financially successful. Her house is spotless. She worries with fervor and loves from a distance. She and my grandfather are in complete solidarity with the Jewish people. A large part of that means not letting Hitler win. Or the Arabs. Or the Republicans. Or the Christians. It means not letting any group that ever oppressed the Jews win. Their Jewishness is very much political.

Harry, my Zionist grandfather, lived next door to us and never accepted the Arab man my mother married. My duty, as his granddaughter, was to uphold the tradition of his enduring religion, of his people. He educated me in the culture, history and language of the Jews; he sent me to a Jewish private day school and to Jewish youth groups and summer camps where I learned Israeli dances and folk songs, made Jewish friends and strengthened my cultural and religious identity. He encouraged me to read from the Torah on the anniversaries of my bat mitzvah. He prepared me, and often harangued me, to carry on his legacy. My mom's and grandfather's greatest fear was that Hitler would win the unending battle by erasing one more Jew from the planet. That meant it was very important that I marry a Jew, or, at least, that I raise my children Jewish. My grandfather did not want to die knowing his Jewish lineage would end in his grave, but I could never make that promise to him. The anti-Nazi narrative was so strong that it scared me and made my Jewishness feel oppressive at times, but I couldn't tell them that. I became sad and angry that I couldn't talk to them about my life and my choices.

When I'd bring home boyfriends, especially the one I ended up marrying, I tried to point out Jewish traits in their gentile selves. One guy had worked on an Israeli kibbutz for a summer and had the T-shirt to prove it. Kurt, my husband, is half-Jewish by blood. But it never seemed to matter. Holt is not a Jewish last name (though neither is Hebshi). My grandfather and mother had a rough time opening their hearts and arms to these boys. Any conversations about my Jewish future made me defensive, and often ended with me in tears and with my tail between my legs.

My mom had known she was marrying an Arab who would not convert to Judaism. Her decision was the seed of the struggle she and I would have over my Jewish identity. I believe she is reminded of that decision by my very presence: my dissent is a mirror in which her religious faux pas is reflected daily. Recently she told me she had dreamt I became a Hindu. It worried her, and she said she's disappointed that I'm throwing away tradition. I'm disappointed she doesn't see how I've created a tradition of my own.

My dad's identity is also based on politics, though his politics are drastically more leftist than my mom's or grandpa's. He began his quest for independence as a teenager living in Mecca. An uncle urged him to explore the outside world, and, according to my father's stories of his break from Islam, Allah wasn't answering his prayers, so he gave it up. When he was ready to enter college, he left Saudi Arabia and landed in Austin, Texas, where he found football games, political science classes and a wonderfully non-religious lifestyle. As he assimilated into American culture, he distanced himself from his family and from Islam, and became an atheist, a Marxist and a labor union organizer.

After the divorce, he and my mom would scream at each other, and I would cry. I didn't want to be like him. I once told him I hated him and immediately burst into tears as I hung up the phone. My mom was standing next to me and I cried on her shoulder. Hating him provoked me to take my mom's side against him in custody battles, in cultural and religious identity, in personality. My mom didn't discourage me since she hated him too.

My mom says she was shocked when she discovered that my father was a PLO supporter. When I was a teenager, she was outraged that he took my siblings and me to intifada celebrations. I had no idea that the intifada was the Palestinian uprising against Israel, though I did know that everyone in the room, including my dad, hated Israel. I thought that if they hated Jews, they must hate me. So I hid that part of my identity and stayed close to my dad and the food tables.

During the first twelve years of my life I was immersed in Judaism and not interested in exploring my Arab side. I wasn't very aware of the other religions around me or even that I was a minority since all my friends were Jewish. Then, in sixth grade, I entered public school. All of a sudden, being Jewish made me different from everyone else. All my new friends were Christian, and I thought they'd hate me and cast me out if they knew I was Jewish. So I attempted to hide it, and as I did so, I began to question God's existence and what role Judaism played in my life. My schooling no longer involved a half-day of Torah or Hebrew instruction, and in the secular world I'd entered, my Jewishness slipped away.

It was only in studying for my bat mitzvah that I was able to stay religiously connected. Every Saturday during sixth and seventh grades, I attended morning Shabbat services with my grandfather. I simply told my new friends I was "busy" until noon, rather than that I was studying the Torah. Passover Seders were "family dinners" and Hanukkah was just like Christmas, only without a tree. All I wanted was to fit in. As I hid my Jewishness, it became easier to let it go. I began to question my understanding of religion, despite the fact that my grandfather and mother continued to bathe me in Jewish experiences.

In seventh grade I attended a Catholic Sunday mass with a friend and her very religious, very large family. It was my first time in a church, and I was awestruck. It was a beautiful sanctuary: stained glass, white plaster walls and a two-story-high ceiling. I gazed into a bronze bowl filled with holy water and wondered what would happen if I touched it, and I marveled at the priest's and altar boys' costumes. It all seemed so devout. I wasn't allowed to take Communion, so I sat, hoping no one would notice, in the wooden pew while my companions took their turns. Although it was beautiful, I felt nothing spiritual that day and was glad not to be Catholic because all that kneeling really hurt.

Family pressure and conflict and my sense of difference from my non-Jewish friends were not the only reasons I began to stray from Judaism. On the day of my bat mitzvah, the rabbi himself actually helped. He pulled me aside, as he did with every thirteen-year-old boy or girl who went through this rite of passage in his synagogue. He told me, hands placed on my shoulders, that he'd seen God. We couldn't even write or say the word "God" because of its holiness, and he had *seen* Him? My rationalization for my disbelief in God, HaShem, *A-donai*, was that I couldn't see Him. When this rabbi, who I'd always felt was a ridiculous clown, told me he'd seen God, my questioning came to an end: I knew God could not possibly exist. Maybe it was because I didn't like or trust the rabbi, but it now felt okay to believe that.

During my high-school years, my relationship with my dad was strained. I was still angry at him, and our conversations were brief. When he asked me, "So, why do you want to be Jewish, anyway?" as we drove the five miles from my mom's house to his, all I could answer was, "I don't know." I was annoyed and put off by his question. It felt like an attack against me, my mom, my grandpa, my upbringing. Looking back, I'm not sure I could have answered that question any differently if someone else had asked me. I really didn't know. I had begun to wonder how I could be Jewish and not believe in God. My dad wasn't an atheist Muslim, after all. I knew he was incredibly bitter about religion in general, and he had never been supportive of my Jewish life.

It wasn't until I moved 350 miles away to college that the Arab part of me began to emerge from my subconscious. As I became more aware of its presence I began to see my dad as a man who had wisdom, experience and support to offer me as I grew into an adult. Distance gave me perspective.

In the WASP-filled college town of San Luis Obispo, Cal Poly University was just like all the other public schools I'd attended: the majority of the students and teachers were white, conservative and Christian. Still not loosed from my grandfather's pressure to remain Jewish, I set out that first month of school to involve myself in the Jewish group on campus, Hillel. I immediately found I had little desire to socialize with these traditional Jews. It wasn't just the persistant phone calls I received by the group's leaders urging me to attend a Shabbat dinner or another meeting. I just discovered I couldn't relate.

As my relationship with my dad became closer, I became more interested in exploring my Arab half—his roots, his family, his culture. As I let him into my life, he let me into his, and I found a wealth of experience to draw on. He accepted my decisions, and didn't seem to judge my intentions as he once had and as my mom continued to do. He supported me in my life's exploration. I began to love him and listen to him. I began to trust him.

• • •

Though my relationship with my dad was mending, my Arab and Jewish halves continued their internal struggle. I began to acknowledge myself as half-Saudi when people would ask.

"Are you Jewish?" my non-Jewish college friends would ask. "I was raised Jewish, but I'm not really practicing," I'd respond, embarrassed by the pressures of anti-Semitism. There were few Jews around, and most of these did not flaunt it. My grandfather continued to apply pressure: "You should check out the local synagogue," he would say when I came home for visits. "Yeah, maybe," I'd respond, unable to tell him that I was really not interested in pursuing Judaism in that way, afraid of his disappointment and rejection. But because I could never tell him of my growing separation from the structured Judaism he'd raised me to practice and carry on, I began to separate from him as well. Our relationship became distant and cold. Our talks were short and left me feeling like the disappointing granddaughter—a black sheep.

When I graduated from college I decided it was time to meet my Arab family. My dad returns to Saudi Arabia for a visit every ten years or so. His last trip, in 1999, we took together, upon my request. The moment I stepped off the plane alongside my dad and my brother, my Saudi relatives embraced me as family. We feasted, and talked as much as we could through broken English and the five words of Arabic I know. I felt loved and, more importantly, welcomed. I had a new family and was now confronted with a new side of my identity.

The ultra-Muslim Hebshis living in Jeddah and the holy city

of Mecca do not know much about my dad's life in America. They do not know he's heavily involved in progressive politics and has given up Islam. He prefers to keep that a secret. But my dad's family knows my mom is Jewish, and one cousin even asked me to confirm it when I visited.

"Your mom is Jewish, right?" Lemya asked me in her broken English. I quickly nodded, wondering what my positive answer would do to our budding relationship. She drew me a family tree and said the Hebshis are related to the prophet Muhammad. Religiously, this is a very good thing. My Jewish mother didn't seem to be an issue. I was relieved about that, but was still unsure whether they would silently hold my Judaism against me or continue to accept me into the family. I didn't tell them about my Jewish upbringing; all they were concerned about was introducing me to their world of Islam.

I looked the part of a Muslim woman. I went through the motions of their prayers, visited the Great Mosque in Mecca and wore the traditional, oppressive women's garb. They were having a heat wave. It was humid, in the 80s or 90s, and we had to cover our heads and bodies in black wraps. I learned the ritual of washing before praying. Was I cleansing my spirit? It all seemed so silly to me, but I prayed, behind the men, kneeling, touching my forehead to the ground and saying, *"Allahu Akbar* (God is great)."

It was interesting, but beyond my whetted curiosity, I felt no connection to the divine. When I toured around the Kaaba stone in the center of the Great Mosque, the center of Islam, I was curious. Hajis on spiritual journeys travel from all around the world to touch the stone, to feel touched by God, closer to God ... or something like that. But as I stepped closer into the middle of the rotating circle of Muslims, my brother holding one hand and my aunt the other, a woman fell down and screamed in pain, another smashed down on my foot so hard I thought it was broken, and a small mob was created as everyone around me pushed one another forward, backward, to the ground, like vultures, to kiss the holy stone. It was madness. *A metaphor for religion,* I thought, and hobbled to the outskirts of the circle, vowing never to get involved with an organized religion again.

Human behavior killed something in me that day. I could not return to the Judaism of my childhood. I could not explore Islam or Buddhism or Christianity or any other religion that comes with a stiff set of rules. I began to understand why my dad had left it all behind.

As an atheist, my father always criticized religious people praying to the Almighty. It made no sense to him. But because my mom tried her best to sculpt me into something different from my dad—who she perceived as flighty, pro-Arab, financially irresponsible, radically liberal—I refrained from labeling myself an atheist. "You didn't get this from me," she said when I decided to give up my burgeoning career as a reporter to "find myself" in the redwood forests of northern California with my non-Jewish, once-Buddhist, German-surnamed future husband. I was like my dad in that I didn't follow the religious path I was born into. I became "non-practicing" or "nothing" when people asked my religion. I'd say I didn't believe in any sort of "organized" God.

It wasn't until my grandfather's death that I came to a place of peace about my Jewishness and about my relationship with him. He died two days after his ninetieth birthday. I was twenty-six. The last time I saw him, before a series of fatal strokes debilitated and then killed him, he explained that he wanted his family to know the Mourners' Kaddish so we could say the prayer for him when he died.

The cold stone and marble of the mausoleum engulfed me. My two aunts, mom, stepdad and brother created a semicircle around his final resting spot. My grandma didn't want to walk down the two flights of steps to the site, so she and my husband cried and talked about a life gone by, while we all said our final goodbyes. We ripped pieces of black ribbon pinned to our shirts to symbolize the Jewish practice of ripping a piece of clothing while mourning. After his coffin slid into his crypt the presiding rabbi began the prayer in Hebrew and I eagerly joined in.

Yeetgadal v' yeetkadash sh'mey rabbah . . .

Saying those words connected me again, temporarily, to something larger than me and my struggles. Was God watching? Was grandpa's spirit still alive? I knew religion was there to answer these questions. But my grandpa had said Jews don't believe in heaven or hell. He thought when a person died, he simply died. The spirit is left in the memories others continue to hold and the contributions the person made to society. I remembered countless Saturday mornings when I sat in one of the blue pews of the synagogue looking up at my grandfather while he said this same prayer for one of his many deceased relatives. The prayer sounded just as mystical and beautiful when I said it, now, for my first deceased relative, my teacher, Harry Ruja. My grandpa was always standing next to me, coaching me. I was always his pupil. And like a good student, I take his teachings and make them my own and I pass them around to those who will listen. I don't need to be a religious Jew to carry his spirit inside of me. My grandfather, who had nourished me in his beliefs and traditions, was getting a proper burial because of his dedication. Fulfilling my grandfather's wish by reciting this prayer was the best way I could say goodbye.

And though I could never, while he was alive, mend the rift that my stray from Judaism created between us, I felt closer to him and to my Jewish core in his death. As I concluded the prayer, I felt my Jewishness for the first time in my own way, without anyone telling me what it was or why it was wrong or right.

Oseh shalom beem'roh'mahv, hoo ya'aseh shalom, aleynu v'al kohl yisrael v'eemru: Amein

The traditions and religious beliefs my grandfather and mother hammered into my young mind are still ingrained in my bones, my core, and hidden in my pain as I try to lift the weight of their expectations. But they are rarely exposed.

I have started building my own traditions and sense of spirituality, which include elements of the traditions of my childhood. It is important to me to carry on traditions and feel connected to my spirit and my people. But my people aren't Arabs or Jews, they are my family and friends.

To explore my spirit I take long walks and contemplate the world around me wonder about where I fit, marvel at nature, the sky, the moon, smiling faces. I practice yoga to clear my thoughts, connect with my body and mind and feel centered and grounded.

As I explore the meanings of the Arab and Jewish blood that flows through my veins, I become more calm about my warring sides, something that seems impossible in the world I read about in newspapers. The pressures I feel to practice, ignore or reject my spirituality lift further away with every breath of fresh air I breathe. I can explore my own sense of spirit without the constraints of my upbringing.

The Last Conversation
L. A. Miller

When I entered the hospital room my breath left me. I'd never seen him like that—not even remotely close to that—an oxygen mask covering his face, IVs everywhere, his skin wrinkled and gray. He looked so small. My mother was in a tiny heap in the corner of the room, all fragile bird bones and frosted hair. I began crying. I had intended to be strong—for my mother's sake—but instead I just crumpled, whispering, *"Oh God."*

I went to his side and stroked his face, his arm, willing him to open his eyes and say he felt "terrific," my father's automatic reply whenever someone asked how he was, his answer no matter how he was really feeling. Instead there was just the hiss of the oxygen and the *beep* of the heart monitor and the quiet mewing of my mother from the other side of the room. A nurse entered and took readings off the various machines surrounding my father's body. I waited for her to say he looked better, that he would be "just fine," with a chipper nurse's smile. She frowned instead, and said his morphine level was too high—she was worried he was under so deep. The nurse left and returned with an injection of Narcan—the anti-narcotic emergency-room doctors give junkies who've OD'd—and stuck my dad's inert form with the needle. He startled awake with a gasp, his eyes bright and confused, like a newborn's.

"Hi, dad." He just looked at me with big, scared eyes.

• • •

My father had been taken to the ER the day before because of back pain. He had a long history of disk problems so I wasn't too surprised when my mother had first called to tell me. But it was simply a matter of hours until they diagnosed the staph infection that was causing his back pain, a matter of hours until his body went septic as the infection raged in his blood and his organs began to shut down. A matter of hours until I couldn't remember the last conversation I had had with him, and wasn't sure I would get another opportunity to say anything else. He was scheduled for emergency surgery the morning I arrived at the hospital—they were going to remove his artificial hip where the staph bacteria had lodged and were multiplying.

After he was prepped, I rode the elevator up to the surgery unit with my middle brother, who is a doctor, and his wife, who is a nurse. I was comforted being there with Erik—he is the least emotional of the four siblings in my family, a staunch logician who speaks plainly. He is also the only atheist besides me. With no false hope to spur him on and a medical degree to boot, I felt certain he could tell me what was really going on. And I really needed to know what in the hell was going on. He cleared his throat.

"Les, you have to listen to me. No one else wants to hear this but his chances aren't very good."

"How not good? Fifty-fifty?" I searched his face for clues. He looked impassive but serious, and I understood he was being a doctor now, a doctor delivering news like *it's very advanced*, like *we tried everything we could*, like *his body simply isn't strong enough*. "Is he going to die?"

They both looked at me, his wife's face the telling one. "The normal survival rate for staph infections like this is about 20 percent," he said. My father was dying. I started to pray.

My family on my mother's side is Swedish and Norwegian and German—it is redundant to say they are Lutheran. My father was a Baptist as a kid but our family was always Lutheran—that Catholic offshoot known for bland, white food; a certain humorlessness; and hymns sung in impossible keys, all sharps, grating and jangling. Our family went to church every Sunday, the 8:30 service, though I tried everything to get out of it: feigning illness, hiding in my room, watching the minutes tick by on the clock and hoping against hope that my mother would sleep in, that instead we could read the comics in our pajamas while my dad made waffles. Sometimes I even prayed that we wouldn't have to go to church.

Our church was an ugly 1960s building, shaped like an overturned ark and filled with a sea of blond heads. Everyone's last name was Christianson or Jorgenson or Mueller. Sometimes there was a hand-bell choir but most of the time there was silence—just shuffling feet as we stood and sat, stood and sat and sang those terrible hymns in time with the organist with a tight perm and a no-nonsense sneer. The pastors were bland and non-threatening, like midwestern food, potatoes and cream. The service itself contained neither joy nor fire and brimstone—either would have been impolite—so instead we sat with our legs crossed and our hands folded and gazed blankly at the pastor like a herd of Jersey cows. When it was all done, my brothers and I went on to Sunday school, where we memorized passages of the Bible and heard about how the Mormons and the Buddhists were all going to hell. Once, during prayer, I locked eyes with the Sunday school teacher. "Jesus does not hear you if you pray with your eyes open," she said. She didn't address that hers had been open too.

Needless to say it was never a place where I felt comfortable, or comforted, and when I was ten years old I made a deal with my parents. I would keep going to church until I was confirmed, then I was free to make my own religious choices. So I began my earnest journey toward confirmation—learned more about the Bible, donned a white acolyte's robe, lighted candles, and carried incense on big days like Palm Sunday and Easter. I think we had a test. Then one Sunday a group of us—burgeoning adolescents all pimply and nervous, the boys' voices high and strained, the girls trying not to giggle—became confirmed members of the Lutheran Church. I thought then that I was free.

The surgery seemed to take an eternity. I waited with my mother and my husband for my other brothers and nephews to arrive. We sat in the waiting area of the small hospital in the small town where I had grown up, where my parents still lived. I drank percolated coffee and cried some more—eliciting sympathetic looks from passersby, instead of the usual glares I get in that town for my primary-colored hair.

As we waited my parents' friends drifted in and through. I wondered if so many people would show if I were dying. Was that the benefit of living here—in this tiny city full of fundamentalism and Republican ranchers and last year's fashion—for forty years? Right then they didn't seem like small-town people, as they had when I was growing up, when anyone who *chose* to make their home in Yakima was automatically suspect. They just seemed solid; they held me and looked me in the eye—didn't talk about the stretch of good weather as though we'd all run into each other at the grocery store. They knew sorrow—more than a few were battling cancer; they'd weathered divorces and deaths and drug-addicted kids. Underlying all of this, I knew, was a deep current of faith that held them all together, that motivated them to comfort others and allowed them to deal with whatever tragedy life flung at them. This was the draw of church, of faith, I guessed, the magic potion that made you strong. I was simply grateful they knew how to comfort my mother. I'd never had to. I didn't know if I could.

A couple of them prayed with her right there, and they all said they were praying for my father. I was grateful for that too, though I felt uncomfortable in the presence of their joined hands and whispering lips. Where did I belong in all of this? Usually I reveled in my difference whenever I came home—my off-dress, my off-hair, my off-politics. I'd made it out. But suddenly the differences loomed large and I wanted some commiseration. Where were my people—the godless ones? I looked to Erik, rolling his eyes at the prayer circle, still angry, I could tell, at the level of denial operating within the room. I looked at my husband, intent on a *Newsweek* beside me.

Desperate for solace, for something to do other than wait, I closed my eyes and tried not to cry and then, silently, I tried to pray myself. But I didn't remember how. Lutheran prayers were quite formal—lots of "thou's" and "Heavenly Father's"—words that felt like paste in my mouth. And I hadn't prayed since high school, those desperate kid's prayers, bargaining prayers—get-me-out-of-this-God-without-my-parents-finding-out-and-I-won't-ask-for-anything-again. That didn't really count. I fumbled, trying to figure out whom to address. It was like trying to pray to the great Oz though I'd already guessed he was just a man behind a curtain with a little smoke and mirrors.

Dear God, please don't let my father die. I'll do anything, just don't let him die. I wasn't convinced it would do any good—why should God do me any favors? I didn't believe in god. In truth, I thought of him as a little like Ronald Reagan, if he existed at all.

My parents didn't keep their promise. Confirmation came and went and still I was forced to get up every Sunday so I could be dragged to church. I didn't have to go to Sunday school any-more, little consolation since I'd started ditching to go to 7-Eleven with the two cool kids anyway. I was thirteen and raging—raging against my parents, against all these hokey Min-nesota transplants who had the pastor for supper and baked cookies for after service, against the confines of the tiny, tiny town where I lived.

That broken promise, and the fact that my ability to deter-mine my own spiritual path had been taken away, guaranteed that Christianity, and Lutheranism in particular, would come to symbolize the prison in which I found my teen self trapped. One more joyless, perfunctory activity steered by adults who didn't care to know what really made me tick, who didn't really want to discuss religion—just dictate it. One more place where disagreement was synonymous with argument, and polite people didn't argue; adults certainly did not argue with children.

It became unbearable to me that America was so Christian. I refused to say the Pledge of Allegiance in school. I tried to have a church group banned from meeting on school property after classes were done. I declared myself an atheist and allowed all things religious to sting me like holy water thrown on a demon.

I tried to talk religion with my father. I wanted him to understand it was all a dangerous hoax, and he still seemed salvageable. Every Sunday he'd pick up the little golf pencils in the pew and rate the pastor's sermon on its application to everyday life, humor and persuasive rhetoric. If he gave it a high rating he passed the card on to the pastor as we shook hands on the way out. He never passed on low scores. Either way, it demonstrated to me that at least he was thinking critically about the whole matter.

So one Sunday, after church and over waffles, I pressed him. How could he believe what they were saying in there? I mean, *creationism?* He was a man of science, after all. My dad said he thought creationism and Darwinism could both be correct—it was simply a matter of timing, of playing creationism in slow-mo for a few billion years. He said he believed in a Supreme Being, and that's about all he knew. He believed most religious traditions shared similar ethos and he was just trying to be good, to live a good life. He said church reminded him to be a better person. In short, he wasn't a Lutheran (really), but he had faith. I understood then he was lost to the dark side.

• • •

The surgeon, my parents' next-door neighbor, came out to tell us the surgery had gone a little tougher than anticipated. My dad's hip replacement had knitted so well that they'd had trouble chiseling it out, but it was good they had. A huge septic pocket lay beneath that joint—another half-hour and he would have died. I wondered at this reprieve, and sneaked a look at Erik. I shouldn't do cartwheels.

I was torn between preparing myself for my father's death and holding out the same hope as all these guileless supporters clustered around us. But they had that same something I didn't: faith. They actually *believed* he wasn't going to die, that their prayers were making a difference. I believed in percentages, in my atheist doctor brother who had seen these cases before, who didn't see many miracles in the emergency room—just the odds played out again and again. I felt like a traitor for not believing he would pull through, but I felt ridiculous trying to convince myself he would. I had no idea how I would handle his death, I had no map for this, no plan. I needed to start getting ready.

My father was transferred to intensive care, and we all began our vigil. My parents' friends gently reminded us to take my mother home, to make sure she had something to eat. My father wouldn't wake up from the anesthesia for hours, and at that point probably wouldn't be lucid anyway. My mother was terrified to leave the hospital and I understood why. What if it happened when you were at home, in the minute you relaxed and talked about normal stuff, while you were finally eating dinner or downing a second glass of wine? What if it happened then?

The next day I had to return to Seattle, go back to work. I said I'd be back a few days later, on the weekend. When I left my father was still barely conscious and on high doses of morphine. I tried to say goodbye, but he didn't recognize me. There was a terrible odor to his body, a crust on his dry lips from the oxygen and lack of fluids. His feet were encased in spaceman booties that inflated every so often to keep his circulation going. A monitor measured his oxygen level—when it dipped too low an alarm would go off and we would all have to beg him to breathe deeper, breathe harder. He tried sometimes; most of the time he didn't respond. They poured an antibiotic cocktail into him intravenously. They said we had to wait.

My family called me two days later and said I needed to come home that day. When I picked my husband up from work he said they'd called him too while I was on my way over—they'd said to come quickly. Never had traffic been this terrible—it was 4:00 P.M. on a Friday afternoon. Matt swerved and cut people off, drove on the shoulder for a stretch. I didn't say a word, but instead stared at the fir trees and the mountains and the snow still clinging to the high hills. I looked at the sunlight on the water and thought of how much my father loved the Northwest—the forests, the water, fishing. I took a mental picture of the land-scape, a snapshot for my dad. *This is how the world looked on the day my father died, I thought.*

Every minute for two hours I conjectured if that was the minute he'd slipped away. I felt cheated that I wouldn't know when it happened, that despite our closeness there would be no current through my body, no shudder to let me know, like in the movies. Did I envy the rest of my family crowded around his bedside waiting for his face to change? Waiting for the spirit to leave him and float skyward? I wondered what would happen to him once he died, if he would join the air and the sun and the trees. To me, death simply echoed the laws of physics: matter can neither be created nor destroyed. I wondered where his energy would go, displaced from his body, from us. I thought of my dad's wishes for his funeral.

He'd been explicit with me because he knew I would do whatever he wanted, that I didn't care what was proper or what people would think. *I want a celebration, Les—lots of good champagne, and play* Godspell. *Then I want you all to tell stories about me—what you remember the most. My legacy.* I didn't know if I would have the strength to organize this, anything.

I thought of the Lutherans, the Presbyterians . . . almost everyone we knew was Protestant. They were good at funerals. They knew when to send flowers, when to pray and when to arrange for services with casseroles after. They could say to the widow, to the children, *Now he is with God.* What could I say? *I think his matter has been released to take hold elsewhere. I will see him in the river and the cottonwoods, but really he is simply gone and I am still here and so angry.*

It sounded so much less certain—it *was* less certain, because I was unsure of what happened upon death: knowing he wouldn't go to heaven didn't offer a concrete answer in return. God sounded so much grander than a burst of freed molecules let loose on the Yakima Valley but, in reality, whichever my vision of the afterlife, neither one changed what seemed inevitable, neither made me feel less victimized, less orphaned: *I am still here and I am so angry.*

I looked at my husband, another atheist, intent on delivering me to my father's bedside—I envied him; he had a task. I surprised myself by praying again, reflexively, like scratching an itch, or blinking. Reduced to a six-year-old girl who still believes God answers prayers, and the Easter Bunny delivers chocolate, and that fathers are immortal. *Dear God, please don't let my father die before I can say goodbye.* I was learning to ask for less.

He had improved by the time we got there—another reprieve. Shaking, I went to his room. The sun was shining brightly on this side of the mountains too, and it streamed through the window of my father's room. His eyes looked rheumy and glassy, like he was drunk. He brightened as I came in, and beckoned me close. It was then I saw his arms were strapped to the bed. "Undo the straps," he whispered conspiratorially, "I just want to go outside for a little while." I told him I couldn't undo them, that the nurses said he kept taking out his IV. "Just loosen them, I want to go on the roof," he begged.

Through his delirium and the terrible reek of the ICU he could sense that Spring was asserting herself—cherries blooming and crocuses nodding their heads—and he wanted to go outside. I thought of that snapshot I'd taken for him. He said my name and I started—was he was coming out of it? This was the first time he'd recognized me since he'd gone into the hospital. He was coming back to us, to me! Smiling, I again gently refused to loosen the straps while he tugged and struggled and begged some more. "Then what good are you?" he hissed—angry, frustrated, still clearly delirious. What good was I indeed?

Being more "spiritual" than Lutheran, my dad was open to all sorts of New Age-y influences that, since he combined them with work more than with his personal life, seemed harmless and even avant-garde for a fifty-five-year-old dentist in a small town. After one retreat in the mountains he'd returned with reports of fine vegetarian food and inner work and the news that they'd all envisioned their power animals—his was a tiger. A few months later he'd sneaked off to Seattle to have the tiger tattooed on his back, so I was sure that had he been lucid he would have found comfort in the fact that Joan had just arrived and joined my oldest brother and me in his hospital room. She was more than a long-time business acquaintance of my father's; she was also a friend and a therapist, and she had brought with her her most "powerful" objects—feathers, an abalone shell—all wrapped in a bright red cloth. She tucked them under his pillow and prayed with my oldest brother—who shared my father's name, his occupation and his nondenominational belief in God. I'd watched him go from the most rebellious of the four children to a man who took his kids to church, sometimes Lutheran, sometimes Presbyterian. He shopped around, but he always said grace at the dinner table.

I looked on and wondered: I made wishes on eyelashes, didn't

I? I never picked up playing cards until I received my full hand. Was what they were doing any different than enacting these small superstitions—trying to exert some minute influence on fate? Was I failing my father by not trying to do something other than make sure he kept breathing and holding his hand? If he died would it be my fault?

It took me a long time to separate my atheism from rebellion. When I did, it took me a while longer yet to tell the truth, to call myself an atheist instead of the other, gentler *A*-word: agnostic. It seemed so harsh, and clinical, and yes, a little part of me was wondering, *what if I'm wrong?* Would my baptism save me after all? Was the confirmation the kicker?

Truth is, when my father was lying there in that hospital bed I wanted more than anything to be able to *do* something— pray, accept the words of other people's prayer, tuck abalone shells under his pillow. I wanted more than anything to *believe* something—that a loving god wouldn't let him die, that if he died he would be cradled in peace and light. Later, I recognized that my attempts to talk to that old Lutheran god my Sunday School teacher had said wouldn't be saving any of *my* friends was tantamount to begging a man with a gun to my head to spare me. Like this fictitious gunman, I realized, I wasn't begging god to save my father, really. I was begging him not to *kill* him. If god indeed resembled a youthful Ronnie Reagan, I felt simply like what I was: a middle-class liberal, a woman, who could only be harmed by his policies. Really, whether god existed or not was irrelevant—he was no ally, and my prayers were a sign that I had no power, no control, no recourse. I didn't, and that was horrifying, but it was honest.

Many people who have survived a face-off with death finally get right with god, they *believe*. In essence, I think, they equate their salvation with proof of god's power, but isn't faith supposed to operate outside of proof? Isn't that faith's very definition? Through my father's illness I didn't credit god with those beautiful mountains I passed, those first emerging crocuses or the icy waters my dad so loved to work with a graphite rod and 7-pound test line. I didn't believe in god's power to create beauty or bring a new life into the world, so how could I really believe in his power to take it away? In that I guess my faith did turn out to be a little like superstition, like not picking up my cards before the full hand was dealt. I was hoping against hope that if I prayed I'd come up with a straight flush, while knowing full well that the order of the cards was already set. Perhaps instead of praying I should have remembered that other favorite saying of my dad's: Nobody ever said life was fair.

I should tell you, my father recovered, slowly but completely. He still catches bass and works on people's teeth and plays golf in Palm Springs in the winter. He calls his recovery a miracle, and I say he beat the odds. Regardless, I am grateful. I still don't know what happens when people die. I still don't believe in heaven or hell or strict reincarnation, but what I do know is that whatever happens, it's up to those of us left to bear the burden of the loss. I finally understand the grace of my father's funeral wishes—a request more for our benefit than for his. Directives for celebration, for joy; tools to help us get on with doing what we do, doing work in his memory instead of dwelling on the gaping hole where he'd once been. A smart man, my father.

I didn't find faith in the experience—but I found other gifts. I found a new tolerance for the spiritual practices of others, and an ability to feel the mercy of their prayers despite believing they are issued to the air. I envied the community demonstrated by those church-going folk, then realized I didn't need god in order to seek out community. I found comfort in the character of my immediate family—the varying degrees of stoicism and tenderness, strength and vulnerability. In my brothers' sudden gentleness— their startled faces when I cried and their willingness to pour when all I wanted was a strong drink and a cigarette.

At home I discovered my own circle waiting for me right where they'd always been—friends who didn't pray, but who made me coffee and talked about my dad and allowed me my full range of emotions, including fear, resentment and rage. People who simply said, there's no reason this should happen—no purpose, no lesson. Go ahead, feel it. A husband who just held me while I cried. My problem wasn't a lack of people to help me, but that I had never learned to ask, or even make myself open to the offering. Perhaps that's what those fledgling prayers did for me— gave voice to my asking for help, allowed me to say the words first, before trying them out on those surrounding me.

Most importantly, I learned to tell all those people I care about that I love them—frequently, earnestly—so that I'll never again have to wonder about that last conversation.

Glitter and the Goddess

Kara Spencer

When I was eight, my mother confessed that she was a witch. We sat together by an open door watching hurricane gales bend the trees in the forest like elastic. The tempest surrounding us had compelled her to reveal the secret impulses of her soul. A witch, she told me, was not evil. A witch was wise in the ways of magic and knew secrets of the natural world. She described psychic experiences, lucid dreams, folk healing and the power of one's will as a catalyst for change.

She whispered these mysteries to me as if fearful of her prowess. In society, she was a model Catholic. When she divulged her identity as a witch, I didn't realize how heretical this confession was to her practicing religion. I simply thought of magic as a gift or talent, akin to speaking another language. Though she never spoke of being a witch again, a seed had been planted deep within my psyche.

Throughout my childhood, my mother and I took long walks through the forest. We would sit on moss-covered rocks, gather pinecones, flowers and stones, and she would spin fairy tales of nature spirits. On Midsummer's Eve we baked cookies and left them for the fairies and elves in a dewy pine grotto. I read from my mother's collection of esoteric books, which lived on a separate shelf from the Bible and the *Encyclopedia of Saints*. Her tarot deck was wrapped in black silk and carefully opened for divination and reflection. Through my mother's storytelling and intimate relationship to nature, I learned to celebrate the mysteries of the natural living world. Magic was in my blood and the earth was my temple.

Magical tales were interspersed among religious teachings of Jesus, Mary and Catholic saints. I attended Continuing Christian Development classes while my mother designed and maintained the church gardens. While my mother encouraged my belief in magic, she also instructed me to say bedtime prayers to the Holy Trinity. At times, she brought the essence of paganism into her Catholic teachings, such as when we made an altar to each of the four elements during the four weeks of Advent. Pagan philosophy had infiltrated my Catholic upbringing and my mother did not fully understand the lasting implications of this influence. While Catholicism seemed intent upon implanting guilt and penitence in my consciousness, I was inspired by an awareness of divinity and power in the natural world.

I reluctantly attended Catholic junior high school uniformed in the regulation plaid, polyester-wool blend, flameproof skirt (I tried—with a Zippo during geography class). The female students all attended a special assembly on how to properly cross our legs; the Brothers were flustered by schoolgirls sitting with their knees apart.

My parents had enrolled me to ensure I got a "proper" religious education. Through community involvement in the theater and arts, I had begun to meet people outside of my white suburban school, people who were of different religions and ethnicities. My parents were concerned about my associations with non-Christian friends (my mother developed a fear that beliefs outside of the Christian religion were Satanic). Though she herself had introduced me to magical ideas that fell outside of Catholicism, her dutiful-Catholic character publicly scorned such philosophy as fantasy.

Spiritual diversity worked its way into my consciousness. I looked up the definitions of atheism and agnosticism in the dictionary and secretly considered them. Invitations to friends' bat mitzvahs came in the mail, but my parents would not let me attend. At the library, I read through books on Buddhism and First Nations spirituality. I was searching for a theology that would affirm the vital link I knew existed between the universe and myself.

My best friend told me about a Wiccan priestess with whom she wanted to study. We shared books on magic and witchcraft and tested our psychic skills by sending each other telepathic messages. In the privacy of my bedroom I practiced casting spells with flickering candles, improvisational poetry and three slowly strummed guitar chords. Seeking meaning in the chaos and patterns of nature, I created my own internal spiritual refuge. My growing conviction that spirituality could be personally determined defied the authority of the Catholic Church's sacred tomes.

It was in my freshman year of high school that I personally abandoned Catholicism. The dogmatic religious instruction of parochial school left little room for my individual beliefs or philosophy. "If you don't believe in God you're going to hell!" my religion teacher yelled at me, standing before the classroom of straight lined desks. "You can't tell me what to believe!" I vehemently retorted. Of course, that is exactly what they wished to do. At home, when I sought support from my parents, my father verified that if I didn't believe in God, I was indeed going directly to hell. He delivered this sentence as if telling me we would have cream of mushroom soup with peas for dinner.

My mother, meanwhile, had begun to display symptoms of internal struggle. Sometimes she was spacey and would forget the conversations you had with her. My sisters and I made jokes about her poor memory and bizarre behavior. She became irrational and controlling. Coinciding with her mood swings, she began insisting that we attend church every Sunday, something that we were previously lax about between holidays.

I found vodka bottles hidden around the house. I discovered flasks under the La-Z-Boy, between the potholders and aprons and in her station wagon with the St. Christopher medal shining from the visor. As she struggled with her increasing lack of connection to the world and to sobriety, I struggled with the destroyed trust and companionship between us. I didn't know why she had begun drinking, and I never found out. However, I watched as she became isolated, ill, depressed and superstitious.

One afternoon, in my early teens, my mother saw me carrying a book on earth magic. She chastised me for reading a book on witchcraft, even though it was hers. She interrogated me as to whether I understood that it was just "fake" and "make-believe." She hadn't spoken of witchcraft in years, yet I clearly remembered her secret whispers during the storm when I was eight years old. She kept her metaphysical books hidden in a dusty drawer. Witchcraft was no longer an acknowledged part of her life, and she regarded magical philosophy with fervent disapproval. When I refused confirmation at fifteen, she was convinced I had turned to Satan. She searched for signs that I had damned myself to hellfire everlasting. I frequently discovered my personal items, such as artwork, posters and photographs, destroyed and thrown into the garbage—they were evidence of my fall to hell.

After school, my best friend and I would slip away to the little pagan bookstore where we bought candles and Back Off, I'm a Goddess bumper stickers. Daily, I sought escape and solace in nature. I walked in parks and nature trails to avoid going home for as long as possible. The forest, bogs, mountains and sky offered me shelter and rejuvenation. In the circle of land and sky I could forget the calamity awaiting me at home.

From my bedroom late at night I would crawl out the window and climb onto the roof to talk, cry and sing to the Moon. She was my counselor, guide and midwife. I discovered the healing power of being fully present in the natural living world. As the Moon waxed and waned, I swung from manic to depressive, grasping for sustenance at the universal umbilical cord.

My family's dysfunction and my self-excommunication left me wallowing in the wake of destroyed paradigms. A new physical and psychological scaffolding needed to be crafted before I could sustain my spiritual self. In the tumultuous passage I yearned for a childlike knowledge of magic. I watched the tumbling seasons and waited for the alchemical tempest to illuminate my psyche's healing.

• • •

Thump. Thump. Thump. Thump-thump-thump. Thump. Thump.

Two weeks after high-school graduation, I attended my first rave at a warehouse in Portland, Maine. The heavy bass resounded in my ears like the placental *whoosh* of blood to a floating embryo. From the dark pouring rain I entered a glittering womb of wild and ecstatic revelers. I immersed myself in the thousands of people dancing; I merged with the cascading beats. The sensual lights and intoxicating music spun a magical web around the warehouse. The night, the rainstorm and the empty industrial district collaborated to create an invisible cloak around our party. It seemed as if we existed in another time and space, apart from the mundane world.

I danced rapturously until the morning sun cast its glow through the steamy windows. The DJs spun fabulous music all night long from their hidden perch on a dark balcony. Instead of focusing on the DJ-as-superstar, every person present was a participant and performer. Though we were mostly strangers to one another, it was comfortable to meet, talk, dance and laugh. I was empowered by the anarchic revels to claim personal responsibility for my individual experience and pleasure.

That night introduced me to the global underground of ravers who celebrate the primal ecstasy of dance with electronic music. At each party I found out about the next one through hand-distributed flyers and word of mouth. Dancing at a rave wasn't about steps or style. I didn't dance for the DJ or the cute raver in the glitter and fairy wings next to me—I danced for myself. I discovered a powerful place to which I could journey through dance. I became more than myself; my awareness expanded to sense the gestalt of ravers, humanity, bonded in the universal flux of life.

From the dynamic energy of trance dancing emerged a sensual transformation that nourished and healed my spirit. In the rave community I discovered an expressway to the ecstatic. While dancing, I would lose my sense of physical boundaries. I would feel the energy of the other dancers coursing through my body like shockwaves of light. Dance is a language, through which I learned to express my erotic and sensual sides. In the fusion of dance, techno and incense, I rediscovered the magic of living in this world.

When I moved to the Pacific Northwest I immediately sought out my fellow ravers. I attended raves in warehouses, lofts, theaters, mountains, deserts, beaches, forests and parks. Local partygoers drummed and created altars, meditation circles, healing sanctuaries and teahouses. Benefits were held for various global justice actions, and neo-pagan rituals were enacted during parties. With fire and costumes performers called in the four directions and paid homage to Mother Earth. Ancient Greek myths were reenacted with belly-dancing divas and tribal techno beats. We circled and danced from dusk till dawn for full moons, equinoxes and solstices.

Under the stroboscopic lights I received massages and hugs, swayed to the penetrating beats and snacked on organic vegan buffets. I drank chai with college students, radical parents, tattoo artists, science nerds and yoginis. My feet danced for hours on sand, soil and concrete. Whirling fire dancers, skyclad revelers and costumed nymphs, fairies and satyrs were common on the dance floor.

The raver community I found was a special tribe of anarchist neo-spiritualists, different from your typical hedonists in their lack of self-abuse. We were celebrating the mysteries of the universe in our own way, with bubble machines, electronica and herbal teas. We were reenacting the primal ecstatic rituals of ancient goddess-centered and pagan cultures. It was not the half-naked raver boy purifying me with his bundle of sage, nor the pretentious five-hour fire dancing ritual of rebirth that led me to reawaken magic in my life. Our gathering to dance was a ritual itself, and through our celebrations we worked magic to uplift the community. Magic is a conscious intention for change and healing combined with action.

Contrary to media propaganda, raves are not all drug-riddled orgies. Drugs were rarely visible at the events I attended, and if they were, people quickly convened to remedy the situation. Individuals were responsible for their personal safety, and the group intervened if someone was behaving in a way that made others feel unsafe. Psychoactive drugs can open a window to the possibilities outside regular consciousness, but many revelers believe that artificial pathways to ecstasy do not let one pass through that opening. There was an immense communal interest in yoga, bodywork, meditation, whole foods and sacred sexuality, as people worked to uplift their daily lives naturally.

Coming together with the techno-tribal community showed me my own potential for psychospiritual growth. I had been drawn to rave culture because it encourages individuals to create and take responsibility for their own experiences. While I packed my sneakers and water to head to a party, I would think about what else I could contribute. A few gallons of chai, assorted plastic bugs, oversized pillows and an extra tent could be transformed into a relaxation den for outdoor parties. Day-Glo paints and surplus cardboard could be used for spontaneous artistic creations. A rainbow parasol and a box of fuzzy clothing could inspire imaginative costumes. Creative autonomy, both spiritual and political, had been condemned by my childhood Catholicism, which proselytized its dogma as the One True Path to Enlightenment. Finally, I'd found a community in which I could participate however I wanted to. How I found spiritual connection in the world was for me to decide.

As time allowed me to heal and release from my depression and emotional pain, I began to feel an increasing spiritual urgency to connect with the more-than-human world. My sense of unity with the living world solidified, my menstrual cycles became aligned with the lunar dance and I began to experience paranormal occurrences. I started to visually witness people's auras. Whilst in conversation with someone, I would suddenly notice the colorful or glittering glow surrounding her body. Turning my head, squinting my eyes, I would wonder if it was just the light, and whether other people noticed it too.

Shortly after this development, a fellow raver and her mother brought me to a workshop on energy healing and bodywork, where I was introduced to the ancient concepts of centering, grounding and balancing the human energy field for health and vitality. I found a yoga class with a teacher who had studied massage and she interlaced teachings on bodywork into our practice. In my weekly yoga classes we practiced sensing and balancing one another's energy fields between practicing asanas and deep relaxation. When a person's energy felt sticky or thick, it corresponded to stress and tension. I learned to smooth the subtle energy and keep it flowing.

My depression ceased as I concentrated on fostering vitality and balance in my body. I went to Puget Sound's rocky shore and waded into the rippling tide. I watched the phosphorescent algae swirl around me and I submerged myself in the water. The earth was helping me to heal.

My dream life began to intensify. Lucid dreams came regularly and I learned to control my creative sleeping visions. One night I awoke and realized that I was suspended delicately in the twilight stillness above my futon. The realization quickly came that I was experiencing astral projection. The cerebral fog that makes the dream world opaque and hard to discern was not present in this state. My senses were extra-sharp; I was conscious of details I had never seen before. The air twinkled as if dusted with atomic glitter and my being felt buoyant and ecstatic. I tried to sit up and explore further, but I was immobile as if submerged in concrete.

In a change of tactic, I consciously willed myself forward, slipping fluidly through the air. I became overwhelmed and my awareness was snapped back into my body. Now awake, my limbs tingled with fire and electricity. I recalled the stories my mother had whispered to me as a child. The magic skills she had secretly described to me were now coming to light as I transcended the sense of victimhood that had clouded me for years. It seemed that these mystical experiences arose in my life as my subconscious's way of telling me I was safe and on the right trail. I had moved past the depression and onto the path of healing. Through this inner change I was discovering a deeper understanding of the more-than-human world.

Inspired to learn about my unusual gifts, the next week I walked downtown to the local pagan bookstore. The owner greeted me with a booming voice and the wafting smoke of Nag Champa incense. I somewhat hesitantly confessed to her my recent experiences with auras and astral projection. Instead of laughing at me, as I'd feared she would, she shared with me her similar experiences and led me to a collection of books with abundant information about these phenomena.

Searching through the shelves I recognized several of the books as those I had browsed as a child, slipped them from my mother's library. Here again I came across the word "witch," used to describe those who honor the Mother Goddess in the triple aspects of Maiden, Mother and Crone. Though my mother may have only half-believed in witchcraft—with her other half firmly rooted in her more rigid Catholicism—I embraced my own pull toward witchcraft as a path of developing self-awareness and growth.

I found magic within myself, in my body, dreams, intuition and relationship to nature. The transformations I experienced through dance, yoga and dreamwork were a form of magic. With my intention to heal lingering trauma I was awakened to greater awareness of the more-than-human world. In pre-Christian Europe, wise women, midwives and witches believed magic and healing were so intertwined that they could not be separated. The ancient bloods of these wise women course through my veins.

I believe that my mother felt a similar pull toward magic and healing because it is in the collective consciousness of our ancestors. My great-grandmother was a midwife and village wise woman. Her family tree traces back to areas of Western Europe where, before Christ, the Goddess was celebrated and women were priestesses and healers. As my mother turned away from the magic of the earth she marched away from a life of health and empowerment.

A passion to explore the healing arts as a tool for social change led me to move to the city to pursue a career in massage therapy. A desire for health, community and political action grew from my connection to magic. I feel a calling to hold a space for women to heal themselves through gentle, creative and empowering practices. I've applied my education in therapeutic massage toward supporting natural birth as a labor-support doula. While holding a laboring woman's hand, and watching a newborn take her first breath, I feel the connection between life and death, the flow of blood, energy and spirit that sustains us all.

The witchcraft that I practice today is womancraft: feminist healing arts. A woman who knows her body and soul, strength and beauty, has a powerful magic. It is the magic from my blood, my milk and my breath that inspires my healing. Instead of arcane rituals with a coven of cloaked witches, I perform rituals of empowerment and healing through massage therapy, doula care, feminist parenting, Internet networking and activism. I celebrate my menstruation and sexuality as sources of magic and divinity. While meditation and spells are a strong magic, teaching and engaging in activism in one's community are infinitely stronger.

I am a witch, a woman, a healer and a steward of the earth. I celebrate the waxing and waning of the Moon and Sun. I honor the beauty immanent in nature and the divine in all beings. I devote myself to creativity, magic, the healing arts and political action. The spiritual is expressed in my work, through dedication and creativity. In my vision of the world before me, the mundane becomes ecstatic, ordinary action becomes ritual. Whether I am playing games with my son, massaging a woman in labor, writing an essay or dancing to beats under the full moon, I am acting within a sacred space. Within my being, I celebrate communion with the soul of the world.

Million-Step Program

Stephanie Groll

I was twenty-two when I graduated from college, and my whole life stretched out ahead of me. So I swallowed forty-eight sleeping pills. And that was that.

Good thing I didn't believe in God or I might have been headed straight for Hell. Instead, I believed I was releasing my anguished soul from this imperfect life, freeing it up to be reborn as a happier person. My body would be returned to the earth to complete its natural, albeit short, cycle.

Except that, obviously, the suicide didn't work. When an ambulance arrived, I sat in it while the paramedic grilled me. My feet dangled out the back door of the vehicle. They were heavy, pulling down hard so that my circulation was cut off where the backs of my knees touched the bumper.

"My address is 2136 Fair Oaks Road," I mumbled.

"So, you live here," the paramedic confirmed.

I looked up at the house but didn't recognize it. Annoyed that he obviously wasn't listening, I repeated myself. "No, I live at 2136 Fair Oaks Road."

"This is that address. Are you sure you don't live here?" he asked, punctuating the question with a forceful breath.

A second look transformed the unfamiliar view into my child-hood home. "Oh, yeah," I said.

"How many sleeping pills did you take?" the paramedic asked.

"Forty-eight."

"You should be dead."

There was no answer to this. I should have been dead.

With no more questions to ask, he put down the pencil and clipboard. He moved quickly, inserting IV tubes and adjusting knobs on the inside walls of the vehicle. He shook his head as if to shake off nausea. I knew he was disgusted with me, which was a perfect affirmation of my suicidal impulse: I'd known him for ten minutes and already he despised me.

"Why did you take them?" The paramedic didn't just ask it, he accused. My answer was the clearest thing I would say all day.

"I was bored."

In college, a few years before my suicide attempt, I created what I thought was the perfect spiritual structure for me, which is to say, I had no spiritual life. As a Hebrew-school dropout, I was never very moved by God or worship, and my Reform Jewish family didn't think that was odd. Jewish culture has always meant more to me than Jewish religion. I got the holidays and the history, I got the food and the warmth and the conversational bits of Yiddish. I just didn't get the faith. My childhood concept of an omniscient God was that he could see me masturbate and pick my nose. And that's just creepy.

Thinking that only the weak were attracted to the idea of an all-powerful being that could grant or deny prayers, I disregarded organized religion. I thought that if pious people couldn't see the foolishness of what they believed in, then they deserved the blind lives they led. The only reason they needed a god was that they couldn't take responsibility for their own lives. I, however, had my shit together enough to rely exclusively on myself, to have control over my own life. If I was successful, I could thank myself for a job well done; if I felt miserable, it was my responsibility to change it.

And I *was* miserable—desperately, achingly sad. But instead of seeking help, I holed up until the sadness passed. Sometimes I'd rip paper, without realizing what I was doing. Whatever paper was near—a sales receipt or a takeout menu—I'd tear into smaller and smaller bits, slicing frayed edges with my fingernail. The strain in my throat came from choking down my emotions. My mind raced with manic reassurances and reprimands: *I'm fine, I'm fine. Shut up, Stephanie. Nobody likes a downer. Cheer up. Everythin's FINE.*

During my senior year, things got worse. I hated my ugly, boring, eccentric self. But I never admitted that I felt that way because it would be too embarrassing and too painful to deal with. What kind of loser doesn't like herself? So I worked hard to shrink my 5'9", 190-pound body from view. Not by starving myself, but by shutting my mouth. I restricted myself to small talk and slipped away from all conversations that turned the focus on me. I wanted to make people love and admire me by showing them how positive and strong I was.

I was good at this game. The more withdrawn I became, the more my friends would try to reach out to me with a "How *are* you?" or an "I'm here for you." And it wouldn't even faze me. With shallow breath and clenched jaw, I'd give an autistic nod, answering, "I'm fine" or "Yeah, thanks" before they finished their inquiries. No eye contact, tight smile.

They wanted to get at me, but that wouldn't do. I hated to be touched because I didn't deserve comfort. I had to take care of myself and nobody could relieve me of this responsibility—not family, not friends, not some higher being. But it's impossible to shake off a case of low self-esteem by planting a look of serene emptiness on one's face. I had constructed a hard shell around myself, but it only took one tap in the right place to shatter it.

In my corrupted mind, once I had "proof" that the core people in my life were tired of dealing with me, I had permission to duck out. They might be a little sad at first, I thought, but I knew they'd be secretly happy that I had relieved them of the burden of knowing me. I thought I was doing everybody a favor by disappearing.

Fast forward through the pills, a few years of denial and finally, four years of therapy. I had let a select few into my confidence, showed them all the awful things I was discovering about myself. I became a new person with good friends and a boyfriend, Doug, who wanted to be with me despite my stupid deficiencies. Go figure. Best of all, I didn't want to die anymore. But again, I had only myself to thank for all of this.

When Doug asked me to walk 500 miles with him on the Camino de Santiago, a Catholic pilgrimage route in rural Spain, I decided to make the trek. My life had plateaued and I wanted to shake it up a bit. I was making no strides in my career, no decisions about the seriousness of my relationship with Doug and no new breakthroughs on the state of my self-esteem. Surely the repetition of walking all day every day with no technological distractions would make a quiet space in my head for epiphanies. Maybe I'd figure out how to reach my long-term career goals. Maybe Doug would ask me to marry him or maybe it would become clear that we should break up. Maybe the universe would finally make sense to me. So I packed a journal made of fine Italian paper and went to Spain.

For more than a thousand years, people have been walking to Santiago de Compostela in order to pay their respects to the apostle Saint James, whose relics used to be housed in the cathedral. (As a bonus, walkers' sins are pardoned.) Doug, a high-school history teacher, wanted to relive a bit of history, to experience the century-old pilgrimage with me. Praying to Saint James is said to have a healing power over the person prayed for—not that we'd be praying. The modern pilgrimage is made for every conceivable reason, but currently it's a popular cleansing ritual for people in transition. I only met a handful of pilgrims who were Catholic, which suited me just fine. The less Catholic this experience was, the better.

On Day One we set out at 6:00 A.M., with a crisp wind out of the Pyrenees pushing us down a dirt path marked with yellow arrows. Painted on trees and rocks and walls, these arrows would guide us all the way to Santiago. My backpack, heavy with essentials—rain gear, water, a first-aid kit—threw my balance off a bit. But the road was easy to navigate and I reminded myself of my good fortune to be going down out of the mountains instead of up into them.

After ten kilometers we stopped for a break. With an enormous chunk of chocolate in my hand, I turned back to see how far we'd come. Our starting point at a monastery in Roncesvalles was long out of sight and a herd of blond cows stood squarely in my view. Bells clanking, they chewed down the grass. A young calf pushed her nose through a barbed wire fence to get a whiff of us, bringing her big eye millimeters from a barb.

By the time we'd walked sixteen kilometers, the scenery was rolling by like the view from a moving car. My head hung low; all I could concentrate on was the ground in front of me. A little white daisy popped up between some rocks in the road. As quickly as I came to admire it, I saw my heavy shoe come down to crush it. I could not control my steps; I could only witness them. Exhaustion had set in and deadened my mind. My body was on autopilot, moving forward by virtue of momentum only.

I took the day's final five kilometers one shaky step at a time. The downhill slope turned steep and rocky. No smiling, no talking. Heartier pilgrims passed me left and right, while those weaker than I lay splayed out along the side of the road. I wanted to join them for a rest, but stopping now would put me dangerously close to quitting, so I pushed on.

When I arrived in Zubiri, I was limping. I followed the arrows directly to the *refugio* and walked into a ratty schoolroom, found a bed and passed out. I had embraced the Spanish siesta. Three hours later, at about 7:00 P.M., I blinked at the underside of the bunk above me and assessed my lower half: everything was swollen and paralyzed. I was aware of muscles in my feet and ankles that had never announced themselves before. Tender shins prevented me from flexing my feet. Gingerly, I pulled off my shoes and peeled back my socks to discover a blister on the bottom of my right middle toe. I looked away and let out a high-pitched whine.

There I was in Spain, practically crippled by the pain of a blister—the first I'd ever experienced—and I had far more to endure before this "vacation" would end. Thirty-four days, to be exact. 21.5 kilometers had wrecked me; how could I get up and do it all again the next day? Doug observed that Catholics had a built-in drive to get to Santiago, but when things got tough, what was to keep us secular types padding along? We too needed a purpose for doing the Camino. I had no answer at the time, but I did feel a sort of intangible sense of adventure pulling me forward.

For lack of better motivation, I simply started walking. Over the next few days, I felt my rhythms pare down to the very basic. Wake-walk-eat-sleep-write. I had no energy left for self-pity or doubt. It was the first time in my life that I did exactly what I wanted. Doug's strides were longer than mine and he felt hindered by my natural pace. Back home I might have sped up to accommodate him, but on the Camino I couldn't care less about making a good showing. All that mattered to me were my immediate needs. The word "compromise" dropped out of my vocabulary. I slept and ate and rested when it suited me, not because I had turned selfish, but because the walking required all of my energy. There was nothing left over for the obsequious caretaking I normally piled on people.

And I felt good, free. If I learned nothing else in Spain, this alone would have been enough. Before the Camino I based my life on external cues. At noon I would eat lunch, even if I wasn't hungry yet. When I was depressed in college, I tried to squelch it instead of giving into it because I'd absorbed from society that depression was unacceptable. I'd spent most of my life trying to fit myself into a mold that didn't fit, hoping to be accepted. But here on the Camino, that need for external approval dissolved in the face of the extreme physical and emotional challenge of this pilgrimage.

That first week, fatigue prevented me from sitting up straight, and my vision was terribly blurred. The refugios were like factories, checking in swarms of pilgrims and packing us into crowded rooms to sweat while we slept. The sound of snoring drove me to use earplugs every night. Restaurants served mounds of food at little cost, but we always left feeling distended and dissatisfied. And despite moleskin applications, my blister was never given a day off from walking. New ones sprouted every day, always on my right foot.

Before dawn on Day Four, I was dragging my fingers over my laces, trying to tighten them, when I noticed Doug staring at me. He'd already hoisted his pack.

"What?" I said. I knew he thought I was taking too long.

He contorted his face to imitate my demeanor.

My eyes stretched wide open and I said, "It's 5:45 A.M. I'm tired."

He raised his hands palms-out, as if to say, "Touchy!" Then he said, "I feel like I'm walking on eggshells with you here."

"Well quit it!"

He hooked his thumbs underneath the backpack straps.

"I feel like I dragged you along with me on this trip. Now I'm responsible for your happiness and comfort."

"What?" I screamed. "Look, I never asked you to take care of me here. I wash my own clothes every day. I tell you not to wait for me when I walk slowly. I *want* to be here. But you've placed this burden on yourself and it doesn't allow me to feel comfortable if you're going to worry about me. I need you to be cool with me not being cheery all the time. I think you're freaked out by my exhaustion, but I'm not dying. I'm just trying to adjust to walking every day."

He stared at me with his mouth open for a minute. Then he said, "Well, I feel better."

"Yeah, me too."

We laughed and set out to find a yellow arrow.

As soon as we crossed over the border from Navarre to the wine-growing region of La Rioja, the number of yellow arrows declined considerably. We walked for long stretches without knowing if we were still on the right path, relying solely on instinct to lead us. At one point we completely lost the way; we hadn't seen an arrow in hours. I craned my neck to look for some answer in the rural landscape but saw only a few clusters of towns separated by a succession of rolling hills and vineyards. Pounding on an asphalt section of the Camino for several hours had set fire to feet already baked by the afternoon sun. I was sick of Doug, sick of myself, sick of walking.

When we finally picked up the trail again, we were just outside Ventosa, a tiny agricultural community. We stumbled up to the refugio sitting high above the smoldering red-tile roofs, and we knew this was our destination.

The refugio was housed in an old stone building that looked

like every other building in Ventosa. But as soon as I crossed the threshold, I felt a difference. Cool air washed over me. A Brazilian man named Acacio welcomed us and relieved us of our backpacks, which weighed him down considerably.

"Please," he said, motioning to a wooden bench, "Rest." He looked thrilled to see us, as if he'd been waiting for us to arrive. I couldn't match his intense eye contact and felt him willing me to connect when I looked away. He offered us a smile and a bed and carried our bags up to an attic dormitory filled with sleeping pilgrims.

There was no restaurant in Ventosa and Acacio invited us to cook in his kitchen. Made available to all pilgrims, it was stocked with cooking vessels of all sizes and smelled of recently baked bread. We went to the store (which turned out to be one corner of an old woman's basement) and loaded up on *chorizo* and beautiful vegetables she'd grown herself. We slow-cooked sweet onions, zucchini, chanterelle mushrooms, green peppers and tomatoes in fat from the chorizo. After seasoning it with salt and pepper, we ate the whole sautéed feast over rice. After many days on the road with unfamiliar food, we felt rejuvenated by this home-cooked reminder of our regular lives.

After dinner, we sat with Acacio near the fireplace while he told stories of the Camino. He'd walked back and forth to Santiago annually for three consecutive years, he told us, mostly in winter because he helped his friends on the Camino during the summer.

"Oh, are they coming to meet you here?" I asked.

"Yes. You are here. New friends arrive every day," he said. I gave Doug a nudge under the table.

Making what I thought was light conversation, I told him we'd gotten lost on the way to Ventosa, that the yellow arrows seemed to disappear once we entered La Rioja.

"What? They are everywhere!" Acacio said, shaking his head. "You must open your eyes."

Doug then pulled out his map and asked Acacio which towns we should avoid and which ones Acacio recommended—after our experience in Ventosa we only wanted to go to small, personal refugios like this one.

"This," Acacio said, motioning towards the map, "I do not like you to carry this. The Camino is personal. I do not want to affect your journey." But, unable to resist giving advice, he followed up with, "I can only tell you the places I find the magic."

He picked up a pen and stared at the paper for a minute. Then he looked up at Doug, squinting in the dim light. "What is your purpose for being on the Camino? Is it for heart and sense, mind and soul?"

Doug nodded yes, keeping his eyes trained on our host's face. This was our first overt encounter with the spiritual side of the camino. I felt a pang of excitement, hoping to receive spiritual insight from Acacio. He seemed like a fortune-teller who is too authentic to set up shop at a carnival, but who floats through life bestowing verbal gifts on the people he feels moved by.

"It is important for you to get to Santiago but," Acacio turned to me, "you are already on the path. You already have . . . " He held his hand, palm-side down, three inches above his own head and shuffled it a little. "But continue on with him, to help him."

It was my turn to be transfixed. I stopped fidgeting and considered his words. I've been told many times throughout my life that I have a certain "something." Nobody can put words to it, and I have no idea what they're talking about. They never say more than, "There's something about you," pointing an index finger at me like they can't put their finger on it. In the past, I've quickly dismissed this as impossible because I'm clearly not special: I'm horrible, tedious . . . insert hideous attribute here. But coming from Acacio it felt like a compliment that I was finally ready to accept. It also felt like an assignment: to pay attention to life more, to meet his intense gaze and hold it.

Encountering Acacio marked the point of departure for me from tourism to journey. That night, with his encouragement, we slept out under the stars, because he told us that the energy in the ground around churches and a beautiful sunrise would conspire to give us something special. There was a considerable wind, but it added to the sacred feeling of the church grounds. The moon bathed us in silver light. It wasn't until we squirmed down into our sleeping bags that I realized how much I'd missed sleeping next to Doug. In the morning, as consciousness crept in, I snuggled down into the plush warmth of the bag. Breathing in the scent of the grass, I turned my head and saw a moss-covered headstone.

"We're sleeping on graves," my slow brain informed me. If I'd seen them the night before I never would have camped out there. But we got through the night feeling eerily protected. It was the deepest sleep I'd had since we began.

The next morning, rounding the first corner beyond Ventosa, we came upon hundreds of cairns, splashed with yellow paint and stacked six and seven stones high. Many pilgrims had passed this way before. Acacio was right. We just had to open our eyes to find the arrows.

Because Doug wanted to walk faster than me, I started picking a point on the map and telling him I'd meet him there at the end of the day. He took the map because I no longer consulted it. I was wherever I was, and calculating the day's remaining distance wouldn't get me to my destination any faster. Bit by bit, I was learning to give up control.

In Carrión de los Condes, Sara, a Danish woman with whom I'd been walking, offered to treat my blisters. It was Day Nineteen and we were sitting on the steps of a refugio at dusk. I said no at first, out of habit, but accepted her care when she insisted. Cradling my feet in her lap, she soothed me with her light touch and I relaxed my jaw when I realized how good it felt. After cleaning the blister with antiseptic, she gently sewed a sterilized needle and thread through it, pressed out the clear liquid and left a short length of thread in the blister to allow it to drain throughout the night. I watched in a trance, skin tingling, as she performed my little surgery. I didn't want it to end.

Afterwards, she massaged my arches and told me of the scallop shell she'd found on Puenta La Reina, a Roman bridge we'd crossed separately weeks before. The shell is a pilgrim's symbol and she stopped to admire it, reflecting on the thousands of years it must have been perched there, marking the way to Santiago. My breath caught in my throat. But it hadn't been there for thousands of years, I told her, because I was the one who had left the shell there—my gift to the Camino. With a racing pulse I marveled at this woman with whom I'd connected before we even met. She pulled me toward her for a hug.

By Week Three, my body began to crave the walk, so much so that I felt restless if we walked less than thirty kilometers a day. One day in Galicia, I made my way up the verdant hills below O Cebreiro. I'd already walked thirty-two kilometers and the sun was beginning to set. I had eight kilometers to go. Blisters prevented me from walking faster than a snail's pace and Doug was way ahead of me. I heard a car coming up the road and I had evil, lazy thoughts. Then I stopped myself, thinking, *I should do this on my own.* It was only eight more kilometers. But as the car approached I saw my hand reach up to flag it down. When the driver stopped, I felt relief flood through my body. But the relief was tinged with cheater's guilt. Accepting gifts from people around me was still difficult, but I was learning with each step that sometimes I needed help from others.

It took me five weeks and a million footsteps, but I finally made it to Santiago. Just as Doug and I were entering the outskirts of the historic part of the city, we heard a shout from within a bar—my Danish friend Sara and her boyfriend had stopped for a coffee and caught a glimpse of us as we walked by. We squealed at the fortuitous reunion. A series of mishaps had separated us a week before and I had resigned myself to finishing the Camino without them. But in the end, Doug and I walked the final steps of the Camino together with the companions who'd helped us along the way.

I passed under the giant arches of the cathedral and melted into a pew to listen to the pilgrim's Mass. My swollen and battered feet bumped up against the knee rest in front of me. A cool wooden panel pressed against my left leg, and I traced the edge of a scallop shell carved into the armrest. I closed my eyes, but paper-thin eyelids could not separate me from the others, from the sounds and odors of all of the pilgrims who were alongside me, looking for something in that church.

Twelve priests from twelve different countries filed in two-by-two, dressed in somber-colored robes. Seeing them sail past tourists and unshowered pilgrims was the first hard evidence that this was a Catholic pilgrimage. Every day of the year the cathedral holds a noontime Mass to welcome arriving pilgrims. The priests spoke one after another in their mother tongues for all the pilgrims to understand. English was conspicuously absent.

I understood anyway. My Spanish was strong by then. But their voices were gruff and my eyes glazed over. I had felt like a guest in every church along the Camino, taking only a cultural interest in religious art and history. I didn't expect anything different in Santiago.

Then an elderly nun shuffled to the front corner of the dais. She opened her plain mouth to sing hymns, and out poured an ethereal voice that sent a shiver down my spine. Tension drained away. My back softened and I leaned into everything she offered me. Her a cappella voice reached deeper into my core than anything I had experienced on the camino thus far. She didn't ask if she could comfort me; she rushed in like an adult subduing a hysterical child. I couldn't have tuned her out if I wanted to. Her words pulled tears from ducts that had been dry for more than a month. In the nun's presence I felt small and anonymous and worthy. She sang:

Te conocemos
Nos conoces
(We know you. You know us.)

I couldn't believe I was responding to a "God" message. But it wasn't the religious institution that spoke to me. It was the concept of a loving force connecting me to other people. I felt as if the nun were holding and stroking me and I could not fend her off any longer. Tears and snot ran down my face as I forgave myself for grasping so tightly on to my isolation and self-sufficiency. In one blink, the church looked different. The pilgrims looked different; softer, more tolerable.

Te conocemos, nos conoces. I couldn't hide any longer from God, who sees all my foibles and loves me anyway. I used to manipulate everyone into thinking that I was okay when in reality I needed someone to wrap their arms around me and let me cry. Every time I fooled someone, I had taken one step away from humanity, until I was completely alone. But four little words cracked me. Church air filled my lungs. There was no pain in my body. No slouch in my posture.

I blinked through tears at the faces of hundreds of pilgrims around me, some elated, some crying. We all had different reasons for doing the Camino and maybe we didn't even talk about them, but we were all part of the same force. Emotion burst out of me in liberating waves. It wasn't long-controlled sadness that couldn't be held back any longer; this emotion was love.

When the mass ended, there was Doug, quietly searching my face with his eyes for some clue to what was going on with me. He swallowed hard and braced me from elbow to elbow while he lifted me to my feet. I leaned hard on him at first, and opened my mouth to tell him what I'd discovered. But I didn't want to interrupt my emotions by intellectualizing them. So I kissed him. We would have the rest of our lives to talk about it. As soon as we stepped out into the aisle, the crowd of pilgrims carried us along toward the exit. The harsh sunlight seeped through the cathedral doors. I took my time descending the steps, enjoying the sensation of a few deep breaths.

I felt solid, clear. There's the camino and then there's the Camino. My path is undeniable. If I am to benefit from it, then I must acknowledge it. At times the road is rocky and rainy and filled with people I'd rather walk right past. But at other times the walking is effortless, and the path is marked by breathtaking views and meaningful connections with my fellow pilgrims. All I have to do is keep moving along . . . and open myself to help when I need it. I've wanted to give up—I even tried to give up—but now that I've been to Santiago, I want to walk through the pain.

The Practice of Faith

Maliha Masood

"Just stand next to me and do as I do," my grandmother said when she taught me how to say *namaz* (pray) at the age of seven. "But first you have to do your *wadu* so that you are clean." So I went to the little bathroom and filled a jug with cold water. I rinsed my nose and mouth, and splashed my face, arms, hair, neck, ears and feet three times each while reciting the *Shahada*. One of the five pillars of Islam, it translates as "there is no God but God and Muhammad is his last prophet." I covered my head with a large white muslin scarf so that only my face and palms showed. It was a balmy summer evening and my grandmother elected to pray outdoors on our grassy lawn. We laid our prayer rugs side by side, pointing towards Mecca. My prayer rug was cherry red, and I would use it for the next twenty years. It was to become rough and old through years of intermittent use, but that day it was bright and smooth in its newness.

I stood on the right of my grandmother and imitated her movements. *"Allahu akbar"* (God is great), we raised our hands to our shoulders, folded them over our chests and recited the *Surah Fatiha*, which I had memorized in Arabic. "Allahu akbar," we placed our hands on our knees and bowed in humility. "Allahu akbar," we rose and immediately dipped down to touch our foreheads to the ground in gratitude. "Allahu akbar," we rose and sat in contemplation reciting a long Koranic verse.

"Allahu akbar," we rose and stood up again in respect. We repeated the prostration three more times. Then we ended by turning our heads from right to left to salute the angels sitting on each shoulder.

Although we were not supposed to talk during the prayers, I turned to my grandmother and asked her, "Does Allah see us praying?" She nodded vehemently and placed a finger to her lips to silence me. She took out her *tasbih* (Islamic rosary beads), and started counting them furiously while murmuring something under her breath. I watched her and did the same with my own prayer beads. She nudged me and motioned me to open my hands, palms up, and stretch them at arm's length. This was the final part of the prayers, when we asked Allah for forgiveness, made requests, revealed our deepest secrets, professed our gratitude or just had a regular old conversation with Him. This was the part I liked best.

I spent the first ten years of my life in Karachi, Pakistan. My parents were moderate Muslims who expected me to follow Islamic ideals and still lead a carefree childhood. They never pushed me against my will to pray or to fast. Those practices were encouraged but never enforced. We rarely went to mosques to pray; it was customary to do so at home in those days. Only men went to mosques, but even my father chose to stay at home and pray in privacy. Though I learned how to pray at the age of seven, it never became a habit. If my parents had been harsh disciplinarians like many other Muslim parents, they would have forced me to pray, even beat me with a stick if I refused or locked me up in my room until I obliged. But they did no such things. They were tender, caring, loving parents who wanted me to be a kid and enjoy my youth.

But even as a child, I felt a tug of war inside me between Muslim faith and Muslim practice. I felt Muslim, living as I did in a country where 97 percent of the population is Muslim. I had developed strong strands of faith that led me to believe in the existence of God, and I would even talk to Him at night as if to an imaginary friend. In my elementary-school religion class, we would translate the Arabic prayers we recited into Urdu, my native language. Although I believed in those sacred words, I had a hard time sticking to the cumbersome ritual of praying.

In my family the *Maghrib* (sunset) prayers were especially important. When I asked my mother why they stressed it so much when we prayed four other times each day, she explained that it was the only time the whole family was together and it was nice to pray in unison. But to me it was the most inconvenient time to pray, as I was usually off gallivanting with my friends. I distinctly remember playing hide-and-seek in our spacious apartment grounds or flying a kite on the roof when the call to sunset prayers echoed faintly from some distant minaret and I blatantly ignored it. My mother would shout my name from the balcony or send someone to look for me while my friends and I hid in our favorite spots and giggled like conspirators as the poor servant girl searched in vain.

When the sky had drained all its color, I would nonchalantly saunter home, armed with a pile of flimsy lies—my favorite being that my watch had stopped working. Missing the sunset prayers nullified all the other times I did pray, according to my parents. But I only wanted to pray when it was convenient for *me*. "Why do I have to pray all the time even when I do not feel like it?" I relentlessly asked Mom. She would simply respond, "Because it is our duty as Muslims." Although I knew all the rituals and had a healthy dose of faith in God, I was skeptical about practice.

When I was eleven years old my family and I immigrated to Seattle, Washington, where it became harder to practice Islam, especially given the weak foundation I had established. I would wake up for school in the mornings with a low buzz ringing in my ears. It was the sound of silence. In Pakistan, I had been awakened at dawn by the rich commanding voice of the neighborhood *muezzin* singing the *Adhan* (the Muslim call to prayers). He would be joined by more voices, until their collective rhythms began to cascade in a melodious waterfall. It was this human alarm clock that impelled me to get up. After prayers, we would eat a breakfast of bread and English marmalade and fragrant steaming chai. Before I opened the door and sprang outside for school, my mom would make me say a prayer to Allah for protection and safety. It always gave me faith that someone was watching over me.

In Seattle, I rushed to school after a hasty breakfast of bagels and orange juice. It was a chore to wake up so early for dawn prayers. I thought God would understand that I was tired and needed to rest. After school, I babysat for our neighbor, so there was no time to pray. In the evenings, I would do my homework sprawled in front of the television while my parents silently prayed in the bedroom. They would chide me for my lack of practice, to which I would reply: "I will make it up before going to bed." Although it is acceptable to make up missed prayers later in the day, I had no legitimate reasons for skipping them. I simply couldn't fit prayer into my new schedule in America. It never occurred to me how far I had strayed from the principles of my religion because I still considered myself to be a Muslim in spirit. I even gave speeches about it in school and educated my classmates about Pakistan and Islam. I told them about the five pillars, among which prayers and fasting rank highly. When they asked me if I prayed, I replied less than truthfully, "From time to time."

Sometimes, at the request of my grandmother, my younger brother would perform the prayer call. He would stand in our living room and cup his hands behind his ears and loudly recite the Adhan. Our very own muezzin! I would halfheartedly bring out my prayer rug and go through the rituals. With my lenient family and no Islamic community, I had little motivation to change my ways. A few years ago, my parents bought a little clock in the shape of the holy Kaaba. It sits on their mantelpiece, programmed to sing the Adhan at the appropriate times of the day. But the sound felt fake and unbelievable compared to a human voice chanting from the top of a minaret. Whenever I heard the tape recording, I felt obliged to pray, but not moved to do so. "But isn't it better than nothing at all?" my mother would ask. I yelled my response, "It is so unreal!" and stormed out of the room. Late at night, when I was snuggled in my bed,

I would silently recite long Arabic verses and open my hands towards the ceiling and confide in Allah. My faith assured me that He was listening to me.

Two months ago, my parents performed Hajj, the pilgrimage to Mecca that all devout Muslims are expected to perform at least once in their lifetime. Naturally, my mom prayed for me: "O Allah, this daughter of mine knows everything about Islam, she even has more faith than I do, but she does not practice what she believes. O Allah, make her follow the right path, the path of practice, to prove her enormous faith in you." My mother is the most devout practicing Muslim I know. I was astounded to learn that she thinks I have more faith than she does, because I am far from devout.

Faith and religious practice are two separate things, and they are only sometimes related. In my case, my reservoir of faith is decidedly full—it is a living mechanism that I sense whenever I am in need of spiritual sustenance and guidance. When I was torn about deciding between two different graduate schools, I was in desperate need of guidance. So on a bright sunny afternoon, after an exhilarating run in the park, I performed a meditation exercise to get in touch with my inner guide. I did get an answer, one that really surprised me, but I acted on it with full confidence. I realize now that seeking out that guide was an attempt to reach out to God, to hear Him speak to me and to be receptive to His message. During pivotal periods in life, I believe my faith will lead me in the right direction. Faith is the internal radar between my God and me.

I suppose that praying towards Mecca is a form of communicating with God as well. But the highly formalized, ritualistic aspect of it diffuses the immediacy of my connection to God, which I sense so readily in my meditation. At the same time, while I am not a strictly practicing Muslim, and I don't play by all of the rules, my faith is derived directly from Islam.

My father says that without devotion to formal practice, I'm just a "part-time believer." One time when we were standing face to face in the small boutique my parents own, my father seemed to be in a talkative mood. I relish any opportunity to debate with Dad, so I casually asked him the same question that I've often asked myself: "Why do I have to do namaz even though I don't feel anything?"

He looked at me with kindness and, as if addressing the small child I was once, he replied, "Because it is your obligation to show Allah your gratitude for all that you have, for without Him you wouldn't be here!" I furrowed my brow and said, "Yes, but I do thank Allah all the time. Why does it only have to be through prayers?"

He tried to relate to me, "You know, when I was growing up in India, I used to feel much the same way as you. But when I would walk past a mosque and see masses of people praying diligently, I began to wonder if they were all just a bunch of idiots to pray to a deity they could never see, or if I was the idiot not to."

"So you thought there was more to it than meets the eye?" I retorted.

"Of course there is," he replied. "When devout Muslims pray, they are professing their belief in Allah, they are submitting to

His will, which is the essence of Islam. What makes you think that only you can get away with it? What makes you so special?" he countered.

"But I don't always feel the urge to pray!" I nearly cried. "It seems artificial, like an order I must obey or else I will be punished."

"Yes, it is like an order," my father gently stressed, "but once you get used to it, you feel more connected, more complete as a Muslim. If you count yourself as one, then you cannot avoid prayers, or else you are not a true believer."

"That's not true!" I fumed angrily. "I am a believer!"

"Then why don't you pray consistently?" he asked simply.

Why not indeed? I ask myself.

In my early twenties, I struggled to pray at least twice a day, but I still felt like a robot going through the programmed set of motions. At least I felt less guilty. When I was twenty-eight, I developed a deeper intellectual interest in the history and culture of Islam, which left me with more questions than answers about the roots of my heritage. So I departed for a personal quest to the heart of the Islamic world—the Middle East—where I spent over a year traveling solo and living in Egypt, Jordan, Lebanon, Syria and Turkey. I went there to find out if practicing Islam really is the crux of the religion or if there is more to it. I also wanted to know how faith factors into the equation, and whether or not it is independent of practice or intertwined with it. It seemed logical that my immersion in Muslim countries, where the proliferation of mosques and throngs of worshippers are so visible and dominant, would make it easier for me to embrace praying.

Allahu akbar, Allahu akbar!
Ash-hadu an la ilaha i-Allah
Ash-hadu anna Muhammadan rasulu-llah
Hayyia 'ala salah!
Hayyia 'alal falah!
Allahu akbar
La ilaha illa-llah

God is most great, God is most great!
I testify that there is no God except God
I testify that Muhammad is the Messenger of God
Come to Prayers!
Come to Salvation!
God is most great
There is no God except God

One day, in a chaotic covered bazaar in the traditional Islamic quarter of Cairo, the din and the crowds became unbearable, so I dodged into a back alley that faced an ornately sculpted mosque. All of a sudden, a loud crackle emanated from the loud-speakers at the top of a slim minaret and a man's voice began to sing aloud in drawn Arabic syllables. I sat down on the pavement and listened intently to the clear and commanding voice, the heavy and ancient words. I had heard the same melody and the same phrases repeated five times a day from the neighborhood mosques around our house in Pakistan, but this was the first time I was so close to the source itself. It sent shivers down my spine. It made me cry. It had the tone of a divine wake-up call that reminded Muslims to take a break from their business, schoolwork, shopping, exercise or any other daily activity and spend a few minutes with God.

Then I began to notice other things. I witnessed shopkeepers who went through the motions of devotion, dutifully going to their local mosques five times a day, all the while cheating their customers and betraying their friends. In fact, many of the most strictly practicing Muslims I met seemed primarily concerned with an overt display of their piety and lacked virtues such as honesty and integrity.

My landlady in Cairo was a prime example. She was always swathed in a thick white scarf. Whenever she dropped by my apartment unannounced, she gasped in horror at my loose, uncovered hair, sometimes forcing her eyes shut and refusing to look at me in my "unholy" state. To her, as to many fervent Muslims in the Middle East, the *hijab* (scarf) is a huge symbol of Islamic devotion. Without it, I might as well be walking around naked and pronouncing myself a non-believer. I knew right away that for her, the external props of religious zeal were just as important as (if not more important than) my internal faith. She would routinely ask me how many times I had prayed on a given day, and insisted on finding me a teacher for study of the Koran. I knew she looked down on me because I did not bother to put up with appearances like other Muslims. She always went to the trouble of pointing out that her only concern was to "help poor fellow Muslims." But she would insist that I pay rent two months in advance, even when I wasn't sure if I would stay that long. If she just wanted to "help me out," then why would money be such an important matter? But to her, money was everything. Even when I lost my job and decided to leave Cairo earlier than planned, she didn't reimburse me for my unused portion of the rent. Her idea of a "practicing" Muslim did not put much emphasis on practicing human decency and kindness and having faith in others; it was mostly a matter of labels.

I was disappointed. I had hoped to find a wholly faithful and devout Muslim culture. While the struggle between my bounty of faith and lack of consistent practice was problematic for me, it was equally troubling to see people on the opposite end of the spectrum, with a high degree of practice but a low dose of faith. I was sure for the first time that practice isn't the only important part of Islam and that it does not always bring with it a deeper sense of faith.

That isn't to say that I never experienced the intersection of faith and practice during my travels. One frigid spring morning when I was in Bursa, Turkey, I forced myself to leave the cozy warmth of my bed at 5:00 A.M. Outside, it was cold and dark, the city still slumbering, except for those few souls who mustered the strength to answer God's first call to duty of the day. I covered my head with a large scarf and walked across the street to the Great Mosque of Bursa, where I took my place with the other women and began the dawn prayers. Bowing our heads towards Mecca, we murmured the virtues of Allah. It was a rhythmic dance of the devout. And I was among the believers, supremely in harmony with my faith and my practice. It was a moment of wholeness in which I was truly at peace with myself. When I was praying in that Turkish mosque, I felt *spiritual*. I had found that elusive intersection of faith and practice. I don't experience that sublimity every time, but I derive strength from striving for it and some level of peace just knowing it exists.

What I realized from my pilgrimage is that it doesn't really matter if I am surrounded by a hundred mosques or none, or if I live in a Muslim country or not. For me, faith is intrinsic and personal and I will not find more faith simply by engaging in prayer rituals. It became clear that I would have to find my own solution. Muslim countries would not provide me with any easy answers.

After spending nearly two years abroad, I returned to my home in Seattle. The United States. An entirely different planet from where I'd been living. I knew that it wasn't going to be easy to return after experiencing the warmth and simple joys of Middle Eastern culture, but the American in me was longing to return to the land of rugged individualism. I enjoy its freedom, opportunities and choices, even though it is those very freedoms that have fed my struggle between living my life as I please and adhering to the demands of practice imposed by my religion.

The oldest Arab mosque in Seattle is always overflowing with worshippers on Friday afternoons. Though I've lived in Seattle for over twenty years, it wasn't until after I returned from my pilgrimage that I attended the mosque for the first time. As I stood there, wearing the black-and-gold embroidered *abaya* that I had purchased in Damascus, my hands almost detected the fine particles of sand still embedded in this garment that had traveled with me from the Middle East to Seattle. I began to marvel at the universality of the prayer ritual: I was reciting the same Arabic words, doing the same sets of prostrations and wearing the same type of clothes as I had in the Middle East. I realized at that moment that even in America, I could be close to Islam if I wanted to. I could be close to Islam anywhere in the world, as long as I had my inner faith.

Lately, I am starting to notice a slight shift in my attitude towards practice. I try to pray more often just to see how that works out. But I can't and won't force myself. My one and only prerequisite for prayer is desire, which is not a constant. A part of me wishes that I were not so wishy-washy about practice. But that would defeat the whole purpose of praying with meaning. It would return me to my childhood, when prayers were purely a ritual. My new desire to pray stems from a need to heighten my spirituality. Now I pray because I want to, not because I *have* to. I know that I may never consistently pray five times a day, but when I do pray, it brings me a sense of inner peace and calm, as beneficial as meditation. My prayers are becoming less an enforced form of ritual, and more completely the gateway to Allah, which I can access whenever I wish to seek advice, gain comfort or nourish my soul. I'm not forcing myself to connect when I don't feel the need to connect, and, for me, this makes the times when I do pray feel more sacred and less rehearsed.

I'm not here to reinvent Islam. I am simply finding the components within that truly resonate with me. For me, spiritual balance is more important than rigid devotion. Breaking free of that devotion gives me the space to revel in my faith, in a way that forced adherence to rituals never has. The melodious call to prayers, the Adhan, still echoes and vibrates somewhere in the deep recesses of my mind. I have heard it countless times, in dozens of countries—timeless Arabic verses in crystal clear notes, floating high above the minarets. Five times a day, it reminds Muslims of practice *and* of faith, the voice of the muezzin urging the devout to cast aside everything and submit to Allah. It is my call to faith, and I am answering it in my own way.

Daughter of a Preacherman

Andrea Richards

The Father

Just six months ago, I made my family exceedingly happy by becoming an honest woman. I married my long-time live-in boyfriend in a Christian wedding. After five years of "living in sin" we decided to tie the knot, not from external pressures, but for our own personal reasons. (I assure you, even after getting hitched, my husband and I are still real good sinners.) We chose a Methodist church in our home state of North Carolina and I asked my father, a Southern Baptist minister, to perform the ceremony. One of the stipulations for getting married in a Christian church is that all readings must be scriptural. Despite this, I sent my father two secular passages I wanted to use in the ceremony, one from Walt Whitman, the other a poem by Rainer Maria Rilke. My dad pointed out the discrepancy, and I countered his concern by stating that for every gay man in America, *Leaves of Grass* is a sacred text. His chuckle was a good sign, but I worried his initial skepticism would evolve into full-blown offense by the final stanza of Whitman's "Song of the Open Road":

> Camerado, I give you my hand!
> I give you my love more precious than money,
> I give you myself before preaching or law;

117

Will you give me yourself? will you come travel with me?
Shall we stick by each other as long as we live?

I knew my father would approve of the passage's enthusiastic tone and its anti-materialist stance. I knew he would find the metaphor of travel apropos, even a bit groovy. But as an ordained minister, and the type of fellow who treats minor traffic violations as acts of serious criminal behavior, he would have to be bothered by the line about preaching and law. Whitman's eloquent dismissal of organized religion and social order in favor of coupling would simply not fly in the house of the Lord. I readied myself for battle because the piece felt essential to me and my husband-to-be, an alternative vow that we both wanted made at the altar. This wedding was about us, after all, and we believed in love, individual freedom and the open road far more than religious dogma. I committed myself to not compromising. I was getting married with Walt or not at all.

My ultimatum didn't matter. I never even had the opportunity to voice my dissent. I'd forgotten what father I was dealing with. This wasn't the dualistic, sin-obsessed guy I'd reacted to in swellheaded Sunday school lessons—this was my dad, the same man who gave me battered Camus books and a file on existentialism he'd saved from seminary when I, at age fourteen, inquired into the "death of God" thing.

Don't get me wrong, my father is resolute in his Christian faith and devoted to his denomination. He's a Southern Baptist through and through, which is why we agreed to have the wedding completely dry. (You can imagine how perplexed some of the guests were as they looked for the bar.) But he's not the stereotypical tyrannical, self-appointed morality squad, and he's no stranger to religious dissent. In the last thirty years, the Southern Baptist Church has become one of the nation's fastest-growing Protestant religions, and the movement within the denomination towards religious fundamentalism and the political right has been divisive. Ministers like my father who take a theologically moderate position have quickly become a minority in what's been called the Baptist Battles, and like all those who hold minority opinions, they are rarely heard in the mainstream. But such misfit Southern Baptists do exist, and they allow Whitman and Rilke to share the same stage as Ecclesiastes in the holy sacrament of marriage.

My sister is also a moderate Southern Baptist. She's an ordained deacon at a Baptist church in Chapel Hill, North Carolina. Her church recognizes homosexual unions, ordains women ministers and basically makes radical fundamentalists rabid. Most of my extended family members are Baptists of varying degrees. Some are moderates and others are of the don't-shop-at-Wal-Mart-on-Sunday variety. After my grandfather's death just a few years ago, I found out that, although he'd attended a Baptist church all of his life, his official church membership was with a Presbyterian congregation. This revelation shocked me—*but we've always been Baptists,* I thought. If nepotism could secure entrée into religious salvation, my plot in heaven would have been secured a long time ago.

Growing up as the child of a minister makes you a ready-made rehab case. At least that's what preachers' kids are led to believe from a very early age. It's almost like being a Kennedy—at birth you are set up to flounder on a very public scale. But unlike a Kennedy, there's no real glamour to your demise. The preacher's kid is just a pawn, sent to test the clergy in their commitment of living a life close to God—a little horny hellion in the house of the Lord. That's the first and most popular expectation we PKs must negotiate. The second is the B-side success story, which is just as limiting: you will inherit the faith of your forefathers and wind up a hallelujah chorus girl. Thus far, I've failed at both paths. I wasn't suspended from high school or kicked out of college, I never lit a doobie during youth group (because, for the most part, I wasn't there) and I didn't participate in activities that involved prison time. Basically, I was a good kid hindered by an inability to keep a beat and a distaste for group activities.

Let me add another element to the mix. Not only is my father a Baptist minister, he also spent twenty-three years in the military as a Navy chaplain. This double whammy of growing up beneath two potentially repressive regimes really raises eyebrows when I talk about my childhood now. For a while, we lived on base and awoke every morning to the regimented sound of a cannon being fired. At dusk, if the volume on the TV was low, you could hear "Taps" while watching *The Cosby Show*. Interspersed between these regular noises were loud booms of artillery fire. Marines were playing war, often in what felt like dangerous proximity to our standard-issue tract home. For fun, my friends' parents would take us out to fields full of tanks and miscellaneous large pieces of artillery and let us play on them.

But even as a military brat, I was a misfit. Though my father volunteered to go to Vietnam, he hates confrontations. To this day, my mother has to do all the returns after Christmas. There was never a real gung-ho tough-guy sentiment in our home, nor was there the rigid discipline that kept my friends' houses so spotlessly clean. *Their* fathers made them meticulously order the sock drawers and performed a weekly dust-check on furniture by running their standard-issue dress-white gloves across cabinets and dressers. Battered copies of *Please Understand Me* and weekly family counseling sessions were more my family's style. And of course, being good Southern Baptists, there was nary a drop of liquor to be found in our home, which also made our household distinct. My friends all had the luxury of their parents' ample liquor cabinets to sample from. Of course, I eagerly helped them, out of curiosity and out of desperation to do something, anything, wrong. Why desperation? Because instead of a clear-cut despot, the three-headed Hydra I needed to rebel against—church, state and my parents—mostly just confused me.

Though there was never any question that I would be required to attend church on Sunday morning, I was never entirely sure what I'd find there. Religiously, the military is a diverse group, and my father's job was to minister to all of them, even though he was ordained as a Southern Baptist. Sure, there were rabbis, Catholic priests and Buddhist monks on the base, but basically every Protestant—Methodist, Episcopalian, Baptist, Disciple of Christ, Lutheran, Presbyterian and Other—went to the same church. This diversity within the congregation enabled an easy acceptance of religious pluralism. By the time I was twelve, I'd received an eclectic sampling of most Protestant and

Catholic traditions. I could recite the rosary, dance with the Greek Orthodox on their Easter and take Communion in three different styles. Not bad for a Baptist girl.

The Son

As a preteen, I liked poetry, my sister's Adam Ant LPs and Jesus. Though it was the Reaganite '80s, my father was fond of quoting a Kris Kristofferson song in his sermons, the 1972 hit "Jesus Was a Capricorn." Even nowadays, when the spirit moves him, Dad is apt to sing a few stanzas at the pulpit. But my father is a military man, so despite his love of peace, he's no ex-hippie, nor is he especially liberal politically. Theologically, however, he is a moderate who believes that the primary message of the Bible is the revelation of Jesus Christ as the Savior to the world. For him, it is a message of love, forgiveness and social justice. And as a kid listening to his sermons, I thought he made Jesus seem like the coolest guy ever—a rabble-rouser who fed the hungry, helped the downtrodden and had mercy and love for prostitutes, gamblers and heck, even murderers. I knew this Jesus wouldn't bat an eyelash at a tattoo. Yes, Jesus was dangerous: he was a threat to the established powers-that-be, and he challenged the foundations of government, religious practice and social hierarchy. In short, this was the sort of fellow I wanted to hang with.

So at age thirteen I walked up the church aisle and gave my life to this way-cool guy. I accepted the Lord Jesus Christ as my personal savior. That's what Baptists do. We don't baptize babies; there's no sprinkling at birth or confirmation classes. Unlike in other Protestant and Catholic traditions, in the Baptist church you don't need a priest, preacher or any other type of holy person to tell you what the scripture reveals or to serve as intermediary in your talks with the big man upstairs. Instead, you have a personal experience with the Holy Spirit and accept Jesus as an individual, on your own terms and when you are moved to do so. It's very DIY, and, in comparison to other Christian faiths, a little wacky in its non-hierarchical set up. These theological differences may sound slight, but such radical departures got early Baptists a reputation as Puritans-gone-mad, and they were kicked out of the Massachusetts Bay Colony.

When you feel "called" to be baptized, you commit yourself publicly to the faith in a ceremony where you are fully immersed in water. Some folks do this the old-school way, in a creek or river, but nowadays most do it in a small pool located somewhere within the church expressly for the purpose of baptisms. Suffice to say it's not for little quick dips in the hot Southern summers. This ritual washes the believer clean (figuratively and literally if they've chlorinated the pool recently) and s/he emerges from the water as a new person in Christ. At age thirteen, I was ready to be this new person. Of course, I had no knowledge then of how many other new persons lay dormant inside of me. These identities would emerge later in life as new ideologies opened themselves up—religious, political, social and intellectual ones. But I was a Baptist first, though I hardly knew what that meant—a feminist, post-structuralist, socialist, punk-rock-whatever, later.

● ● ●

The Holy Ghost

When my father retired from the military it was difficult for my family to adjust to civilian life. We moved, for the final time, to a small town in North Carolina. The racial and religious diversity I'd grown up with came to a screeching halt and I had to contend with a new high school, populated with what I quickly dismissed as a bunch of hicks. Everyone was white, Christian (if not Baptist) and had known everyone else since grade school. It was horrifying to a transient like me. And unlike the microcosm of the military, this civilian world was marked by vast differences in social class. Sure, officers made more money than enlisted Marines, but it was nothing like the economic stratification in this New South suburb, where relocated Yankees working for IBM maneuvered their new Audis full-speed past decaying mill homes that still housed the sons and daughters of sharecroppers. With the rapid movement of military families from one base to the next, kids never have the time to build cliques in school. You simply hang out with whomever is there, and hope their fathers won't get transferred to Okinawa before your birthday party. This New South was still old enough to have history, families that had known one another for generations, houses that were so old they actually fell down. And the Baptist churches were so big they took up entire city blocks.

I found myself mixed up with a whole new breed of Baptist. There were church groups at school that, since I had no friends, I joined by default. First of all, I found out that there were big differences between my faith and other Christian ones—the least of which was this whole baptism thing. Catholics, whom I'd grown up with, were practically pagan according to these new ideals. They made a big mistake by worshipping saints. And that transubstantiation thing I was so fond of was completely off—Communion was just crackers and juice and it really didn't need to be done so much. Having a relationship with Jesus wasn't about just talking to him when you felt down or writing righteous letters on behalf of Greenpeace, I needed to put my faith into practice by saving souls for him. Plus, I needed to feel the Holy Spirit working daily in my life. (Most of the time, all I felt were hormones.) And oh yes, the world was coming to an end.

It's an odd sensation to wait for an apocalypse more than once. In high school during this Holy Spirit, nearly-friendless phase of my life, my one friend Erin and I waited for the world to end twice. She was reading the book of Revelations in her bible-school class and filling me in on the highlights. We were ready to see some shit go down. My father would have none of this—he'd made one trip inside the church Erin attended and declared it too full of fire and brimstone. I believe it was the preacher's elaborate description of demons devouring sinners during the children's sermon that turned him off. On the other hand, I was comfortable with this extremely conservative theology. Perhaps it had to do with my loneliness, or my lack of patience. As a teenager I went crazy with waiting—to get breasts, to get my driver's license, to grow up. Immediate apocalypse promised a permanent release from the humdrum of daily teenage life. My plea for Erin was similar: she was an undiagnosed ADD case who was happy when anything out of the ordinary happened. Together we were a team hoping for cosmological catastrophe.

Fortunately for us, a particular fundamentalist Southern Baptist "scholar" had assigned a specific date for the world to end, the dead to arise and judgment to be passed on all mankind. We were elated. Hanging out in Erin's bedroom, listening to REM albums, we would discuss pestilence, plagues, Outback Red outfits, the two beasts, the fall of Babylon and how cute Tony Santori was. These were the concerns of good Baptist girls about to encounter their final hour.

Sometime in the late '80s was the first false alarm. Needless to say, we were pretty bummed out when the apocalypse didn't happen—the stress of living as if judgment on our eternal souls was imminent had exhausted us. We felt ripped off. So when news of the next one came, we agreed to be less fastidious in our preparation. Sure, we would try and save a few souls here and there, and not sin quite so much, but the Holy Spirit wasn't speaking to us as clearly anymore. Not without insurance on this apocalypse thing.

Part of our prep work had involved going to a nearby Fellowship of Christian Athletes camp for a little leadership and evangelism training. Neither of us were legitimate athletes, but what we lacked in physical abilities, we made up for in spiritual fervor. We had been chosen by our school's chapter to attend the camp, and spent a week staying in the former facilities of Black Mountain College—the legendary experimental college that closed in the late 1950s. Here, on the former site of one of the nation's most radical experiments in art education, we performed embarrassing icebreakers, communed with the Holy Spirit and learned to be better servants for Christ. Now I like to imagine that each night as we slept in there, the ghosts of Josef Albers, Merce Cunningham, Charles Olson, John Cage and Buckminister Fuller mingled around with the Holy Spirit some. Once again, no apocalypse came our way, although I did get a good tan and develop a mean backhand. By the time I got back home my interest in eschatology was over.

And maybe I did hear the wrong spirits in Black Mountain, because my interest in the avant-garde was just beginning. And this was a hobby my father and I could agree on—until I hit that dharma-bum phase in college. He took me to the art museum after I returned from my Black Mountain trip and I found rapture, though not the kind I was previously looking for, in modern art. Sitting on the hard benches of the contemporary gallery was not unlike the millions of times I'd sat on hard church pews, ignoring the sermon and daydreaming. Here was another sacred space where I could think of things outside of my own tiny existence. There were things I didn't understand—like that Franz Klein painting—and felt I probably never would. This sensation was familiar and unsettling, and before I knew it I was on the verge of another conversion experience. But this time the object and mode for the passionate experience was art. I was looking at a Rothko, no wonder.

My father encouraged my interest in art, which then grew to include literature as well. Reading could provoke reverie too, and like Sunday school class, a good book supplied me with endless questions. My father, the first to admit that he doesn't have all the answers and that in his Southern Baptist worldview there are still a lot of unresolved gray spaces, passed on to me his copy of *Zen and the Art of Motorcycle Maintenance* (which now I think of as a book all hard-up parents give their struggling teenagers). Unwittingly, he launched me into a two-year investigation of all things Zen. From him, I learned that religious devotion is not marred by critical inquiry, and that historical context and current politics inform interpretations of holy texts. So if I encountered an analysis I didn't agree with in a sermon, in an art museum or in the classroom, I should just read and study the primary text to come to my own conclusion. This happened often, and for me, literary criticism took on the power of religious salvation.

I gleaned that there were many ways of reading a single text, and unresolvable contradictions in life and religious belief, and I slowly developed an appreciation of the many mysteries in both. Because of this, I am inevitably drawn to spiritual seekers. I'm not alone in this propensity—all the PKs I know (like alcoholics, we find one another quickly) are similarly inclined towards mystical crackpots, recovering religion addicts and sincere soul searchers. Though most other preachers' kids are, like me, skeptical and questioning of their religious tradition, they nevertheless are even more suspicious of the irreligious—the folks who have no tendency towards belief. Because that's what truly boggles my mind. I may restage my religious tendencies by becoming a zealous vegetarian (not anymore!), a religious studies scholar or an evangelist for the entertainment industry, but there is a core, hot as lava, of religious fervor that I've inherited and continue to feel, in all its transformations.

When I return to North Carolina I am occasionally asked by my parents' more fervid friends to talk about my "walk with the

Lord." I try my best to artfully misdirect these inquiries. My parents' friends certainly know, via my parents' numerous prayer requests, that my faith has undergone many changes, and that as of now, I'm a very unfinished religious project. My father puts it most diplomatically: "You won't find Andrea at the foot of the cross." That is his polite way of saying all the juicy stuff—that I've opted to study religions from a secular perspective instead of a faith-based one, that I choose to spend my Sunday mornings at the farmers market reading the *Times* instead of at any church I always think of Emily Dickinson's riff: *Some keep the Sabbath going to church;/I keep it staying at home,/With a bobolink for a chorister,/And an orchard for a dome.*

I know these choices disappoint my father and family. For them, and especially for my father, church attendance is important, whether or not you agree with the specifics of a particular dogma. Fellowship is paramount to faith. He'd be happy if I went to any Christian church on a regular basis, Baptist or not. But I don't go, and there's no single reason why. My faith, as shifting and shaky as it may be, seems too personal to share with strangers and too in flux to fix at any one religious site. Should I go to the Catholic mass so I can light candles for my loved ones, or should I meditate for an hour at the Shambhala center? Neither feels completely like home, and so I stay home. I read a book or take a walk. I find my own sacred space and ritual, the farmers market and the *Times*. I even find fellowship with all the other geeky newspaper readers waiting in line for their coffee and eggs. The one time I do regularly attend church is when I'm visiting my parents, and I have to admit that when the chorus sings "Just as I Am", "Amazing Grace" or "Shall We Gather at the River?" I feel overwrought with religiosity. It is a homecoming in every sense of the word.

But it doesn't last. As soon as the song is over, I remember how far I've traveled away from this world. Yes, the faith I grew up in is still meaningful to me; it is such a part of my identity that I cannot ever fully separate from it, nor do I want to. I'm a believer all right, but by God, don't ask me to give you the specifics because every day it's changing. I'm not the typical badass or good-girl preacher's daughter, but then again, my dad isn't the typical preacher. And while he may be disappointed in my lack of devotion to his chosen faith, he tries his best not to let me know it. Which is, interestingly enough, a very Baptist trait—or at least a historically Baptist quality—to tolerate and respect all religious beliefs (even the absence of any).

My Dad and I talk shop a lot. I'm interested in his job, and he's always interested in whether or not I have a job. Since he and my mother live in North Carolina and I live in Los Angeles, most of these conversations take place on the phone, or occasionally by email. He is now serving as the interim pastor at a small Baptist church with a usual attendance of about eighty people, most of whom are senior citizens. It's a great gig, and my father seems to be enjoying his ministry. He is often out when I call. If I do catch him at home he is inevitably working on a sermon or prayer lesson—reading or writing, I suppose. Which is just what I'm doing most days too, although our texts do differ considerably. When I tell him he works too hard and that he ought to enjoy his "retirement" he tends to find some way to change the subject or shut me up quickly.

One characteristic that my father and I share in spades is that we hate to have people telling us what to do. Undoubtedly, that's why we both chose professions where the boss is, well, distant and invisible. I'm working on a piece about Eastern mysticism and early Hollywood film stars, and his latest project is to transform my childhood bedroom into a library and meditation cloister, a far less popular proposal than my mother's idea for a nursery for potential grandchildren. My vote is for his proposal. And I have no doubt that, when he gets past the construction phase of this project, he will, with a smile I hope (but at the very least with a smirk), place my old Buddhist texts from college somewhere on his bookshelf.

The Church of Godly Men

Tanessa Dillard

I knew something was wrong with my church when parents starting forbidding their kids to listen to Amy Grant. To our congregation, this sweet, angelic woman—who for years had been singing her heart out for the love of God—had allied herself with Satan by recording some secular songs. In an instant, she went from gospel sensation to heathen prodigal daughter.

In the '90s, my Baptist church still preached against rock-'n'roll. By this time, Christian artists had crossed over into rock and rap music. From what I could tell, they attracted more kids to church than traditional evangelism. Music didn't seem like an issue worth complaining about, and the church's inability to keep up with the times amazed me.

I began to wonder why the church focused on the issues it did. A disproportionate number of the sermons seemed to be about the sins of contemporary American society, things like pop music, sex out of wedlock and, in particular, out homosexuality. Of course, there were plenty of sins occurring within the congregation, scandals on every pew. But we never talked about those.

The holier-than-thou attitude of my congregation wasn't my only source of conflict.

The subtle racism and sexism I experienced within the church began to burden me as well. I endured a some-of-my-best-friends-are-black sermon, complete with a nod to my family in the third row: "We love y'all." It seemed our Southern preachers had brought their conservative values with them to the Pacific Northwest.

The church didn't consider its sexist traditions oppressive. Females were simply asked to be "virtuous women." "We're going to celebrate the baptism tonight, so women, get baking and bring some cakes and cookies." It was God's plan for women to be subservient (which apparently includes performing all food-preparation tasks), something to do with Eve in the Garden of Eden. "Why do the women always have to bring the food?" I'd complain. "Why can't women be preachers? Why are the women in charge of the nursery?"

"That's what the Church believes," my parents told me. It was an issue I'd let go of, because I knew the attitudes would not change. In other words, I shut up and ate the cake.

Over time, the homophobic messages within the church grew stronger. I wasn't even sure what being gay meant. It would be years before I would have any gay friends or meet someone who was openly gay. I felt spiritually drawn to defend homosexuality, not because I knew anything about it, but because I knew my church despised it. They talked about gay people the way overt racists talk about black people. In a weird way, the attacks stung me.

My idea of Christianity did not include hate; my favorite hymn was "They Will Know We Are Christians by Our Love." My parents were teachers. During many summer road trips to Texas, they sacrificed hours of traveling time to help strangers on the side of the road. Even though I'd been brought up in a Baptist church, I fantasized about converting to Catholicism and becoming a nun. I wanted to take a vow of poverty, spend my life in the service of others. I dreamt of becoming a saint.

By the time I reached my teens, I officially hated the church I'd been raised in. After all, this was an institution that once put on a slave auction! I isolated myself from my family in the back pew and only pretended to sing the hymns. My mind was mostly on boys and clothes. Even though I paid little attention to the sermons, I became alert when certain things were said.

"The Bible says . . .
Homosexuality is a sin . . .
They say it's not a choice . . .
We love the sinner, and hate the . . ."

Every time I heard these messages from the pulpit, my head became heavy and twisted.

In our church lived absentee fathers, a child molester and alcoholics, but sermons frequently focused on homosexuality, the sin that seemed not to apply. I fought the urge to shout in protest, while everyone else agreed, "Amen." I was powerless and outnumbered.

My parents did not have such strong feelings about homosexuality. The issue was not a part of our immediate lives. No one in our community, in our church, was gay. My parents insisted I not focus singularly on homophobic messages, but try to find at least one redeeming quality in each sermon. My mom had taught me to put others before myself and suffer silently, and that idea was supported by the Church's belief that women should serve but not speak.

So, in silence, I practiced my own brand of spirituality, which had little to do with church. It was about me talking to God in the school halls or reading a poetic passage from the Bible at 3 A.M.

Before I left home for college, my pastor provided me with the name and number of a sister church in my college town. Little did he know, I had something else in mind. I was longing for a more open-minded community. From time to time, I went home with college friends and visited their churches. The store-front black church where people danced, fainted and spoke in tongues; the Armenian church where people switched over to English when I came to visit; the contemporary church that rocked out every Sunday in a high-school gym. This church had its own band and themes like "Easter Unplugged." I avoided Baptist churches, because I knew they tended to be conservative. Part of me wished to find a black church, or at least a multicultural one, where I would never be singled out for my race. Every church I visited seemed wrong for me. Too racist. Too sexist. Too homophobic. No matter how friendly the people or how great the choirs, sooner or later what I'd hoped was my religious utopia turned out not to be, when a sermon conflicted with my ideals. I packed my spiritual bags and moved on. I did not like the idea of being a church-hopper, but I couldn't seem to find a home.

Even though I couldn't find a church where I felt comfortable, my faith in God hardly wavered. I believed that spirituality meant more than putting on a skirt every Sunday. I devoted my time to volunteer work, playing with children in a women's refuge and mentoring a boy who had always wanted a sister. I read the Bible regularly, seeking my own meaning. If I needed guidance, I closed my eyes and opened the Bible randomly, picking a spot with my finger. There, I hoped, would be my solution. Sometimes life's answers came to me in dreams. But as much as I valued my personal spirituality, I wished to share my private joys with others.

Nearly a decade after leaving my parents' home, I moved to Chicago to perform full-time service in AmeriCorps. I shared a room with a stranger in a housing co-op in Hyde Park, not far from the University of Chicago. There, I ate my fill of the house's vegan meals and slept on a box spring, since I could not afford a bed. My housemates were artists, activists, musicians and students. Only three of the twenty I lived with defined themselves by their religions—Jewish, Buddhist, Catholic. Mostly, the house had an anti-religious, and specifically anti-Christian, attitude. It was hard to share my spiritual side without coming across as the enemy. "Is that a Bible?" someone might suspiciously ask, observing the thick book on a table or shelf. I felt ashamed, both for putting my spirituality out in the open and for having kept it so guarded it surprised people.

House debates frequently involved berating Christianity, and many times I agreed with the arguments made. Over time, I noticed that the people who were most outspoken against the religion were people who had grown up in conservative churches like mine. I never attended church during my year in AmeriCorps.

I worked in a three-story elementary school in an impoverished community. There were security guards on every floor. There, I tutored third graders in reading, and referred to myself as a tutor rock star, because of how the children treated me. Every day, I fulfilled my mission of doing good deeds. Being swept away by the aggressive embraces of children each morning, or sharing my exotic fruits with them at lunch, I felt a little like Jesus, Mother Teresa or at least Arnie, the guy at my church who gave kids motorcycle rides.

After devoting myself entirely to volunteer work, I felt more in touch with my spirituality than ever. I had convinced myself I was doing God's work, not the government's. Leaving the children at the end of the year left me with a spiritual void. I was ready to go to church again, I decided, or at least to start looking.

Early that summer, while walking on the U of C campus, I made an impromptu visit to a bookstore. The bookstore was housed in one of those gorgeous brick university buildings often pictured in campus brochures. Its narrow-pointed roof and heavy wooden doors made me think of an English church or castle. I discovered a chapel upstairs, a small church with stained glass windows and a great portrait of Jesus. On a table by the entrance, I picked up a pamphlet that looked too good to be true: ARE YOU LOOKING FOR A CHURCH THAT . . . cares about the environment, fights for social justice and accepts people of all races, sexual preferences and religious backgrounds?

My internal answer was a resounding "Yes!" I made a note to

myself to visit that church sometime, even though going to new churches always made me feel like I was on display. But within a few weeks, I found the courage to go to the church above the bookstore. Anxious and a few minutes late, I walked in the building and up the spiral stairway. There were no other latecomers, no other people around. The bookstore was closed.

A smiling man greeted me at the door with a hug. He looked weak, youthful but aging fast, with a sunken face and sores on his body. My immediate thought: AIDS. The man seemed happy, which surprised me. If he truly was sick, I wondered how he could find peace. I wondered how he could stand at the door and offer himself so freely. It was a full and powerful hug, the kind people give friends they haven't seen in a long time. Even my friends rarely hugged me that way. It moved me that he welcomed me without knowing me. In all my years of Christian worship, no one had ever hugged me upon entering a church. The man handed me a program, and I found a seat.

I immediately noticed that the congregation was small, not more than twenty people. It seemed even less, with one guy at the pulpit, another playing piano, an amazing choir of five— four men and one woman—and the rest of us scattered in chairs. I started to think . . . *no, it couldn't be.* The multicultural congregation was predominately male; the men were paired off, some holding hands. *Oh my God.* The pianist wore a sleeveless vest and jeans. He and I were the youngest people there. He looked like a calendar hunk, blond spiky hair, tan, probably worked out. Then there was the pastor, a tall clean-cut man in his thirties who wore a red robe. *Everyone here is gay.*

After the welcome, the pastor asked us to greet each other. I stood tensely in my row, hoping this minute would breeze by. I watched men circulate, giving each other hugs or kisses on the cheek. Several people made their way to me in that brief time, including a cheerful black man and the woman in the choir. People wanted to know all about me: where I lived, what I did for a living, how I found out about the church. Their attention empowered me, because it seemed sincere.

The service was traditional. There were prayers, scripture readings, choir selections, offerings and a sermon—just like there always been in the church where I'd grown up. On the surface, the greatest difference between this and the churches I had known was that the people praising God were unapologetically gay. But the members of this church were also more open and welcoming, and they seemed to revel in their faith in a way that I found inspiring and refreshing. I felt more comfortable here than I'd ever felt in the church of my youth.

Like me, these people were outsiders in a society that looked down on them. What made it all the more amazing was that they were devoted Christians. Their gayness made them distinct from other Christians, while their devotion to Christianity distinguished them from other gay men. They marched in gay parades and they prayed for their enemies. Instead of abandoning their spirituality, they created a religious community that incorporated their gayness. Their example inspired me to stay true to everything I believed. They made Christianity seem appealing to me again.

The pastor greeted me after the service. "I enjoyed the message,"

I told him. I had said that to many a pastor as a child, but this was the first time I truly meant it.

On my walk home, I stopped outside a campus dormitory to process my experience. It was sunny and warm, so I chose a bench under an overgrown tree. I felt overwhelmed with joy. Never in my life had I witnessed such sincerity in a church. The congregants' kindness to me felt like a reward for my acts of kindness to others. The church program had read, "Welcome home." At last, I had found a church where my heart could rest.

Every Sunday that summer, I walked to the gay church. I continuously left my house in a rush and arrived a few minutes late, like I had on my first visit. By the end of the summer, the man who had welcomed me with the hug was no longer able to attend services. He was sick, the pastor shared with us, though I never heard more details than that. The people became familiar, and we called each other by first name. I looked forward to their hugs and kisses. Being nurtured in that spiritual environment helped me to be a more tolerant person. I decided to let go of my resentment of the church I grew up in. I focused instead on my gratitude for the church I'd discovered. There, I regained the spirituality I had long lost.

After leaving Chicago, I continued to feel inspired by the men's faith. Because of them, I'm becoming the kind of virtuous woman that I could never have envisioned in my youth—strong instead of subservient, loving instead of judgmental. Each day of my life, I strive to be the kind of Christian that they showed me was possible.

The Playhouse and the Altar: Householder Buddhism

Liesl Schwabe

The alarm goes off at 3:45 A.M. More often than not Pico, my two-year-old son and the world's lightest sleeper, wakes up too. I fold him into a ball and try to get both of us back to sleep, as my partner Justin dresses silently in the dark before going to make coffee in the kitchen and beginning his meditation. Sometimes I can smell the incense in my sleep.

Pushing Pico's stroller through our Brooklyn neighborhood to the park, my mind drifts through the grocery list, the names of friends I should call, the books I wish I had time to read. I suddenly remember that the *Vajrasattva* practice I was doing during Pico's nap was interrupted by his waking up before I got to the 108th recitation that would make a full *mala*, or Buddhist rosary. I exhale and begin to mouth the 100-syllable mantra. It is a practice of purification, of trying to uproot the seeds of negative karma, from this lifetime and previous ones, before they have time to come to fruition. I keep an eye on the traffic lights and the walk signs and Pico's bagel. Just as I do while sitting on my cushion at home, I visualize the Bodhisattva Vajrasattva above the crown of my head and a tranquil clarity filling my body, replacing the heaviness of faults and inconsiderate actions. I see the darkness of hurt and misunderstanding blowing away. I am working on letting go.

Later that night, on my way to table 10, I size up the couple from halfway across the room. I decide she is trying too hard to ride the eighties revival and he is too eager to impress her. I know they will know nothing about wine but act like they do, and all I can hope for is that he springs for an expensive one. I'm also jealous that, presumably, they can go out for $100 meals without having to also pay for a babysitter. Catching myself, I stop. By the time I make it back to them with glasses of water I am focusing on not being so judgmental, so bitchy. I make an honest effort to look them in the eye, to be patient and, as she takes a moment to decide between the blackfish and the cod, to genuinely hope that they are happy and well and peaceful.

Tibetan Buddhism is the foundation on which I try to build my intentions and my actions. It is a dynamic path, as pliable as it is unchanging, as comforting as it is harshly practical. I find the wisdom and the realization that have been passed on over the centuries to hold immeasurable integrity, selflessness and joy. It is my hope that working to ground myself in an awareness of this wisdom will be of benefit to others. Coming to the Dharma has been a blessing that I now cannot imagine life without.

I first went to India as an eighteen-year-old college student and studied the Vipassana, Zen and Tibetan traditions, the three major branches of Buddhism. For several years, before really committing myself to the path of Tibetan Buddhism, I explored and dabbled. I found a meditation cushion small enough to stuff into my backpack. I maintained a half-assed sitting routine for years, but had yet to feel a real connection to any specific practice or teacher. I read a bit, spoke much less and was uncomfortable in my search—always feeling as if I should somehow know more than I did.

The summer after I graduated from college was, probably not uniquely, a thorny time in my life. I wrestled with an overabundance of undirected energy, unsuccessful job hunts and general notions of inadequacy. I was dealing with a heart-wrenching breakup and a fast-expiring sublet. My feet were far away from the wandering and suffering of my mind and I was terrified to put one foot in front of the other. Then one sticky August night, in my fourth-floor apartment, I cried on my borrowed futon and the closest thing I've ever experienced to a vision came to me. Somehow my memory had conjured up the Eight-fold Path, which I had not given much thought to since my return from India several years before.

In Tibetan Buddhism, the Eight-fold Noble Path is a rough outline of maintaining awareness, in the present moment, throughout one's practical and daily life. Right view, right intention, right speech, right action, right livelihood, right effort, right mindfulness and right meditation. I blinked and stopped crying. My mind jerked forward like a rusty gear starting to turn after years of abandonment. I realized I hadn't been giving any thought to my speech or my intentions or my view. If anything, my words had been harmful and my objectives selfish. I'd been obsessing over livelihood, but more in terms of salary and cool title than impact or repercussion. I thought about effort and how I'd been spending every last ounce of it on trying to make things different than they were; holding on tightly to what had been before, but no longer was; and failing to accept that romantic love, like all emotions, is transient and fleeting. I climbed to my Brooklyn rooftop, decided it was time to leave New York City, return to India and make more vocal to the world my need for guidance.

The next fall, on the night the Yankees won the World Series, my cheeks were red with bad airport-bar wine as I paced the Korean Air terminal. I was with an old friend from college who himself was returning to India. Justin was going to continue his own practice of Tibetan Buddhism, which was already quite regimented and focused. He spoke to me about his connection with his teachers and his commitment to the Dharma in a very approachable, practical way. Nothing New-Age-y, nothing exclusive, nothing spacey.

As we flew away from the sun and through twenty hours of night, he was turning from transcontinental chaperone to close friend, as well as the first person I had really been able to talk to about spirituality in terms of what to *do* and not just what to *think*. I began to recognize that *doing* is ultimately what spirituality comes down to for me. Nothing going on in my head mattered at all if it wasn't translating to how I lived, what I did. There was a spark of wanting to make change happen. I scrapped my plans of making it to Calcutta alone and went with Justin to meet his teacher, a reincarnate Lama, or *Rinpoche*.

It is a necessary thing, I believe, to admit to not knowing. I realized over the next few weeks, while attending the Rinpoche's teachings on the foundations of meditation, that I really had no idea what I wanted at all, in my life, of myself, in the bigger picture or the smaller. I had always been on the go, moving with the seasons and preoccupied with travel plans. Living in the future tense, every makeshift mattress on the floor was a stepping stone, but there had never been a river bank on the other side where I could stop to dry my feet. I never took the time to be still, though no matter how fast I went, it was always the same anyhow.

I also realized that I was standing on the cusp of adulthood, perhaps even already in its throes—making my own decisions, aware of my accountability and quite unsure what all of that should mean. Aiming to embrace and deepen my understanding of Tibetan Buddhist philosophical cornerstones like compassion and impermanence was, I quickly came to believe, the way for me to grow up with some sense of priority.

I remember saying to Justin one night as I was deciding all of this, that I had not yet in my life experienced any real times of sadness or loss. I thought that perhaps it was wise to become more familiar with my own mind and attachments now, in order to make dealing with unforeseen trouble later on easier to handle. He looked up at me with a grin.

"Not only that," he said. "Practice enhances your ability to take in joy." I thought of the Dalai Lama and of his infectious laugh and of Bokar Rinpoche's gentle smile and obvious lucidity. I knew Justin was right.

Perhaps on some level I had been skirting the issue for years. I'd always considered myself "spiritual" (whatever that means). I'd come to India twice now on the proverbial quest for enlightenment—or at least the path towards it. Here, following the steps of the Buddha, I felt the devotion I'd known my whole life surge and grow and begin to take root. As much as everything was new, nothing felt unfamiliar. I had told myself during my first trip to India, maybe as some kind of procrastination, that I would know when the time was right to commit to one teacher. Even as an eighteen-year-old, my eventual arrival in the Dharma seemed inevitable. This pull towards the teachings of the Buddha had been snowballing for years. I'd been talking, talking, talking about all this *stuff.* Finally I was in a position, with the guidance of a teacher and a community to support me, to dive in and be quiet.

My decision to begin practicing the teachings and philosophies I'd been toying around with intellectually for years was definitely a beginning, but it was not so much a departure. It made sense to me in a way I have a tough time chopping up and squeezing into words. There was no revelation. There was no one, single moment of clarity or discovery. It felt more like an unfolding, like trying to begin to learn how to use a tool with which I could become more true to myself and more understanding of others. I needed to back up, to start at the beginning, to accept that I was alive on this planet and no one was going to tell me what to do next or how to find fulfillment in the weighty blessing that is this lifetime.

While the activity of quiet meditation—in which one allows one's mind to rest in its natural state of expansive clarity while regarding thoughts as waves in the ocean or clouds in the sky— is the ultimate essence of Tibetan Buddhist practice, Tibetan Buddhism also involves using mind, speech and body in conjunction *together* to cultivate more awareness and devotion. To try and be still with one's own preoccupied, afflicted, wild-monkey-in-the-jungle mind is a rather sweaty, boring, crazy, pins-and-needles mess. There are tools, like mantras and visualizations, that help keep people like me, prone to impatience and distraction, more focused on the task at hand.

My first phase of intensive practice was the start of 111,111 prostrations. For monks and lay practitioners alike, prostrations are the first part of what are known as the "preliminary practices." These four practices are specific to Tibetan Buddhism, though they build on the insight-meditation efforts of watching one's mind that are common to all traditions. Prostrations are physically demanding. One begins standing, with hands together in prayer above one's head, then moves the hands to the mouth and then to the heart before lying down completely, nose to floor, and getting up again.

As this is happening, one also visualizes one's enemies and one's loved ones, as well as all sentient beings, limitless as space, prostrating simultaneously. This helps to break down the preconceptions and emotions that prevent compassion and wisdom from dawning. The visualization focuses on the Refuge tree, which is an enormous tree with branches and limbs enough to hold up all the Buddhas (there have been many, over all the eons and in all the directions), Lamas, Bodhisattvas, Protectors and written and spoken words of the Dharma.

During the course of each prostration one recites, in Tibetan, the Refuge prayer. Essentially, this provides acknowledgment that we all tend to look for protection from the things that scare us—sickness, death, loneliness—but that ultimately, no one can protect us. Only as individuals practicing the Dharma, devoting ourselves to realizing interdependence, can we begin to see the endless cycle of attachment that causes suffering brought on by sickness, old age and death. This is why it's called Refuge, because we arrive, as one does when seeking refuge, as if our life depends on it. We come to the Dharma joyous, grateful for its truth. We come to the Dharma determined to embrace and actualize in full awareness of the Buddha (enlightenment), the Dharma (the path) and the Sangha (others who help along the way).

During this time I spoke very little. I was more alone and less lonely than I'd ever been in my life. As I went up and down and up and down in the frosty pre-dawn darkness, through the sunny mid-afternoon heat and into the mosquito-filled dusk, I began to accept myself. As someone who'd grown accustomed to trying to do ten things at once, without the attention span to last for even one, this was a very new way to live each day, repeating a single activity over and over. I did not know at the time how long it would last, how long I would last. I purposefully tried to stop looking ahead. This time provided an immeasurable understanding of the way each day can become so much more important when one is rooted in an ongoing awareness of the preciousness of human existence.

37,000 prostrations into it all, I found out I was pregnant. In some ways, this is where my practice really began. Or at least got put to the test. All of a sudden practicing Buddhism was no longer just about being on retreat, in India, far away from responsibility, living off a small savings account and having the luxury of spending my days alone at the temple. All of a sudden notions of interdependence were no longer theoretical. Interdependence in action was making me fat and nauseous, as I tried to understand that something that was part Justin and part me was growing inside me completely on its own, separate but not. Suddenly, thinking about the idea, as one does when trying to understand the breadth of reincarnation and karma, that we are to treat every other being with gratitude and compassion as if they had at one point been our mother was very different, as I tried to imagine myself as a mother.

I had known Justin for over five years at that point, but we'd only been romantically involved for a couple of months. While I felt his soundness and his wit would make him a dedicated father, I also knew that his understanding of the Dharma would be what would ultimately make becoming parents together the single most important and beautiful thing in my life. Determined to remain open in the face of uncertainty, we relied on the teachings and the blessings we'd received. Faith proved crucial. I started to realize that practice, like parenthood (as I would soon learn) is a work in progress, with an impermanence all its own.

We came back to New York City and went to work, Justin as a house-painter and I in an office. We got an apartment, set up camp, built an altar. Pico was born and we came to understand a whole new kind of unconditional love. We gave him his own last name, Dorje, which means "immutable" in Tibetan. We want him to know that as so much changes and unravels, there exists the indisputable clarity of mind, and that this clarity can be his. We stayed put for a year as our baby got big and learned to walk. Then, just after his first birthday, we took Pico back to

India. We wanted to return for our own continuation of instruction, but we also wanted to return for him, to further his own connection with the place where he found us. We wanted to offer our gratitude for the way karma had brought us together with our son precisely as we were trying to navigate and find the path of Buddhist practice.

Justin and I both believe that we can be Buddhist and maintain a close tie with our Lama from any place in the world. We chose to come back to New York because we want to raise Pico close to his grandparents and we want him to go to school in the United States. We have felt it best to have jobs and stability and a sense of home. Now that Pico is old enough to need his own plane ticket, it might be a while before the three of us get back there all together. But our life in the West is a delightful one, and the opportunities for practice are bountiful. The challenge is the same here as it is anywhere: to keep our practice grounded in our lives and to keep our lives grounded in our practice. New York City ought not to inhibit those intentions. The mind is the same despite geography.

Buddhism was brought to Tibet from India around 800 C.E. Since that time, along with the prevalent monastic and yogin traditions, there has also been a tradition of lay practitioners or householders, of husbands and wives and their children. Awareness of this history helps me to feel some sense of continuity, some sense that I am not too far off the mark. Right now, there is a Blue's Clues plastic playhouse set up in front of our altar, because that's the only place there's room for it. Pico knows how to prostrate and does so before playing with his playhouse, after putting his toy pots and pans inside to free up his hands. This is the integration I am striving for.

Just before leaving India last year, all three of us went to talk with Bokar Rinpoche. Both Justin and I had been spending time with him individually, to discuss the changes in our practice and the specific questions that had arisen. This last time though, we went to him as a family, to talk about what being a family meant. We hadn't even had the chance to ask when he started speaking.

"You have been very fortunate that you have been able to return to India and visit such auspicious places, to go on pilgrimage. But now," he continued, "it's time for you to go home. Maybe sometimes you will worry about money, but remember that for people who have more money, they only have more worries. Keep up with the practice you are doing, every day. Be good to one another." This last part got me. He couldn't be more right. We needed to remember this. Above all else, this is where the challenge could be the most difficult and all our practice would be for nothing if we could not be good to one another.

Tibetan Buddhism calls for compassion and wisdom in every moment. This means that while the quiet solitude of meditation is necessary for evolving as a practitioner, it is also essential to practice on the subway, at the playground or while waiting tables. In some ways it's easier to have compassion toward everyone while I'm sitting alone, in silence, on a cushion. It's challenging to feel compassion toward anyone while I'm carrying a stroller up three flights of stairs in a crowded subway station at rush hour and no one is stopping to help and the kid is screaming because he threw the Cookie Monster toy onto the train tracks and I know once I get above ground it's going to be raining. . . . But this is where compassion is necessary. This is where it's possible for me to grow.

The visualization maintained while doing prostrations changes the experience from simply going through the motions and muttering the words into a true embodiment of devotion, conviction and joy. I have found the same to be true in everyday life. Making cookies or pouring wine, I can see my actions as offerings. Taking a shower, the water and soap not only wash away the smells of restaurant work and changing diapers, but my anxieties over the way things should be as well. Going to sleep and envisioning my Lama at my heart, all of his teachings and all of his insight are with me, part of me, right here.

Raising a Family the Good Old-Fashioned Way

Juleigh Howard-Hobson

"Look—there is the Bee Goddess!"

My children run ahead of me, pointing to their favorite deco-
ration as we head towards a large labyrinth marked with bright
yellow string that coils upon itself in the warm spring sunshine.
I walk behind them, watching them waving their vegan corn-
dogs, trotting along on their skinny legs as they approach the
circle. It's mid-April, the sun is warm and the Earth Day festivi-
ties are in full tilt. We have already painted flags on reclaimed
cloth, made masks from recycled paper and eaten everything
from soy ice cream to organic Indian curry. We have saved the
labyrinth for last, as usual.

It is not just any labyrinth—we walk a special Goddess
labyrinth created by a local group of midwives. We wind
through it, walking a path around the outer wall, then entering
a spiral, then taking a series of turns that shift and re-shift our
direction as we approach the center. As we turn and re-turn, we
pass pictures of the Goddess in all her forms—as Brigit from
Ireland, as Isis from Egypt, as Hel from Scandinavia and as the
Great Mother from Malta. Sacred symbols of spirals, crescent
moons, bees and Celtic knotwork dot the area. I trail along,
savoring the warm sunshine, letting my mind and spirit sink into
the here and now of where I am and what I am doing. My

children stream ahead, now stopping to look at a blue ceramic coiled-snake figure, now darting off to inspect a piece of silk embroidered with images of three phases of the moon. They don't have to ask me what any of this means. They know. They have known the Goddess since they were babies.

Since before they were babies, really. When I was anxious to start a family, it was the Goddess to whom I turned. And she answered me very clearly.

Six years ago I belonged to a San Francisco Goddess circle that met once a month to create ceremony in the Ancient ways. This particular meeting was held under an oak tree, in September—the wind was starting to pick up a chill and the sky was just beginning to darken. We were meeting to meditate on deep questions—to look inside ourselves and find the Goddess within, holding the answer.

It was an emotional ceremony; the depth of unspoken questions cloaked the evening in a subdued tone. We stood first, holding hands to gather our women powers, and then, as we sat down, we were each given a thin glass-corked vial to hold. It felt crisp and brittle in my hands at first, like a cold interruption—but it fit so perfectly in the hollow of my hand that its chill melted to warmth in a matter of seconds. A small wooden bowl of seawater was passed, clockwise, from hand to hand. The bowl was deep, the wood was solid and the water was very cold and fresh—collected that day from the Pacific Ocean.

Each woman dipped her vial into the bowl while silently presenting an issue to the Goddess for clarification. For some women the issue was a single question, for others it was a mental struggle; still others offered simple wishes. As she did this, each woman collected some of the water, some of the essence of the Great Mother herself, to take away with her. My turn came and as I touched the vial to the water words rose unbidden, unplanned—"Am I pregnant? Am I pregnant? Please let me be pregnant." I had thought up so many lovely ways to present my issue . . . but these words came from my inner well and they sprang. They would not be stopped, so I let them pass from me to the Goddess unhindered.

A basket of colored ribbons was passed next, counterclockwise this time: purples, blues, yellows, blacks, pinks. I capped my vial and took a ribbon. The ribbons were to signify the answers—each one as individual as the woman who drew its colored length. As I wound my ribbon around and around the glass container of seawater in my hand, I had my answer. My ribbon was pink. It was a strange, electric moment. There was no sense of having "found out"—all of a sudden, *I knew*. I knew that I was pregnant. I knew, also, that the baby was a girl. The fact that medical science backed me up some weeks later was anticlimactic—for that golden moment when I held that pink sateen ribbon in my hand, I felt something on a molecular level that I had never felt before. I felt a certainty that spread from my mind to my soul without any lingering doubts or misgivings.

Mallory Nicole was born exactly eight months, three weeks later—call it old-fashioned faith, but I just knew she would be.

Since then I've had two more children—boys—and my life within my Goddess/pagan path has changed, twisting and turning like the labyrinth itself. I was very close to the Goddess before I became a mother—I was a member of a Goddess circle, I observed equinoxes and solstices with reverence and joy. But it was not until I entered parenthood that the power and significance of who and what I was—and what we were as a Goddess-centered family—really entered my life.

I planned my children's births in accordance with my Goddess-based beliefs. We were to have earthy, natural births, at home, in quiet celebration of the life force within and without. When the labor contractions that I'd read about (and supposed would be a little crampy) hit my body, I felt like I was being torn in two. The midwives, two pagan women whose Goddess labyrinth this baby would one day walk, rubbed my back. They turned off the overhead light and they lit candles and incense. A huge sense of peace and calm hummed above them, interrupted—faster and faster—by my huge roiling contractions. I fought, I fumed, I didn't like that something so uncontrollable could happen to me—to me!

By the time I was told I could push, I was mad, too—nobody said it would hurt like this, like pressing down on broken glass inside my own self. Where was the beauty of birth now? In the midst of all that jumbled electric pain the words of the midwives came through: "Let her go, let her go . . . let the baby go, Juleigh, let her go . . . she wants to be born now." They fell like a thick balm, these words, these words that included "she." These words that acknowledged that we all already knew the Goddess had given me a daughter, a daughter who needed to be born. A great yellow energy surge seemed to shoot straight down from the ceiling into my body—I pushed. I pushed and the energy shot itself through me. I could see the continuum of existence, I could feel the magnificent power of life giving life. I reached out and I touched the Goddess. Mallory was born in her arms.

After that, my relationship with the Great Mother, the Goddess, changed. I no longer merely admired Her. I had met Her.

I'm not saying that we live, happily ever after, in a state of heightened spiritual sacredness—we don't. In fact, when push comes to shove, sometimes there is very little of the ritualistic or the observant in our day-to-day lives. My husband and I get up and drink our coffee while the kids pile out of their beds and jump on the couch. We wrangle with questions about more cookies, who's got the right to use the Thomas the Tank Engine track first and who may skip a bath (usually no one). Sometimes, in the crazy day-to-day chaos of raising three kids, it seems like we only celebrate our spiritual path on our holy days. Luckily, the pagan path has plenty of them. Eight times a year (at least) we acknowledge our faith in some way—on the solstices, equinoxes and cross-quarter days, which fall on or about November 1 (Samhain, our new year), December 21 (Yule), February 2 (Brigit), March 21 (vernal equinox/Eostar), May 1 (Beltain), June 21 (summer solstice/Litha), August 1 (Lammas) and September 22 (autumn equinox/Mabon).

Our celebrations now are usually quiet ones, private family observances of the circle of the year. For some, our children help make small personal altars. For our ancestor altar at Samhain, we gather up acorns, dried cobs of corn and mementos of late family members. Framed photographs provide a backdrop, and the children add other elements: their great-great grandmother's pin cushion, my grandfather's wristwatch, a family spoon, an academic medal. The altar is small, we place it on a tiny table by the fireplace—but it serves as an annual reminder of those who have made us who and what we are, those who are now departed. It helps mark the passage of one year into the next; it helps keep the thread of life from fraying.

"I look like Great Uncle John," says Andrew, closely studying the old-time paratrooper portrait of his great-great uncle, who died in World War II.

"Well, you might look like him," Mallory concedes, "but Grandma says that Ian acts like him."

Our children are growing up fluent in the names, faces and personalities of their heritage. It is a strong anchor in a world that sometimes seems hectic, connectionless and lost.

Some of the altars are impromptu, as in Mallory's dresser-top tableau of winter. She removed her Hello Kitty clock, her ballerina jewelry box and her collection of cat figurines from her dresser. In their place she put pine cones, a branch of a pine tree and small shiny things (to represent ice) such as an antique perfume stopper, a cut-glass bowl full of clear marbles and silver bells on a white cloth. She placed a full row of rune stones (as they come from Norse Scandinavia, they are well-acquainted with chilly seasons) around the glass bowl and arranged a small brass reindeer, a plastic snow rabbit and the Hindu god Shiva (well-wrapped in a small "cloak," as he is used to warmer climates) around the stones. She did this in full knowledge of the symbolic reasons for each item; her little brothers watched her.

There was more reverence and love in her altar than in any crèche scene I had ever helped my non-pagan parents assemble. It was amazing, it was holy, and it was the best Yuletide observance we have ever had.

A particularly personal celebration for our family is the summer solstice, Litha, in June. Traditionally, this longest day in the year was marked by burning bonfires, or sending flaming hoops of wood spinning down hills. The Goddess (sometimes with her son, the Sun) was welcomed like this by groups ranging from Hopis in North America to ancient Egyptians in Northern Africa—a hot celebration for the swelteringest day of summer. We don't do that, but we do have a barbecue in the yard with a few of our pagan family friends. It so happens that Mallory's birthday falls right around the solstice (again, I must marvel at the ways of the Goddess, to whom I looked for this child) so we have a birthday/solstice party day of it. We use the sun as a theme and so far Mallory has been enthusiastic, although last year there was a request for a Barbie ice-cream cake. We compromised and decided that Barbie could, maybe (just maybe . . .) fill in for the Goddess, if the icing was yellow to symbolize the sun. It was a smashing success, even if the Goddess did look a tad skinny and sallow.

Still, sometimes I worry that, even with the solstice and equinox celebrations, the children are not absorbing enough of the old ways. I worry that we don't celebrate or observe our spiritual sides enough, on a day-to-day basis, living as we do in the midst of so much new-worldliness. Sometimes I wonder if it is possible to raise earthy pagan/Goddess-centered children in a world where my own actions compete with things like grandmothers bearing Christmas gifts of robotic puppies, Barbie dolls and Disney-themed sweatshirts (and yes, I said "Christmas gifts"— they do that—they even say, "Merry Christmas . . . oops . . . I meant Yule" with dependable regularity), and where even pagan birthday parties yield American Girl dolls, Hot Wheels and the inevitable videos.

But then, all of a sudden, the children will do or say something that makes me realize that under the trappings of contemporary life, beyond the mundane day-to-day childhood stuff, they do have a firm hold, a deep inner grasp, of exactly what we have tried to give them.

"Mom?" Andrew asked me recently, "Would Luke Skywalker know the Goddess?"

I thought for a moment. He'd caught me unawares: there I was, mundanely peeling an onion in the kitchen, when suddenly I had to think back: Luke Skywalker . . . Jedi Knight . . . Yoda . . .

"Of course, but they would call Her 'the Force,'" I answered.

"Oh yeah," Andrew said, going back to whatever it was he was doing.

Mallory then turned to me and said, in the conspiratorial whisper of the eldest child: "Mom . . . you told him they would call the Goddess 'the Force' because he is only four, but when he is six, I'll tell him that really there is no Force, only the Goddess, okay?"

"Okay," I told her.

She smiled—and I went back to the onions, smiling too.

Of course, we exist in a diverse world and inevitably, sometimes we just bump shoulders. Take, for example, the time that the serene holiness of Mallory's winter altar did not prevent it from disturbing, visibly, a mother who happened to attend a playdate at my house. She'd just joined our homeschool co-op and asked if she could join in on our regular playdates. "Of course!" was our reply—and so she came, children in tow.

My house was full. Two pagan/hippie homeschooling families and one Waldorf-school family were playing at full tilt by the time she arrived, so I didn't notice her reactions to our Goddess flags on the patio, the sweet collection of South American Goddess figures lined up on the mantel or our huge stone Buddha of Compassion, who contemplates in the flower bed much like I do. As a matter of fact, I thought nothing of her arrival, except—Ah! More kids!

At first she sat on our couch and chatted a little. After a while she got up and walked over to our bookcase (hard to miss our copies of Monica Sjoo's *The Great Cosmic Mother* or Merlin Stone's *When God Was a Woman*). Then she walked into my daughter's room, where her kids were playing with the others.

All of a sudden she was making excuses to leave, her face marked by frosty, frantic determination as she hustled her brood into their jackets and out our door. She barely remembered to crack a smile when she said her goodbyes.

Mallory later told me that this mother had asked what "the stuff" on the dresser was, and somebody had answered that it was an altar to the winter spirits (that must have been one of the

Waldorf-school kids). We later found out she was similarly troubled by the Harry Potter LEGO set. She has since joined the Christian homeschooling group.

Luckily, the kids were merely amused by her reaction. I watched them carefully, fully prepared for questions about intolerance or fear—but they had none. Long, long ago we discussed the world and its religions and how some people—individual people—just don't like things that are unfamiliar to them. Some people even hate or fear anything that is not the same as what they're used to.

"But there's so many different things in the world," Mallory puzzled, "countries, skins, food, goddesses . . . "

"Winter altars, Samhain altars . . ." continued Andrew.

"Yep, well, that's the problem—there're a lot of things out there and lots of them are going to be different from you. You can either like it or lump it, really," I said.

"I guess that lady lumped it, huh?" answered Andrew. Then, before I could answer, I figured he had already dismissed it from his mind because he asked, "Mom, can you read us a book before we go to bed?"

"Sure—which one?"

And with an actual twinkle in his four-year-old eyes, he said "*Harry Potter,* we're up to chapter fourteen."

And that was that.

Mostly, the world's diversity is great. We have been very careful to show the children both the loveliness in their own lives and in the happy faith of their spiritual ancestors, as well as the great splendor of the human spirit. Every human spirit. And the children have responded well to this. My daughter has a small wooden Shiva (spouse of the Great Goddess Parvati) in her room. He reminds her of her dad, she says. She knows he is a Hindu interpretation of God, and she likes that. Our son keeps a very rotund ebony Maltese Goddess figure on his dresser. She was brought in there one night (taken from her more prominent place in the center of our living-room mantel) to help him feel safe from "scary things," which might or might not be lurking under his bed. He calls her Baba. Seeing as she now lives in the room of a four-year-old, it's not uncommon for bedtime to arrive with Baba missing from her post, only to be found sitting in the dollhouse or next to a Luke Skywalker action figure on the toy shelf. The calls of "Baba!?" are regular night sounds now, and I think she smiles every time she hears them.

The other night as I was tucking the kids in, Mallory said to me, "Baba is pretty old, huh?"

"Very old," I said.

"So she is eternal?"

"Right."

"Is Shiva?"

"Oh yes, we all are, really."

"Mom?"

"Yes, babe?"

"I like that the Goddess is eternal and that we are eternal—even though our bodies die."

"Me, too."

"Mom?"

"Yes, Mallory?"

"Will you tell me about when I was born, and when the boys were born?"

"I think you are leading me down a merry path, young lady—it's time for bed."

"A merry path—like the labyrinth!"

"Yes, exactly like that, go to sleep."

"I like the labyrinth, Mom."

"Good night, Mallory."

"I like the labby-inth, too, mommy!" shouted Andrew from his room.

"I like it, too, I love you all, good night, no more talking."

"Goddess bless, Mommy!" sang out Mallory.

"Goddess bless, Mommy from me, too!" added Andrew.

And when the baby added his own: "godda blegh" as I carried him around the room in ever-slower sleep-inducing labyrinthine turns, I thought to myself:

Goddess bless? She already has.

The Sound of God

Lisa Schiffman

I was a frog. I was a bird that squeaked. I could not, for the life of me, sing. My vocal range spanned approximately three notes. My voice was small, like a chicken's. Whenever I tried to sing I stopped again almost immediately, in mid-note, embarrassed by the weak, uneven, out-of-key trickle of sound that came from my mouth.

The whole issue came to a head on a Friday night. I tried the Shabbat service at Chochmat Halev, a center for Jewish meditation and learning whose name means "wisdom of the heart." I knew I'd have to peel off my shoes, sit cross-legged on the floor, meditate on command. By the end, I'd probably have to hold hands with strangers.

The place was packed. A boisterous crowd spilled out the door. Mounds of worn shoes blocked the entrance. Coats were mashed into all kinds of places. Inside, congregants covered the floor, sitting, squatting, and kneeling knee to knee.

I arrived just in time for the guided meditation, sat near the back. A woman in white tapped lightly on a drum and told a story about the Baal Shem Tov, the founder of Hasidism. Periodically, she'd pause and ask us to check in with our bodies: we'd concentrate on our breath, our posture, the way our weight shifted lower as our bodies relaxed. The room itself seemed to settle after awhile. The people around me began to sway, almost imperceptibly.

Then the prayers—songs, really—began. The energy in the room shifted. I've seen this phenomenon before. People seem to come into a service as individuals. They're separate, distracted, disconnected even, from the people around them. Then a choreography begins. The rabbi, or the cantor, or the layperson leading the service motions to the congregation. Folks lean over, pull out their prayer-books, flip to the proper page almost in unison. They stand up, clear their throats. They open their mouths and sing.

During the songs, a change happens. These individuals become something more. They become part of a whole, a community. They become part of a heritage, a civilization. They're connected by voice, by sound, by melody. Sometimes they become part of each other, part of whatever they call God.

I grew up in a family that denied God. When I was five and curious, my sister, stamping her foot, told me that God didn't exist. She was thirteen and both of us thought she knew everything. God was a lie, she told me, a fiction, something people a long time ago had made up.

Later that day, my father confirmed her verdict. He put his hand gently on my forehead. "My sweet, the idea of God is ridiculous," he said.

I'd inherited atheism. It wasn't a tradition I'd come by honestly, after struggling with and then rejecting notions of God. For more than thirty years, I'd lived without questioning that the world existed, that I existed, that beauty and sadness and pain existed without God. As amazing as it sounds to me now, I'd never thought to experiment. I'd never decided to live—for a week or a day or a moment even—as though God just might exist.

The man on my left leaned back then forward, lost in song. His voice was sweet, like a young boy's. On my right a woman held a sheaf of prayers to her chest as she sang. Her face was flushed, her voice throaty.

I tried. I really did. Every few minutes I'd screw up my courage to sing, only to stop, moments later, when I became aware of the sound of my voice. It came from inside me, from my most private place, and it was flawed. It was ugly. It was sour, like milk gone bad. It was me. I closed my mouth.

After the service ended, as I was rising to leave, the man next to me began talking. "The singing was really beautiful, you know?"

I nodded.

"The songs are what always brings me back," he said. "They touch me. They always have, even when I didn't know what they were all about.

"I guess you could say," he continued, shrugging his shoulders and talking more to himself than to me, "that they make me feel connected to God."

As I left the building, a small knot blocked my throat. Voice. Melody. Song. Each held answers. Answers about a deeper part of myself, about the essence of Judaism, about being human— and perhaps even about something called God.

I can't escape my New York roots. When I'm low they rise up

within me, yelling their wisdom. This time was no different. I was blue, a bit listless and unmoored for a week after the synagogue incident. At home, I realized that the only thing I couldn't do in front of David, after all these years, was sing. In the privacy of my car one day I took the plunge. I shut the windows, turned the radio up full volume, opened my mouth, tried to belt out a Van Morrison tune. No go. Midstream I heard myself, became conscious of my lousy voice, and shut down. I sat there, gripping the steering wheel, in a funk. That's when the voice of New York came to me. *When in doubt*, it said, *hire someone.*

Anna. This woman was a professional. Her flyer, which had the words *Life is Short: Don't take it too seriously* on the cover, described her as a voice and bodywork therapist. She did something called rhythm and flow work, along with sounding, healing, holistic drumming, and tantra. I had plucked the flyer from a bulletin board at the Transformative Body massage school, a place where people go with the hope of merging their spiritual and physical bodies—in the nude, usually, and surrounded by others. Their practitioners have excellent, if far-out, reputations. Anna had spent seven years as a bodyworker at the well-known Esalen retreat, eight years studying African drumming with a Ghanaian master, and eight years teaching voice and movement classes in the Bay Area. Could I trust her with my own voice?

I tracked down the head of the Transformative Body school. Waving the flyer, I said, "Hey—will you vouch for this woman?"

He looked up from his desk. Nodding, he stubbed out the end of a clove cigarette. "She's a standout," he said, as a thin stream of smoke began to rise from somewhere in the middle of his desktop. "Trust me."

I took home the flyer. I kept rereading the copy, which mentioned breath, healing, energy, and something called our primitive voices. Each time I'd finish reading the flyer, I'd toss it into the trash next to my desk. *Nope,* I'd think, *it's not for me.* Then a few hours later I'd walk back to the trash from wherever I was, sheepishly thrust in my arm, and retrieve it.

I finally called to make an appointment and soon enough found myself at her door. A tall, thin, graceful woman met me, introducing herself as Anna. She guided me inside her house, past conga drums and giant gourds, past a single whale vertebra so large I mistook it for a coffee table, past sunflowers that had dropped yellow dust in the shape of a perfect circle on the floor.

In the massage room, under the poster of Buddha, I stepped out of my clothes. When Anna turned to me and began to talk, I fervently wished I'd left on my clothes for a few moments longer. I tried to make it to the massage table with some semblance of grace but managed to bang into it before mounting.

She slipped a long silk scarf over my body. "I usually say a short prayer before I begin the session," she said. Her accent, I realized with a start, was German.

I felt her fingertips on my back. "Shall I say the prayer out loud or to myself?" she asked.

Oh no, I thought, *not a prayer.* I ticked off the possibilities: she'll invoke goddess energy, call upon spirit animals, or make an appeal to the universe.

"Out loud," I said. I wanted to hear it.

She began her prayer. "I pray that this body I'm about to touch has the wisdom to find what it needs. And I pray that I have the wisdom to step aside and allow it to happen." Her voice was melodious, as gentle as her touch. My breath deepened. My shoulders lowered.

Then she cut to the chase. "Every time you breathe," she said, pressing down on my feet, "I want you to let out a sound."

My chest tightened. "I don't breathe all that often," I said. "Bad allergies."

Her hands leaned into the backs of my calves. "Right," she said, laughing. "Look, all I ask of you is to exhale so that I can hear it," she said. "You'd be surprised at what can happen. Your breath is powerful. It gets things moving—energy, spirit, sound—it all begins to open."

She exhaled, ending with an ahhhhhh.

"Try it," she said. "Let out your song."

Silence.

"Go ahead," she urged. "Entertain yourself. Experiment. Play with the tones, pitch, and loudness of your voice."

My hands were ice-cold. My voice, like a pill caught in my throat, was stuck. Finally, a few sounds—nothing more than groans, really—escaped with my exhalations.

"Good," she said. "I heard that. Now keep going, keep breathing, keep making your sounds."

She let loose. Her own sounds were a form of enlightenment, or perhaps a kind of zoo. Trills, warbles, low moans, quivering growls came from the center of her body, from a place my voice had never been. I thought of a dog's growl, a crow's caw, a hyena's laugh. The effect was at once beautiful and unnerving. It was, I thought, a little bit insane.

"No way," I said, shifting my weight on the table. "Can't do it."

She bent over me, her palm on my forehead. "You should experience your entire range," she said.

I was startled. Voice had just become a metaphor for self-expression. When was the last time I'd played with the range of who I am? I concentrated, breathed in and out through my mouth, then reached for the breath in my gut. My voice escaped quietly, then unfolded together with Anna's, becoming louder, higher. Soon she took off alone, an infusion of sounds. She was a wind instrument, then a single plucked string.

She took her hands from my body but continued to make sounds. A strange thing happened next. My body moved as though there were small waves within me. Every sound she made invoked from me a physical response. It was as though my body was no longer connected to my brain. It was connected to her voice. We cycled through this odd, spontaneous call and response, with each of her sounds piercing me, then traveling like a ripple of water up and down my back, my neck, my arms, and my legs, making them undulate. Nothing existed for me outside of this moment. I was fully present.

Years earlier, a young Lubavitch man in Crown Heights had introduced me to *niggunim*, prayers sung without words. It was impossible to tell me about this, he said at first; it was something I had to experience. He pointed to my video camera and invited me to tape him. With the glare of lights on him and the camera a silent judge, he closed his eyes, opened his mouth, and sang. It was the sound of an ancient terrain, of escape from the everyday world. Words would have been an afterthought.

I realized then that voice has the power to enter your body. It connects you to yourself. It transports you to the intuitive world, to the divine.

After the session with Anna ended, she tried to tell me what my body movements had looked like from her vantage point above the table. She frowned, said she couldn't think of the English equivalent, and spoke a word or two in German. I stared at her blankly.

"Primal," she said suddenly, snapping her fingers. She swirled her arms in the air like snakes. "Your movements, they were reptilian," she said. She was beaming. I wondered if I should be pleased. Was this a compliment? I looked up at her, confused.

"You were in a state of grace," she said, nodding her head in affirmation.

Right. I'd just had an ecstatic experience. Either that, or I was going nuts.

Months passed. I saw Anna a few more times. She always began with the same prayer. Although my voice hadn't yet found its range, each session ended with the feeling that I'd just had a religious experience. Had I? A kabbalist, a Jewish mystic, might say I was receiving divine knowledge.

Rabbi David Cooper, in *God is a Verb*, talks about *tzippiyah*. The word was used by a twelfth-century mystic called Isaac the Blind to describe mystical awareness, the state we experience when the sense of past and future dissolves and we're totally in the moment. Cooper says that tzippiyah, when we ponder it, can lure us into a new way of relating to the universe.

Anna. She had brought me to a place where the past and future could dissolve into the present. She had touched me both physically and with her sounds. Through her, my body and my voice were becoming connected to my spirit. I began to believe that Anna could be my conduit to a momentary experience of God.

Artists—singers, dancers, painters—have always known these momentary experiences. Take the painter. All concentration might be focused, for example, on the act of dipping the brush into a palette and sliding it over the canvas. An hour of such concentration passes, and then, suddenly, the act becomes easy. A light enters the painter. For a moment, he actually feels that he's part of something larger than himself. Rembrandt spoke about these moments as times when he could feel a divine spark. He often painted ordinary people with an extraordinary light emanating from within them. Everyone, he said—every single person—has such a spark.

I went back to Anna.

In the massage room, as I took off my clothes, Anna began telling me about a disappointment. While she talked, I climbed onto the table, rolled onto my stomach, let my legs grow heavy. I lifted my neck, tilted my head upward to make eye contact with her. She was talking about Ben, a man with whom she'd been falling in love. She'd spoken about him before.

Her face was troubled. "It's over," she said. "Last night he told me he's committed to right breeding, to building a community of the right kind of people."

"Right breeding?" My stomach tightened. "He's obviously not Jewish."

"No," she said with an exhausted sigh, "he's not." She looked at me. "Are you?"

I nodded my head yes. "Didn't you know?" *Does it show?*

"I wasn't certain," she said.

"Yup," I said. "So just those two short words—right breeding— make me tense. I think of Hitler."

We stared at each other. "Exactly," she said.

She stepped back from me. "I want to tell you something about my past," she said. "I spent my whole childhood in a household of silence. I was born in Germany just after the Holocaust ended. It was a country of destruction and devastation. It had no soul. No one I knew spoke of the Holocaust, yet it was there. It was everywhere. You couldn't get away from it. I wanted to know what had happened, what really had happened, but no one would tell me. At home, I learned that I wasn't to ask questions.

"I grew up in a house of secrets," she continued. "It wasn't until I was a teenager that I learned the truth about my father." She leaned forward. "He was a Nazi officer during the Holocaust. High up. Powerful. After the war ended he was sent to prison in another country as a war criminal. I was born sometime after he was released.

"My parents always seemed worried, haunted. I could only guess at why. Were they afraid other secrets would be uncovered?

Always, there were whisperings I wasn't a part of. Always, I wondered what, exactly, he had done. And had my mother taken part? In any way at all?"

Her eyes became wet. "They were my parents, and I loved them. My father hadn't killed anyone. How could he? How could he be evil?" She stopped, looked at me. She was waiting for an answer.

The question assaulted me: How could anyone—Nazis, ordinary Germans even—have participated in the systematic torture and slaughter of six million people? Daniel Jonah Goldhagen, in *Hitler's Willing Executioners: Ordinary Germans and the Holocaust*, tried to answer that question. Early on in the book, he asked readers to imagine, just as an exercise, changing places with those Germans, performing their deeds, acting as they had. To do this exercise, he said, "... we must always bear in mind the essential nature of their actions as perpetrators: they were killing defenseless men, women, and children, people who were obviously of no martial threat to them, often emaciated and weak, in unmistakable physical and emotional agony, and sometimes begging for their lives or those of their children."

Yet these were ordinary men. Mornings, they shot Jews for sport, as though picking off rabbits in a hunting game. They held children by their legs and spun them round, smashing their small heads into brick walls. They made people dig their own graves. They turned the word *shower* into something unspeakable. Evenings, they went home, kissed their wives, drank their beers, tucked their daughters into bed.

"Your father killed people," I said. "That was his job, and that's what he believed was right. He was purifying Germany. You want to know how he could kill Jews? He believed that we were less than human. We were subhuman. We were animals." I said this as though I were reporting the weather. *The temperature will be fifty degrees today. Winds from the east.* Where were my emotions?

I have touched someone who has touched a Nazi. Her palms which have cradled my head, smoothed oil down my spine, been offered in pleasure, have been held by hands that kept a crematorium running. Or signed death orders. Her voice, which has merged with mine, entered me, has said *I love you* to a Nazi. We have shared not only touch and voice, things we could feel and hear, but molecules, atoms, energy too, the essential elements of ourselves.

I wasn't sure what to do, so I did nothing. Anna was still speaking—telling me the story of her parents, which was the story of herself and of a particular time in Germany—but I was only half-listening.

A tape was running in my head. I heard my father telling story after story of relatives, those who'd died in the Holocaust, those who'd survived Auschwitz and Dachau. Now he was describing the time his cousin Moses had looked up from the fields outside Cracow and seen smoke rising from the city. Moses had known at once that the Nazis were setting Jewish homes aflame. He hadn't yet known that the soldiers had first prodded families out of each house and shot them. It wasn't until he arrived home, breathless, that he saw his house burned, saw his family dead—his young wife, his two sons fallen side by side.

I was still naked. Anna seemed not to notice. My back was

getting cold. My breasts were crushed against the table. I pushed myself up onto my elbows. Why didn't I sit up, get off the table, and get dressed? Get the hell out of there? I was afraid she'd stop talking. Stop telling. The moment was delicately balanced. I was receiving a kind of confession. Did Anna want absolution? The whole scene could have been classified as alternative therapy: *Trained nude female listener wants to hear your painful life story. See her nakedness as a metaphor for your own vulnerability. Bare your soul. Nonjudgment is our specialty. Call for appointment.*

The air was charged. "Maybe everyone—each of us—has a capacity for cruelty," I said. It sounded bland, half-hearted, even to me.

Silence. We looked toward the clock and realized, with surprise, that more than an hour had passed. I wasn't going to be getting voice or bodywork today.

I had committed an enormous, undefined act of cultural disloyalty. The spirits of my cousins, my aunts, and my uncles would come back from the dead. They would visit me at night, their eyes large with dismay.

A sudden thought consumed me: *Anna, too, has suffered because of the Holocaust.* This thought was somehow one too many. I didn't want to examine its implications. I wanted to leave. I got up, finally. Got dressed. She hugged me, thanked me. She looked into my eyes, paused, and thanked me once again for listening.

"Of course I listened," I said, smiling tightly, still in her embrace. "What else could I do? You had me there, trapped in the room, waiting for my treatment." Something was wrong. I didn't sound like I was teasing.

I know why we tell stories. They consecrate moments, illuminate the dark. They make sense of our random lives. They teach us things we may never understand.

Anna and I looked at each other, uncertain, then broke the hug. I said goodbye to the woman I'd once thought could lead me to God. Then I left.

I couldn't go back. Something intangible had become perverted. Something that had been right now felt wrong. The few times I'd tried to call and make another appointment, my gut had resisted. Uncomfortable, I'd placed the receiver back in its base without dialing.

I ended up at congregation Sha'ar Zahov in San Francisco, Rabbi Litman's synagogue. The congregation offered niggunium services twice a month. I'd heard that these services were short, quite beautiful, and open to all comers. I arrived early, sat down, waited for the others to show up.

About ten other Jews came. We sat two or three to a pew, with dozens of empty rows behind us. We weren't a large force. I didn't expect we'd have a large voice.

Two women, Jhos and her life-partner, Bon, led the service. They sat up front, facing the rest of us. Jhos, straightening her prayer shawl, got right to the point. "We'll sing for about fifteen minutes; then we'll be silent for awhile; then we'll sing again. These niggunium, these chants, they'll open you up. You'll see."

She looked at Bon. Bon closed her eyes, leaned back in her chair, and began to sing two lines over and over. The sound was eerie, haunting. It was old Jerusalem. It was a bearded old

Hasidic man in a crumbling synagogue. It was a trail that I began to follow.

I joined in. I listened to my own voice. At first it was weak and sounded wrong. When the woman one pew ahead of me turned around I fell silent thinking my voice had somehow thrown her off. Not the case. A moment later I realized she hadn't been looking at me at all, but instead had simply turned to stretch her neck.

I began again. The tune caught me. I became interested in my voice, in how loud I could be, or how long I could hold a note. I noticed the roundness of it, heard when my voice began in my stomach and rose up, rather than starting somewhere in the back of my mouth. I sang high. I sang low. I breathed through some notes, held my breath for others. All I could hear was myself.

After a time, Jhos gave the signal and we softened to a close. Silence. For a minute I heard nothing. I noticed the inside of my head, the way it was pulsating. Then I found myself listening to the room. It was silent. Or was it? The emptiness was filling in bit by bit. I heard the creak of wood. The *shush* of clothes against a pew. From outside, a motor kicked in. A bus hissed. A woman shouted in Spanish.

There is no silence. It is all inhabited. It is dense with sound.

This is the sound of God. It will come at dawn, or at the first scattered signs of night. It will reveal itself in your body, true as an electric current. It will intoxicate you. It will be a point of punctuation; the beginning, middle, and end of an impossible narrative. It will be as fluid as yourself, forming and reforming, being born and then being born again.

Outside, the sky was dark. Outside, people were passing by the door of the synagogue. I began to hear their voices, each of them. In front of me, Jhos nodded and a new chant began. In front of me, a slender woman sang and her voice was a rose. Behind me, a large man sang—and his voice, it stretched the length of the city, it streaked the sky.

There, in the synagogue, I chanted. My voice raised with the rest. We were—each of us—lamps, inexplicably lit from within.

Worshipping In Color

Bernadette Adams Davis

For months I've been visiting a local Unity congregation, trying to figure out what they're about and whether the church's belief structure and teachings can help me break out of my spiritual rut. The church is predominantly white. I am black. But it doesn't seem to matter to them—I'm welcomed whenever I show up on Sunday mornings.

It is important to me to have a place to show up on Sunday mornings. While I can meditate, study and pray on my own, I miss the sense of community found in a church. I want from church the kind of connections and community not found in subdivisions and car-dependent towns and cities. And I know myself well enough to realize that I need some leadership for my spiritual growth and structure for my worship, praise and prayer. In searching for a space that offers that sense of community and structure, I've been caught between the sexist but culturally comfortable church tradition of my childhood and the often isolating option of crossing racial lines to join a more liberal spiritual community.

Even though I was raised in an African-American Baptist church, my visits to the Christ Church Unity congregation are not my first experiences with predominantly white, liberal churches. I started switching off between white congregations and African-American churches while in college in Atlanta. At my predominantly white alma mater I began attending the university's nondenominational chapel. It was there that I had my first regular contact with a female minister and a mostly white congregation.

A woman with authority in the house of God! Aside from her sermons, which were appealing because they weren't focused on punishment and sin, just seeing her in front of the assembly did so much to release me. I didn't have to watch every word for messages of submission and how I was not meant to lead. And, instead of acting as an unapproachable voice of authority, she was among students regularly. Hearing her message on Sunday, then having lunch with her on Thursday or seeing her at a women's retreat, made it easier for me to be a part of the community and think of church as a place of free, rather than submissive, women.

In the decade since, my most active period of church membership was with a Unitarian Universalist fellowship, where I joined the women's group, participated in services and built social connections in spite of its being a white-majority congregation. After college I moved to a small Southern town much like my hometown. Well aware of the racial dynamics of small southern towns, I was a bit wary those first mornings in the U.U. fellowship, because I wasn't sure how open-minded the people were. My concerns were assuaged as I was embraced as part of their community.

That church also had a female minister, whose egalitarian sermons allowed me to listen and think, not police and react.

Within weeks of my first visit to the church, I had lunch with the minister. At some point in our conversation she recommended I talk to another writer who was a member of the fellowship. I did connect with that writer, and the resulting friendship provided the sense of community I crave from a house of worship. I became involved with the women's group, participated in services and social events and was content to have the church as part of my life. I had found an open and friendly church, with a female minister and a feminist approach.

There was only one problem—race. It isn't that other members made an issue of my racial difference, because they didn't. It was my own desire for just a bit more comfort that sometimes distracted. I missed the ease of a familiar culture and a more diverse environment. Still, until I moved out of state, I let that longing take a backseat to hearing a positive spiritual message in a welcoming community.

My spiritual routine has fallen short of fulfillment in the years since I moved and left that fellowship. Once I identified my longing for some cultural comfort, it was harder for me to immerse myself in the Unitarian fellowship near my new home, so I spent a few years visiting black churches and sometimes just skipping worship altogether. But I had been hearing good things from African Americans about Christ Church Unity, so I began visiting a local Unity church.

During my first visits I found the church to be very open. Smiling faces and outstretched arms greeted me each Sunday. I felt peaceful in the church space. The prayer, meditation and messages in the services also helped foster a sense of openness.

The church itself is a bright place with two sanctuary walls of floor-to-ceiling windows. As I listened to the songs and messages, the view helped me remember the interconnectedness of God, the Earth and humanity. And yes, there's also a woman in leadership. She serves as an associate minister.

I feel an affinity with this church's broad view of where spiritual lessons and inspiration can be found. The Sunday-morning solo may be a Simon & Garfunkel song; the minister may to a mainstream film to make a point. This use of secular texts is important to me because I do not accept that everything that is not explicitly religious is harmful or destructive to our quest for enlightenment.

Still, although there are more families of color in this congregation than in any liberal white church I've experienced, I remain one of a minority in the congregation, and it was one of the first things I noticed. I am working on releasing my concerns about race and listening for the universality of the lessons, yet sometimes incidents wrench my focus back to what color means in that setting.

One incident that stands out happened in the church bathroom, between the message and the closing song. (In month six of my first pregnancy, I couldn't hold out until we held hands and sang our benediction.) As I washed my hands another woman joined me at the sink. She complimented me on my hair, which I was wearing very short and un-straightened. She was in the midst of saying how easy it looked and that I was wearing it well, when her hand was suddenly near my face, then touching my hair, right above the hairline. I drew a sharp breath and she took her hand off my head. I cannot remember what faux pleasantries we tossed as I walked out of the church's ladies' lounge, but I do remember this: my first thoughts were that she had just patted me on the head and was probably surprised at the softness of my hair. I remembered that my mother had told me years before, "you know they think it's like Brillo," as she explained why white people are astounded by the curly softness of a real-live black person's hair.

In that short exchange I felt my skepticism about being a minority in the sanctuary come rushing back. Instead of contemplating the sermon's message, which I can't even remember now, or staying to greet other worshippers, I walked into the sunshine with my mind stuck on some stranger. A woman who probably has no idea what little black girls are told about what it means to be a black girl and woman. Or what stories we've been told about what is and isn't acceptable in relations across the color line. In my mind there's a stash of stories about what white people think about our hair, and how they think we can all really sing and dance and get the spirit. Then there are the white liberals and their fascination with "black" culture, celebrating and exploiting once-bitter stereotypes and caricatures. And so I walked on, not wanting to become trapped in somebody else's idea of who a black woman is.

Am I overreacting? Is my own concern with race pushing me to a misreading of some woman's kindness? I thought about those possibilities after this and other incidents, and I have concluded that it is not an overreaction or some absurd hypersensitivity. In thinking about the dreaded hair-touching incident, I remembered myself complimenting someone on a hairstyle or some other aspect of their appearance. Only in the case of very good friends would I ever touch someone so intimately. Yet a stranger felt she could cross that line with me.

Such attention to race and the underlying messages in others' words and actions leaves me still outside, unable or unwilling to shift from a physical focus on the earthly identity of race to a focus on my spirit and whatever higher purpose I'm supposed to strive for. And as I struggle to be true to my black female self without separating from the diverse world, I always stumble when someone else's words or actions bring me back to the real racial differences that we face on Earth.

That racial divide was very clear to me growing up in a mid-sized Southern town. Though I started public school after integration, social and political issues about race still shaped the school system. And our churches were distinctly black or white, in addition to being Baptist or Methodist or any other denomination. Most of them are still that way, even though our schools and workplaces have been desegregated.

My mother and I were members of the same black Baptist church throughout my childhood. It is a central part of our community, and it is the space where I was baptized and married. The joyous praise of God, familiar liturgy and sense of community still draw me back.

The African-American congregation that has most recently drawn me—I am a two-church visitor—is a 3,000-member Baptist church that was founded in the late 1800's. Even in a congregation of that size, I felt at home right away because of simple comforts. I know the songs; the black Southern tone and traditions make it seem less foreign than the majority-white churches I've attended, more like some distant cousin of my childhood church. And it is still wonderful to me to join in a joyous gathering of African Americans, especially when I interact with so few people of African descent the other six days of the week.

This African-American mega-church makes full use of its size by filling the space with music and praise. Most Sunday mornings its contemporary black gospel (yes, even in gospel music there are differences that fall along racial lines). But sometimes a minister or member will lead us into an old song, something I might have heard at my great-grandmother's church, where the floors weren't carpeted and feet and hands sometimes provided the only accompaniment. I have often cried as the music or a fervent prayer reached its peak and reminded me of just what a blessing really is or how far I have come from some past valley of emotion. And in that context, where most of us share the same race, I don't have to worry about how my actions might affect or fit into someone's overall perception of African Americans. It's just us and we know one another.

One of the things I know from my black church experiences is that, joyous as the environment may be, there is often an attitude that women are the backbone of the church but cannot be the head of it. While I love the church of my childhood and the historical and cultural role of the black church in general, I am often uncomfortable with what is taught about women. Even today, in the congregation I grew up in, women hold none of the top leadership positions. They are trustees (deacons have the real power), deacons' wives, secretaries and Sunday school teachers, but never pastors or assistant ministers. It isn't too hard to figure out that the church's philosophy holds that we are somehow lesser.

In college I thought more and more about how the black Baptist church has a certain tendency to treat women as the lesser half. Women were not to preach in some churches, or hold certain offices (the ones that really make decisions, like deacons), and were expected to submit to male leadership. That made me angry, especially because women are so often the majority of the congregation.

In some sermons I found myself losing the message altogether because of one reference to women's place or proper role in the Church. Recently, at the African-American church I visit, I heard a minister preach that a man who finds a woman who will have sex with him outside of marriage "might as well put an apple in her mouth, because that's not a woman, that's a pig." I was shocked that he would make so clear his disdain for women and support for a double standard—there was no condemnation of the single man looking for a woman to sleep with, only of the single woman who consents.

What was more upsetting was that both men and women shouted amens and applauded his comments. I wondered if there were other women in the congregation who felt as sick as I did upon hearing his sexist words. Again, I was swept away from any focus on spirit and thrown back into my physical self;

this time, to my gendered self. How could I think about anything other than how biology makes me a dirty, wallowing creature who stands below men? I spent the rest of the service fuming, arguing against the minister in my mind. How can we accept that when a man and a woman have sex, she's the pig and he's just some innocent bystander? If we must continue to demonize sexuality (and I'm not saying we should) shouldn't we at least hold both genders equally culpable? But my hearing of such sermons has taught me that the same standards aren't applied to men and women.

The strongest messages I've received from some African-American churches are that women can be whores and Jezebels, wickedly sexual and disobedient, or we can be saintly pillars of the race, raising children, working hard and praising God, even when we don't have a partner's support. I find it impossible to believe that I'm more wicked than my male peers or that I succumb more easily to temptation. And I'm offended that women are supposed to wear themselves thin to be upstanding sisters, while we're still locked out of leadership in many African-American churches. And while I don't doubt this is also the case in more traditional white churches, those congregations don't have the cultural draw that makes me try black churches and even tolerate some of the woman-restricting rhetoric.

American obsessions about race keep most of us apart on Sunday mornings. The worship hour is still one of the most segregated times of American life. Even in the 1970's and 1980's, it was rare to see even one white face in my childhood church. In spite of everything that has changed, we still like to worship with our own people—and we tend to define our people as those of the same race.

My experiences tell me this is true for most churchgoers, but it is changing slowly. In some communities the churches are more diverse and in some denominations, where diversity is a priority, there are blended congregations and ministers are assigned without concern for whether they share the same race as the majority of their congregation. Still, I've yet to find the right mix of progressive rhetoric and diversity in the same sanctuary. Many of the more integrated churches I've visited or heard of seem to have very traditional approaches to religion that do not appeal to me.

I didn't experience predominantly white congregations until I went to college in Atlanta. I would not have considered going to a white church in my middle-sized southern hometown, especially not after years of learning about the civil rights movement and how white segregationists had followed slaveholders' lead in linking oppression with their perception of the will of God. But I had a vision of Atlanta, the black Mecca and New South capitol, as a more progressive city. And being on the college campus, which was fairly liberal, helped me not worry about whether the church would be some bastion of fundamentalist reactionaries conservative on race and gender issues. And so, in the early 1990's, I attended my first mostly white church. It felt less bizarre than I had expected, but ultimately issues of racial difference affected my ability to fully connect with the services.

• • •

Still, as much as I find fodder for race- and gender-based discomfort in the black and white churches I've attended, I must admit that some part of my barriers to connecting in any church are self-constructed. In many ways it is easier to focus on the earthly faults of the men and women around me than to challenge myself to reach a higher spiritual ground. If a minister slights women in his sermon, I find it easy to write off his message and that church's attitudes toward women. And when I feel isolated in my difference at a white church, it is easier to walk away than to push myself to focus on the spiritual messages or challenge church members' assumptions.

I fear that until I can release concerns about other people's assumptions, my praise and worship are empty, no matter where I'm sitting on Sunday. And my struggle is not limited to how I deal with being stereotyped by other congregants. In the black church I feel that my belief in my equality as a woman is not affirmed, and in white congregations I am so preoccupied by racial difference that I am closing myself off from a full spiritual experience. What I really long for is a spiritual place that helps me face and deal with these issues, rather than making me obsess about them even more. After years of wandering, it's my internal battle to find and express an authentic voice that keeps me swinging back and forth.

Or is my spiritual lesson more about not expecting too much? Is it even possible to find a congregation that fits all my specifications, or is it time to settle down, practice some Christian love and forgiveness and create my own space within a church? I will always miss something of the church I've imagined, where cultural comfort, positive ministry and egalitarianism exist simultaneously. Yet my constant border crossings have left me without a safe space. Instead of standing outside the church, waiting for somebody to take me in and make it right, I'm beginning to think I will have to walk myself in and *make* it work in my heart and spirit.

Making myself an insider will require some vision on my part. It's easier to point out all the things I don't want in my church than it is to visualize my dream church or accentuate the elements of a church that's almost there. I do know that I want the church to be diverse, with more than a handful of people of color. I want it to be so diverse that all of us are learning new things about culture and spirit from one another. In my vision the congregation would also be quite active, coming together not only for Sunday-morning services, but also for social and spiritual events throughout the week. And, knowing that diversity can sometimes present challenging situations, I would want us to face such things head-on. It would truly be a step toward unity if we could openly raise and address such issues, whether it's some perceived slight or a suggestion about modifying the service to include multiple cultural traditions. I'm still looking for such a place, or at least for a church that's close enough to my vision that I am comfortable staying within it and helping to make it the kind of spiritual space I've dreamed of.

Pilgrimage on Mission Street

Griselda Suárez

The temple of the Great Mother Goddess was destroyed during *La Conquista* of Hernán Cortés. In 1531, the Goddess appeared to her people and demanded a new temple. This was the beginning of a new spirituality for many natives and, hundreds of years later, for Xicanos as well. It has been a long journey of reclaiming.

It's 3:30 A.M. and I wake up to the beeping cell phone alarm. I get out of bed and walk to the bathroom. I set everything out last night: clothes, towels and flowers. I begin my ritual here. I am going to walk a pilgrimage on Mission Street. My destination is 24th Street and Alabama. I speak silently of my promise. It is December 12, *día de las mañanitas*—the day of celebration for the Virgen de Guadalupe. I pray to Tonantzin, Our Mother.

After I shower, I comb through my long hair and pray to her. The women in my family taught me that if I ever wanted to ask something of *la Virgencita*, I had to give something in return. As hair is highly respected in my culture, I chose to grow my hair when I moved to San Francisco as an offering for courage, enlightenment and patience. I wanted the courage to grow in a city away from home. I asked la Virgencita to guide me through my journey as an artist and help me find the path of *floricanto*, the enlightened way of my ancestors. I wanted to give in to my inner desire to write. I asked for patience when dealing with my family.

Now, in gratitude for my progress on all of those fronts, I chant a litany of praises to her:

> Oh Mother, guide me this morning as I walk to your temple. Protect me. Help me realize my compassion. This year you have helped me learn about love with my mother, my lover and myself. I have developed the gift of words that you have given me. I have survived in this cold city away from my family, and you have given me a new family. Praise you *Virgencita*, you have helped me give birth to myself. With your love I know that I am not alone. With your love, I wake up every morning.

While I pray, I arrange my hair in tight curls around the crown of my head and insert fresh flowers into them. I decorate myself for her. I am her daughter, and she is the Mother Goddess—we are an endless circle of life and love.

I moved to San Francisco almost three years ago, but I have no one to go with to today's celebration. I can't remember a December 12 during my childhood when I did not wake up at the break of dawn. It has been almost eight years since I last celebrated this day, and I am nervous to go on this pilgrimage. Is the celebration of la Virgen de Guadalupe the same everywhere?

Before I leave my apartment, I kneel in front of my altar and offer the braid of hair I cut off two weeks ago, when I visited my family home. I bless it with *copal* and then stand up and salute the four directions to bless my room: my north first, then my south, my east next and my west last. I give the braid to my Virgencita to honor all that she has given and taught me. I go to the kitchen to get my other offering, a bouquet of roses, which I will leave at the temple.

Outside it is dark and I see no one like me on the street. There are only three other people outside, and their hands are free of offerings. I tuck the huge bouquet of roses awkwardly under my arm and wonder if I am in danger. It's 4:00 A.M. and I am walking alone on a foggy San Francisco morning. As occasional cars drive past, some slow down to inspect me. I keep my eyes forward, and I feel safe, for she is with me.

As I walk I have a distinct memory of myself at seven years old, coming home from school and telling my grandmother that the school cafeteria was filled with tissue-paper roses; they were like rainbows on our lunch tables. My grandmother put me to bed that night before *las mañanitas*, and I interrupted her during our prayers to ask why we were going to get up so early to go see the Virgencita the next day. She told me the miraculous story of la Virgen de Guadalupe. I knelt beside my bed and my grandma sat on a chair by the nightlight so that I could see her in the dark.

"Do you know why la Virgencita likes roses?" she asked me.

"No, I don't know *'buelita.*"

"Well, a long time ago, when the people of Mexico were suffering because they were slaves and there was no food and no hope, la Virgencita appeared to a humble Indian named Juan Diego," she told me.

Her long braids lay against her chest, and she waved her finger in the air as if drawing the story for me to see. "The Virgen told Juan Diego, 'Oh my son, you my faithful son, I want you to go tell the bishop that I have sent you to him on my behalf. Tell him that I want a temple to be built here.' But, you see, Juan Diego could not believe that she was real or that the sound he heard was the music of the heavens. She told him, 'Am I not here as your Mother? I see my people suffering. You are my faithful son and I know you will do this for me.' But, when Juan Diego went to tell the bishop, the bishop would not speak to him."

"*Abuelita*, why didn't the bishop want to talk to Juan Diego?" I asked her.

"*M'ija*, just because you are a priest does not mean you do the right things. Everyone makes mistakes," she replied.

My grandmother went on to tell me how la Virgencita appeared once again, and again Juan Diego followed her instructions, but after another refusal from the bishop he gave up.

"She appeared to him again when he least expected her. Juan Diego could not find the words to tell her that the bishop wanted nothing to do with her. But he knew that he must tell the truth, for she already knew everything. 'My Mother, my beautiful Mother, I have tried to tell the bishop your message but he does not believe me. He just sends me away.'"

My grandmother would switch back and forth between the soft voice of la Virgencita and the deep yet humble voice of Juan Diego. At my young age, it entertained me and I wanted to hear more of the story. I moved over to her and played with her braids while she continued with the story.

"La Virgencita told him to go to the hill of Anahuac and that there he would find a gift for the bishop. This gift would be a sign that she was there and that she wanted a temple to be built. Juan Diego had no choice but to go and see what was on the dry hill. When he got there he saw roses of all colors and he knew that this could only be the work of Our Great Mother. When he got to the church, he asked for the bishop and wouldn't leave until he saw him. The bishop said 'Don't tell me that you have seen our Virgin Mary again? Now can you tell me why she would want to talk to a plain Indian like you?' Juan Diego knew that he had seen her blessed image and so he let go of his cloak and the roses fell to the floor."

My grandmother pulled her shawl off of her shoulders and showed me how Diego's cloak might have fallen to the ground. She stood tall with the nightlight shimmering behind her.

"Do you know what happens next?" she'd taunt me for an answer.

"No, what? *Abuelita*, tell me."

My grandmother's eyes lit up like stars in the dark night when she told the magical conclusion.

"The bishop and his priests immediately knelt down in front of Juan Diego because they couldn't believe their eyes. Painted on his cloak by the colorful petals of the roses was a brown woman with the features of an Indian, wearing a shawl of stars and standing on the moon as the sun shone behind her, surrounding her with rays of light."

"Does the cloak still exist? Can only the priest see it?" I asked her.

"Of course it still exists, it was made by the heavens and everyone can see her, she is the Mother of the people. But most importantly, she got her wish for a temple and now every year we celebrate this miracle. This is why tomorrow you are taking roses to her. She loves roses and so every time you see roses you must thank her for them."

Remembering my grandmother always makes me feel connected to my past and to my mother. I look at the roses under my arm and I thank Tonantzin. When I reach 24th Street, I see a group of people on the corner outside of a McDonald's restaurant. As I get closer, I see mariachis. Walking toward me is a woman in a *gabán* with the image of our brown Mother radiating on her chest. She says, *"Buenos días."* An elder welcomes me, and I become a part of the group getting ready to march to our destination. The public aspect of this journey is particularly important to me, because it shows that as Mexicanos and Xicanos we have maintained our essence as a people from the land of the eagle perched on a cactus to a hilly peninsula where fierce wind blows the sun's heat away.

A man wearing a red cap decorated with a black Aztec eagle and a drum strapped to his back hands out sheets of paper that are printed with the lyrics of our Goddess'. His companion, a woman wrapped in a rainbow colored shawl, greets her friends by kissing them on the cheek and speaks in Spanish with an accent that is only heard in the land of *mestizos*.

The front of our group begins to move forward, holding up a banner of Guadalupe. We are more than 200 people and we are taking our streets, our indigenous land. We walk in faith for her. We assemble not caring that there are cars behind us. Since the Spaniards arrived in Tenochtitlan in 1519, we have resisted giving up our ways of expression and have survived a continuous cycle of oppression as many of us migrate to northern lands. We still honor Our Mother the only way we know how—through music and poems. Our pilgrimage is to Saint Peter's Church, a temple with murals of Moctezuma. Standing among these strangers on the cracked sidewalk, I feel at home, finally.

My search for spirituality began when I was very young. I was instructed by the local archdiocese from the age of five, and during twelve years of Roman Catholic education, my faith often swayed back and forth. Spirituality was not part of this education; it was the routine of when to stand and kneel that was imbedded in my subconscious. To this day I can go to any Catholic service and my body will automatically respond.

In high school, I was faithful to the religion because I had met my first spiritual person, my ninth-grade religion teacher. She taught me the history of the religion my parents had passed on to me the day they cleansed me of my original sin. However, my faith was tested as soon as I went to college, away from the environment that had kept me practicing. At the end of my first semester, I attended the Virgen de Guadalupe Mass and volunteered to read from the Old Testament. I was uneasy for the hour I spent in the chapel, and I did not feel that my actions were natural. I left Roman Catholicism behind.

Sabbath worship became a chore, an obligation to fulfill when

I visited my family. The day my mother forced me to go to confession was the day that I reached deep within myself in order to save myself. By the end of my first year in college, my mother had found out, through rumors, that I was not a virgin. I chose not to betray myself by lying and admitted to not being pure. My mother took me to confession the next day, insisting that I needed to cleanse myself. We had missed the scheduled time, but she was determined. She told me to kneel in front of the Virgen de Guadalupe. As she whispered behind me, I was yearning for unconditional love. While I looked at the image of the Virgencita that glowed above lit candles, my mother was reciting words about forgiveness and promises to resist temptation.

All I did was ask the Virgen silent questions that somehow seemed answered in my mother's litany. "Why does my mother think I am bad? What have I done that has changed me in her eyes? Why do women oppress women? Can you help my mother understand? Virgencita, I kneel here before you a strong and brave woman." At that moment, I lost my Virgen de Guadalupe and found my goddess Tonantzin. I lost the image of the pure woman that I was supposed to be until I got married. I gave up the idea that I was born for a man. I found a goddess who told me that she would love me without limits. Tonantzin is not the Virgin Mary; she is an Aztec goddess with power. She talked to my heart in a familiar voice, my own.

Since then I have been on a spiritual journey and have found my roots beneath the veils of a religion forced upon me. I found the earth and the heavens in Tonantzin and she gave me the fire to learn more about her. I was not a pagan. I was an *indigena*, in search of ancient ways. I learned about her story from the other side, the indigenous side. I looked beyond the Roman Catholic legend and found an indigenous goddess. I had to reach back through a history that was fabricated to another that was lost in bloodshed.

The trumpet blares a song of exclamation. It is 5:00 A.M., and we are asking everyone to wake up with us. With songs and poetry we ask our neighbors to get ready to greet our Mother. I look up to the sky and see a lonely star. Her cape shines in the dark blue night above us. She is with us and we sing to her. I cannot resist the cry that wants to come out of me. I am choking on words in my throat. Through me pass my grandmothers, great grand-mothers, great aunts and my mother. I cry and I let go of a rope of silence that has been tying me down. I see myself in the elder beside me and in the baby in front of me.

I keep walking and feel an immense emotional tie to every-body in my life. I think of my mother and everything she endured in order for me to be born in this country. I feel her pain in my heart and I visualize her also crying at this very moment, at the celebration back home. My eyes tear and I share this moment with my mother, so many miles away. I now know that loving my mother involves understanding where she comes from, a Mexico she left when she was twenty-four years old. For so long I rebelled against her rules and expectations, but they were all she knew to give me as a woman. I cannot blame her for loving me the only way she knows how. I can, however, show her how to love me the way I deserve to be loved. I have found peace with her religion by realizing that it is not my faith. Yet, I enlightened myself by acknowledging my womanhood through Tonantzin, and I know that my mother finds herself in the same way.

A woman yells, *"Qué viva la Virgen de Guadalupe."* I find it difficult to respond with *"¡Viva!"* while I am still crying and I have lost my breath. My Goddess, may you live forever in my heart. For Tonantzin, and for my own mother, I yell *"¡Viva!"* Once more the woman recites, *"Qué viva Nuestra Madre."* My Mother, may your spirit thrive in me and may you always live in me. With all the air in my lungs I yell, *"¡Viva!"*

I look up to the sky and smile to Tonantzin as we begin to sing our next song. I sing to express how I would like to be sunrays so that I could greet her at dawn. How I would like to be birds and sing the music of the heavens. But, I am just a humble woman who comes with her voice and flowers to wake Goddess from her sleep. She is the earth and sky, thus she gives me life. The songs I sing praise her heavenly presence. I venerate her as my Goddess, who helps me survive every day just as she helped my ancestors endure a time with no hope. Her story is full of resistance. As a Xicana, I face many obstacles and she inspires me to persevere.

We reach the church and as I enter the temple, I no longer feel the repression I have associated with Catholicism. Worshippers have been waiting for us to bring the music, and they greet the bearer of the banner with applause. Here, we all sing and ask her to wake up and give birth to the sun, once again, just as she did yesterday.

"¡Qué viva la Virgen de Guadalupe!"

Long live the Virgin of Guadalupe.

"¡Viva!"

"¡Qué viva Nuestra Madre!"

Long live Our Mother.

"¡Viva!"

"¡Qué vivan las Américas!"

Long live the Americas.

"¡Viva!"

"¡Qué viva la mujer!"

Long live woman.

"¡Viva!"

Long live.

The priest comes out from his room behind the altar and recites his own chant:

"¡Qué viva el verdadero Dios que reina sobre nosotros y su madre, Jesucristo Rey!" He praises the one true god that reigns over us and over his mother, Jesus Christ, and I refuse to chant. I realize that I still face the same harassment my ancestors endured when they continued to worship their gods within the Catholic Church that was imposed on them. The priest is blind to the fact that for Sunday masses the church is never filled like it is this morning. I am here because I believe in the Mother, not in Jesus Christ. The priest refuses to acknowledge that a tradition honoring the Mother Goddess has survived.

I go to her altar, a framed replica of the sacred cloak atop a hill of roses, and place my offering near the bottom. In the name of Tonantzin, I pray for her blessings and guidance as I allow myself to enjoy the love of women again. She has already taught me how to love myself by appreciating the sacredness of my indigena body, and now I would like to share that love with someone. I know she will continue blessing my spirit's love for words, thus allowing me to pass on my family's history. Lastly, I ask her to guide me with the strength of a warrior so I can continue in the struggle for justice. I leave her blessing myself, for I am *mujer*.

I walk down the crowded aisle and head for the exit. As I walk through the large wooden doors, my hand involuntarily reaches out for the holy water. I dab my fingers in the basin and bring them to my heart. The sun is beginning to rise and I turn up 24th Street towards Mission Street. I see parents with their children buying warm sweet bread and hot chocolate. I see smiles and glowing faces that look like my own. Mission Street is no longer empty. It is now bursting with music blasting from cars and laughter shared between friends walking to work. It is like the boulevard back home.

I arrive in my apartment and I am drawn to my desk, where I write for two hours before I go to work. But it is not only Tonantzin that has given me new strength—it is also the community that surrounded me for two hours this morning. I finally feel at home in this city, after three years of feeling like just another temporary, anonymous citizen. I salute my directions one last time before I leave for work. I step out of my front door once again and keep the shirt with her image on and the flowers in my hair. I open myself to all the experiences she will offer me this new year. It is a sacred day for me; it is the day of my Goddess.

Just Another Anarchist Antichrist Godless-Commie Catholic

Sonya Huber

In the summer of my twenty-first year, I spent a month at an anarchist institute, and then took a road trip to visit my aunts: three nuns living at the St. Scholastica Convent in Fort Smith, Arkansas. The Sex Pistols were in the tape player, with Johnny Rotten singing about being a punk-rock antichrist. Much as I wanted to be, I wasn't wild-eyed Johnny Rotten—so who was I? A true anarchist would certainly have no soft spot for the ladies in black and their days of prayer.

When I was sixteen, that Sex Pistols album sounded like secret instructions for escaping my life. At eighteen, I announced at a Catholic youth service camp, "I wish I'd never been admitted as an adult into the Catholic Church." I think we were passing around a candle or a wooden cross, and everyone was sharing reactions to the week's work of weeding and bagging garbage for invalids and the elderly. I liked the work, but I hated the nightly Bible discussions. The church's spirituality, I decided, seemed like a selfish relay race to save the soul, in which we racked up service points without doing anything to stop poverty. And I hated the shame I'd learned in church, the assumption that I was always sinning and that the way to avoid sin was to say and do as little as possible. It was with that blunt announcement at a Catholic camp that I gave up Catholicism.

But I had taken years of Catholic education very seriously, and I still needed to *do* stuff, to help people. When I got to college, I walked into the volunteer office and signed up for shifts at the local food bank. The leap into activism, from the food bank to the hunger-and-homelessness task force, was the next logical step for someone serious about getting rid of hunger. I'd learned in many Masses to put the ideas of religion into practice, but I hadn't learned in church about organizing for social change, which became my passion. On Sundays in college, you'd find me on a long ride home—not from church but from a demonstration, maybe against the clear-cutting of forests in northern Minnesota, or denouncing police brutality in Minneapolis. I spent the Gulf War months completing many more anti-war activities than homework assignments. I learned how to be the opposite of a good Catholic girl: I learned how to be a troublemaker.

Some of my fellow college activists were still religious: Unitarians, Reform Jews, Quakers or Buddhists. I marveled at the progressiveness of my friends' childhood religious experiences. I visited a Quaker meeting, but the quiet simplicity felt too foreign. On a car ride up to a rally against the School of the Americas, a tiny blond organizer who was also a religion major told me about Liberation Theology, in which the ideas of the Catholic Church are used to support revolution and major social change in latin America. A window opened in my heart—what a wonderful idea. I sighed, thinking I couldn't practice Liberation Theology because I didn't live in latin America.

When I was twenty—about six months before my convent visit—I took vows of my own: I was inducted as a member of an anarchist collective in Minneapolis. We organized a street-theater piece protesting a nuclear dump south of the city. We read theory about radical democracy, most of which I didn't understand. But the rebellious stance and the desire to live a life opposed to greed and materialism—that clicked with me. Although I'd left Catholicism, I was living what I recognize now as a monastic lifestyle: I shaved my head, worked for almost nothing at a coffee shop, and ate raw and unadorned food, mostly simple grains and vegetables. I was part of a community where I knew I belonged. We smelled of the earthy funk of food co-ops, soy sauce and unlaundered clothing, and we glowed with happiness. There were activists who were Buddhists, and others who held drum circles and lit incense, but nobody who would admit to attending something as backward as a Catholic church. For me, drum circles were too corny. I tried to find my faith in revolutionary books and pamphlets, anarchist bookstores and coffee shops. Those institutions became my new church, where, I thought, love and hope lived.

When I went home for Christmas right after joining the collective, I went with my family to church. I hadn't been to Mass in three years. I guess I went just to test myself. I sat with my family in the wood pew of St. Jude's Church. All that gore: the drops of blood, the crown of thorns, the eyes rolling back in Christ's head. Why were we all worshipping a narrative of human cruelty and pain, eating symbols of flesh, only responding by rote to the standard questions? The smell of incense was as thick as rotting flesh. I couldn't wait to get out into the cold, clear night, to go home and read feminist theory, to cleanse myself.

When I turned twenty-one I decided to save my pennies to attend an anarchist institute. It was supposed to be heaven on earth: an ecology-focused summer school in the green hills of southern Vermont.

Some of my classes were fascinating, and the organic food at the cafeteria was wonderful. But I didn't find political paradise. The anarchist guru, an elderly man who'd penned several convoluted volumes of theory, didn't tell me anything I hadn't heard before. Like Catholicism, his strand of visionary theory spoke about millenarian deliverance, when there would be food for the hungry and power for the meek, and as in conservative Catholic churches, there was no discussion at all about how that revolution would come to pass or be built. It would just appear, like the Rapture.

I had expected a liberated zone, but I learned that Catholics don't have a monopoly on intolerance. There were a few mean hippies at the camp—aggressive, squinty-eyed anarchist boys who made fun of me because I didn't smoke weed, because I went to all my classes. It was anarchist-revolutionary high school. I was sick much of that summer with a urinary tract infection, and in the midst of real pain, all that theory wasn't comforting at all. The only thing that calmed me down was a daily walk alone in the pine-filled woods.

While I was at the institute, I found a quasi-spiritual focus.

One instructor wanted to organize a silent meal, and as I loved the idea of creating time to think about food and where it came from, I joined her in planning it. As we explained our event and asked people to participate, we were met with an impromptu protest. A few people guffawed, rapped on the table, shouted about ridiculous, repressive claptrap and otherwise refused to participate.

My strongest positive memory of the institute is a vision not from the classroom but from the cafeteria. One night I started talking to an older woman with short, grayish hair and sun-weathered skin. She had such a calm about her that I wanted to stay near her to absorb it. She said she was a nun and had stopped at the institute to give a talk about her work.

"My aunts are nuns," I said. That was my way of telling her that I was raised a Catholic, without having to say anything about my current feelings for the church. "They're at the St. Scholastica Convent in Fort Smith, Arkansas."

"I belong to the Maryknoll Order," she said. "I've been living in latin America."

I smiled, thrilled to be standing next to a very political nun. She described, in a few sentences, the way nuns in her order lived with people whose lives had been devastated by civil wars and U.S. foreign policy.

I was shy, maybe also in awe. I didn't even know what to ask her about her work, or her religion. I repeated the word "Maryknoll," making sure I wouldn't forget this vital clue. I was officially and emotionally not a Catholic anymore. But this nun was, refreshingly, the opposite of the unforgiving and judgmental academics I was learning from all summer. She was putting radical love into practice. I felt a hunger for that presence in my life, but at the time I labeled it only as a fascination with something from my past.

On the way back home that summer, I visited New York City, and a friend took me to St. John the Divine Episcopal Cathedral. She told me the church leaders had declared the church to be under construction until poverty is eradicated; the building was covered with layers of scaffolding like a spider's web. In the dark church, lit only by candles and stained glass windows with blue starbursts as vivid as acid-trip visions, I felt something loosen in my chest. We explored the cathedral and found aquariums, displays of fossils, art and an altar for people who'd died of AIDS. The church billed itself as a place for people of all religions to come together, a beacon for ecological and social wisdom.

I went to the church two or three more times during my visit. It was my guilty, secret vice, the most twisted sin of an anarchist. I could have been sitting in hip coffee shops or lounging in Central Park. Instead I read Marge Piercy's *Woman on the Edge of Time* by the dim light of candles and the recessed spotlights on the statues of the saints. All the while, I wondered about my revolutionary commitment. After all, any church, even this church, was the ultimate symbol of hierarchy and patriarchy, right? Or maybe, just as Piercy envisioned new worlds, I could envision a new church.

It *was* comforting—it was quiet, I told myself, if nothing else, and I needed comfort. It had been a horrific year, never mind the

bad summer: I'd run into a load of medical and personal problems, I'd had major fights with my family and I'd had to leave
school temporarily. I was in the midst of rebelling against and
rejecting everything, turning my belief system inside out. I was
also gradually forming myself into a new person, a political
organizer. I was getting my first taste of the heartbreak that
comes with that calling: the daily monotony and pressure, the
lack of social acceptance or status, the defeats and insur-
mountable odds, the personal costs. And I'd been in motion
constantly—I hadn't really thought about taking time to
recharge or to think about "spiritual" stuff.

I knew there was something wrong. I was under a lot of stress
from my political work, and I was desperate to find some way to
fill myself back up. I had been raised in a conservative church
that focused on hellfire. But the quiet and the candles of St. John
the Divine and the five minutes with that sister from Maryknoll
had given me a feeling of safety and acceptance that I hadn't
been able to find in any corner of the anarchist institute.

If the move into adulthood is marked by the decision to take
one's life into one's own hands, that was my summer of growing
up. The previous few years had been filled with rebellion and
reaction of all sorts, but the disappointments and pain of that
summer showed me that I needed an anchor—something like a
St. John the Divine—in my life, because there was no liberated
zone I could emigrate to and leave my problems and concerns
behind. I hatched the idea for the road trip to Arkansas because
my parents' preoccupation with another relative's move would

give me a chance to visit my aunts without parental involvement. It was probably the first time I imagined that building a relationship with the church could coincide with taking responsibility for my own life. The two journeys were similar, though I didn't see that then. I was crossing old, familiar terrain while steering my own course, standing up for my beliefs and my adult choices.

The sun was warm. My sixteen-year-old sister sat next to me with her heavy-metal hair, putting Poison and Warrant tapes into the tape player whenever the Sex Pistols or Dead Kennedys clicked off. It had been three or four years since I'd visited the nuns, and I looked completely different: shaggy short hair, unshaven legs, hiking boots. I wish I could say that I felt proud of this new look and identity, but I was ashamed, feeling inadequate both as a Catholic good girl and as a revolutionary bad girl. I felt like the Devil herself, rolling up the gravel drive in a Toyota. As we rang the bell and waited in the sitting room for our aunts to be called from their rooms, I felt as though my presence there was a violation. If they only knew what I'd been doing all summer, what I'd been doing with my life, what my eyes had been reading instead of the Bible.

When my favorite aunt, Sister Rosarita, appeared with tears in her eyes and hugged us, that fear disappeared. I had expected something out of *The Exorcist:* maybe the holy water would boil when we walked through the chapel on our tour. Instead, we walked through the cafeteria line and my aunts said to every black-clad nun in attendance, "These are Stanley's girls, our nieces." We got welcomes and exclamations of happiness, a group of women waiting to pat our hands and peer into our faces in search of a family resemblance.

An old woman in a prairie-style sunbonnet greeted us in the humid greenhouse, her leathery hands pointing a trowel at the rows of vegetables and flowers as she named each one. Another old woman, thickly built, climbed a tall ladder without fear to replace a lightbulb twelve feet up. Women joked with each other, fed each other and helped each other die when it was their time. It seemed like a different kind of "institute," very feminist and woman-centered. I was happy to be there, I had to admit it. I felt more relaxed at the convent than I had in any liberated zone.

That visit helped me to accept Catholicism as a cultural influence, something I could never pull out by the roots. Fully embracing a new spirituality, one I could claim as my own, would take many years, but the process started when my sister and I turned onto the highway toward the convent.

Anarchism's chaos slowly lost its appeal. But my desire to learn about economics and Marxism, to get more of a structure for my political work, thrust me into an environment where spirituality was the biggest taboo. At twenty-three, I fell in love with and planned to marry a socialist. He was an adamant atheist who had been raised Catholic and despised any trappings of religion. When his eight-year-old daughter sat at the kitchen table and told him she believed in God, he laughed sarcastically and asked, "Where is Heaven? People in the space shuttle haven't seen a guy in a white beard lying around."

When I attended socialist meetings with him, I saw other members roll their eyes when they talked about the religious activists they ran into at demonstrations. My fiancé called them deluded reformists, drugged by what Marx called "the opiate of the masses." The socialists in this group seemed to want to convert all potential activists to atheism—as if achieving a workers' state in the United States wasn't enough of a challenge.

I thought of my religious, conservative, lower-middle—and working-class roots in the Midwest and South, and realized suddenly that that's where I was meant to work. I know those folks, and God's a part of their lives. I thought about the pogroms against Jews in Russia, all the intolerance that paved the way for the Communist gulags. I broached the subject with my socialist sweetheart: if we're trying to work with the working class, and so many of them are religious, how can we be so anti-religious? "It's a crutch," was the most thoughtful contribution he could make to that discussion.

I felt judged, just as I had in anarchist circles, as if I had to be pure and free of any religious "delusions" in order to be a true revolutionary. I was offended by this group's arrogance, and I rebelled against it, believing more and more that spirituality wasn't something that any political ideology could eliminate from a person's soul.

As I began to pull away from my fiancé, I found myself doing all of the forbidden activities I could think of, like picking up my old books on Buddhism and attending a queer-friendly Catholic Mass. I began a lifelong research project, launched by typing "progressive Catholic" into Internet search engines. I learned about the Catholic Worker Movement, Catholics for a Free Choice and the Catholic-Labor Network. I gathered up the strength to leave him by sitting in the back of churches, using the silence and calm I found there to think and resolve my questions. Tired of the judgment I endured in my relationship and that particular socialist group, I found more and more that I needed a non-judgmental space in my head for those mushy things he deemed irrelevant: faith, quiet and hope.

Just before my thirtieth birthday, I joined the Immaculate Conception Church in Columbus, Ohio, where I attend Mass about once a month. The priests in my parish are actually sympathetic to social-change issues, and it shows in their homilies and urgings to live one's faith. I'm also active with a faith-based organization that fights for low-income housing and healthcare. I like being a church member partly because many rank-and-file union members and fellow working-class and middle-class activists go to church. In the Midwest, church membership says that you are rooted in a particular neighborhood and community, that you're more than a college-kid migrant activist. To tell people that I am a socialist Catholic offers them something surprising, challenges Cold War notions of socialists as Soviet-style automatons. I don't mention my church membership often, but when I do, it is often to other activists who are also religious, and it helps to build trust.

But it's not all about the practical benefits of showing solidarity with my neighbors and religious activists. I've been doing social justice work for thirteen years. There are so many negative messages in our culture about activists, and also about anyone who doesn't love capitalism. For me, one of the only refuges from American political and economic culture is church, where materialism is questioned (even if some church members don't take that questioning to heart). I sit in the wooden pew and learn how habits of tolerance, humility, listening, connecting and expressing gratitude can be developed—all skills I need for my activism and for myself. I rewrite parts of the Mass in my head, untangling the analogies. "Life in the World to Come," for example, to me means life after major social change. If I keep my mind open, a lot of what's said by the priest has interesting application in my social justice work.

The priest ends the Mass by saying, "The Mass is now concluded. But the Mass never ends; it must be lived." And I feel like I do live it, as much as I can. Here in church, I am appreciated, and I am reminded to give myself credit, because I have been trying to live my faith—the faith of social justice—and, as the church recognizes, it's a hard path that can be wearing on the soul. I'm at peace now with the fact that many Catholics would think I'm a total heathen. I have no guilt about the fact that I've been having frequent sex out of wedlock since I was sixteen. I swear like a trucker. I'm rebellious and loud and opinionated. And when I dab my forehead with holy water or take the Eucharist onto my tongue, it is a sacrament.

After years of despising myself for my rebellious ways, it's a good practice for me to say to myself and the church: I belong here, and I am just as important and whole as anyone else. Maybe it was Catholicism that put those ideas of self-hatred into my head, but reflection and adulthood have shown me that nobody is perfect, and that walking into church with some "crazy" ideas about social justice is not really a sin at all. I'm getting my hands dirty with honorable work, and I believe that God would approve.

A Flash of Lightning

Diane Biray Gregorio

In 1988, I took a semester off from my sophomore year at the University of Pennsylvania to live and study in the Philippines, the country of my birth. As a typical eighteen-year-old from the suburbs of America, who had not lived in the Philippines since I was a baby, I was completely unprepared for the shocking images of poverty and injustice that I encountered on the streets of Manila. I lived in a tiny apartment with thirteen relatives, slowly realizing the daily struggles of living in a country where the vast majority of the people live below the poverty line. The experience utterly transformed me, personally and politically; I returned to the States a very different person. The life plans I had harbored before—to become a millionaire by age twenty-five—seemed less relevant, not to mention self-centered. I felt a passionate responsibility to use my education to address the injustices I had witnessed.

By my senior year, I was saddled with heavy student loans. Many of my classmates were heading toward Wall Street investment banking or management consulting with one rallying cry: "Show me the money!" Yet the memories of my time in the Philippines rang in my conscience. After much soul-searching, I decided to try out the corporate world for a few years in order to pay back some debts, save a little money, and then, I promised myself, I would work in the nonprofit sector. With my diploma, a brand new, navy-blue business suit, and my first briefcase in hand, I ventured into the wilds of Corporate America.

I was making an obscene amount of money for a twenty-year-old. I worked insane hours: over twelve hours a day, six days a week. To balance the pressures of work, I got caught up in a pattern of living large, partying wildly and spending carelessly in the few hours I wasn't in the office. In spite of fervent attempts to numb myself with work, play and consumption, I could not erase the fact that I had become profoundly unhappy. I felt as though my soul was drying up inside, disconnected from a sense of deeper purpose.

In order to reconnect with the inspiration I felt upon returning from my trip to the Philippines, I started volunteering for Oxfam America, an international development organization committed to long-lasting solutions to hunger and poverty. I felt an immediate charge from contributing to what I really cared about: greater equity and justice in the world. Eventually, I realized that I had to make some drastic changes in my life in order to be true to the sense of purpose that was reawakening within me.

Although I realize that it is possible to live a life of wisdom and compassion in whatever profession—whether a CEO, lawyer, car mechanic or an activist—during that stage of my life I needed to shift my course dramatically in order to feel alive again. I quit my corporate job and took a position at Oxfam for half my former salary. I began to confront my unhealthy patterns of spending and partying. I broke up with my boyfriend that I had been with for nearly three years. I started training in martial arts, became a vegetarian, and tried to teach myself how to meditate. I also came out as bisexual. Fittingly enough, it was during this time of living in a more authentic way that I discovered Buddhist teachings.

Anushka was my first dharma friend. She had just returned from a two-year spiritual journey in Asia—doing meditation retreats, visiting monasteries and ashrams. She was a bona fide dharma bum. Here was someone to whom I could relate. She wasn't some sort of distant sage, an old man in a long robe and a scraggly beard, sitting on top of a mountain. She was a woman of color, a lesbian about my age, who was deeply committed to the spiritual path. She too had been raised Catholic. I liked her outlook on life, her joyful demeanor and the way she carried herself with calmness and positive energy.

Through this friendship, I began seriously practicing meditation at the Cambridge Insight Meditation Center, and later at Insight Meditation Society and Abhayagiri Buddhist Monastery. Devouring the dharma through as many retreats, classes, sittings and books I could get my hands on, I felt I had finally found my spiritual home. I began to experience firsthand the natural reservoir of peace, clarity, compassion and wisdom that resided within me.

My work at Oxfam was also taking on a spiritual dimension. As my heart and mind were opening to the suffering within me, I also began to open to the vast suffering across the world. Over the course of five years, my job took me to twenty-five countries in Asia, Africa and Latin America, as well as to poverty-stricken parts of the United States. I marched with women demanding their human rights in Northern India. I visited an indigenous

Mayan village in Guatemala struggling against the exploitation of the coffee industry. I met with a black community reclaiming its land in post-apartheid South Africa. I trekked to a refugee community in the mountains of the Philippines, living on desolate land ravaged by deforestation. I worked with small family farmers struggling to survive in the heartland of the United States.

Yet, no matter where I was on the globe, the same questions weighed on me. Why is it that in spite of endless efforts we still live in a world where nearly 1.6 billion people live below the poverty line? Why does the gap between rich and poor continue to grow? How is it that the oppressed sometimes turn around to become the oppressors? Why are those of us in wealthy countries unwilling to face how our own patterns of consumption, corporate domination, and weapons production contribute to these problems? I began to suspect that social, economic, and political change were not enough to remedy these intractable problems. The root of these ills was much deeper.

Ironically, new insights into these questions began closer to home, in a cabin in Maine during a snowy retreat, December 1994. I had brought along a copy of *A Flash of Lightning in the Dark of Night*, His Holiness the Dalai Lama's commentaries on the Mahayana classic *A Guide to the Bodhisattva's Way of Life*, by Shantideva. True to the title, the beauty and truth of these teachings struck me like a bolt of lightning, straight into the core of my being. Embodied in the ideal of the bodhisattva—a being who realizes buddhahood not just for her own peace and freedom but for the benefit of all beings—I saw for the first time the connection between my spiritual practice and my work in the world. It slowly dawned on me that, although I was treating them as separate, these areas were one and the same. They both sprung from the same source—the yearning to understand suffering and experience freedom—whether in myself or in the world. It was that New Year's Eve, sitting on a riverbank blanketed by the hush of falling snow, that I knew from the depths of my being that I could never turn back.

Shantideva's exquisite passages and the lucid wisdom of His Holiness's commentary reverberated throughout my life. Indeed, over time, I found that my work and my practice fed each other in a mutually reinforcing cycle of awareness. The more I saw suffering in the world, the more I was inspired to understand suffering in myself. The more I understood suffering in myself, the more I could begin to understand it in others. The more peace and clarity that flowed from this understanding, the more I could offer in service. In the ongoing dance of dharma practice and social action, it became clearer that what I had suspected was true—social, economic, and political struggle *alone* would not be enough. These teachings sparked in me the firm belief that, in order to strike at the true roots of poverty and injustice, we need a radical inner transformation of the greed, hatred, and delusion that resides in our own hearts and minds as individuals and as a society. The introduction to His Holiness's book, *Essential Teachings*, explains this clearly:

None of the major terrible problems that threaten survival of the earth can be solved by merely institutional or political methods. *Humankind to survive has to undergo a massive and unprecedented change of heart, an ordered and passionate spiritual revolution that changes forever our relation to each other and to nature.* It is only from such a revolution that the new vision the planet so desperately needs can arise—a vision that sees the connections between every thought and every action, the relations between the obsession with the individual self and its hunger for false securities and every kind of exploitation that is ruining the world.

While there is no turning back, there are endless questions. I continually ask myself, "What form does my service need to take right now—meditation retreat or social justice activism?" So far the answer to this life-*koan* has involved taking the time for each at different points, but also experimenting with the integration of dharma practice with social justice work. I completed an internship with Dr. Jon Kabat-Zinn's program on Mindfulness-Based Stress Reduction (MBSR), working in an inner-city clinic that teaches meditation and yoga to a diverse population including people struggling with addictions and homelessness. I started an MBSR program at Oxfam, engaging my colleagues in an exploration of mindfulness in the workplace and in our work for social justice. I launched a chapter of the Buddhist Alliance for Social Engagement (BASE) in Boston. With my partner, Robin, I am about to introduce meditation and yoga to an after-school program and to a cooperative working with low-income immigrant women. I maintain a daily meditation practice and set aside time for longer retreats. I try to live a life of simplicity and mind-fulness and act in accordance with Buddhist ethical precepts—a formidable task in the midst of busy urban life. My challenge is to continually remind myself that inner revolution and outer revolution must go hand in hand. As Mahatma Gandhi implores us, "We must be the change we seek."

Although I feel a strong draw to a simple life in a forest monastery, I have chosen to go back to graduate school, pur-suing a Ph.D. in Sociology and Organizational Behavior. Entering the academy may seem an odd choice for someone committed to social change. Yet it is not difficult to see that when debating the great social issues of the day—whether it is poverty, drug abuse or violence in the schools—we often attempt to solve the problem using the same logic that got us here in the first place. Is there a fresh perspective that can offer us a more pene-trating explanation of why things are as they are, one that cuts to the source? Like all the great wisdom traditions, Buddhism points to the possibility of being free from the cycle of unen-lightened existence. It is my hope that I might add, in some small way, to the growing chorus of voices who are demon-strating the power of a dharma lens to uncover the underlying truths at play in contemporary social problems. Perhaps this might help in the creation of solutions that address the origin of social ills where they actually lie—at the center of the human heart. Following humbly in the spirit of the great teachers and socially engaged Buddhists before me, I hope somehow to con-tribute to an emerging culture of awakening.

A Yogini in New York

Deborah Crooks

The greater New York population was just beginning to stir when I met Tony in a Chelsea coffee shop at 8:30 A.M. on September 11, 2001. We'd both been up more than three hours, having risen before dawn to make it to a 6:00 A.M. Ashtanga yoga workshop taught by the master of the form, Sri K. Pattabhi Jois. Because of the intensity and discipline required in Ashtanga yoga—a highly specific series of postures in which each bend, jump and twist is synchronized with a corresponding inhale or exhale—an instant camaraderie often springs up among its practitioners. Energized by two hours of deep breathing and flowing movement, Tony and I enthusiastically compared the paths that had led us to New York from our respective homes in Georgia and California.

An interest in improving my health—led me to that first 7:00 A.M. Mysore-style Ashtanga yoga class. After noticing a sign for a yoga studio a few blocks away from my home, I ventured inside thinking it would help me get back in shape. I had no idea I would one day fly across the country to study yoga, let alone have a spiritual awakening. But I soon found out that practicing Ashtanga goes far beyond practicing physical movement: it is the practice of liberation of the soul.

The teacher, a lean man with a long dark ponytail, cleared a space for me and began to talk me through the series, one asana (posture) at a time. Morning sunshine filtered through a south-facing wall of windows onto two rows of people standing or sitting on green, blue and purple yoga mats. Everyone moved through the sequence at her/his own pace. One woman stared at the tip of her nose as she balanced on her forearms and curled her feet up and around to graze the top of her head. A man sat in a cross-legged position with his eyes shut while ten other students inhaled and floated their arms skyward to begin a round of sun salutations. The only sounds were those of breathing and the occasional murmurs of the teacher's voice. Instead of leading everyone at once, he circulated around the room, giving tips to students on an individual basis, modifying or adjusting a posture, then moving on.

Ashtanga calls for performing a specific series of postures, evenly inhaling and exhaling five times in each pose before proceeding to the next one. Regular practice results in an increased sense of calm, fitness and closer alignment with the self. As I went through that first practice I was immediately struck by how little I had scrutinized my body on such a focused level. My left hip could barely open, whereas I found it easy to bend forward and touch my feet. Surprised at the amount I learned about my habits of movement during just one class and motivated by the healthy glow of the other students, I returned the following day.

As I began to attend class six days a week, I discovered that steadying the breath, regardless of comfort and discomfort, pain or pleasure, was the real focus of study. But I often stopped breathing in response to a tight muscle, immediately jumping to the conclusion that I couldn't go on. Surrounded by more advanced students, I doubted my place in the room. But if I were to get anywhere near yoking together my body, mind and spirit—the union for which yoga is named—I would have to transcend such beliefs and judgments about my capabilities.

"Each time I give you an adjustment I'm creating more room for your breath," my teacher explained as I tried to inhale deeply into my tense shoulders. His adjustments took my limbs past their usual limits, expanding both my range of motion and my sense of the possible.

Slowly and ever so slightly my flexibility increased with each passing day. Sending breath deeper into my body was stirring up a well of repressed feelings. Soon the challenge of practice was more emotional than physical. It became obvious to me that I had spent much of my life suppressing my feelings. Learning that I could fully experience them and survive was revelatory. I often spontaneously burst into tears as I "detoxified" past experiences. Sometimes I wanted to bolt from the room in sheer terror. And other times, practice felt like pure bliss.

If there is a "goal" to yoga, it is to cultivate equanimity or equal, non-reactive regard. This is why Ashtanga is a "practice," as opposed to simply an exercise routine. Tears might be running down my face and my teacher would simply say, "Breathe, here," tap my sternum and move on to another student. The challenge is to "be" with myself, whether I am uncomfortable or ecstatic, and complete the practice with the utmost attention I can muster. My emotions are a part of the action, but they don't have to control the show.

Despite my frequent emotional discomfort, I invariably felt more at peace with myself and with the world around me by the end of class. The tears not only provided new insight into my habits and history, they also freed up more space for the present. As I expanded the range of motion of my physical body, my ability to perceive and receive information, both physical and energetic, increased. The world looked, smelled and sounded more vivid and I felt more connected with both myself and others. Everyday challenges seemed less stressful, my appetite and digestion began to improve and my sleep was sound. Life seemed far richer than I could have ever imagined and my continual self-discoveries motivated me to get to the studio each day.

It's considered a rite of passage to travel to Mysore, India, to study with Jois, the eighty-seven-year-old Brahmin who devised and refined the Ashtanga system. After a year of regular yoga practice, it was clear that Ashtanga was becoming central to my life, and I wanted to make the trip to its source in Southeast Asia. But as I began to plan an international pilgrimage, my father's health began to deteriorate precipitously. My commitment to Ashtanga had coincided with my father's diagnosis with non-Hodgkin's lymphoma. Instead of finding myself wandering the exotic streets of India after yoga practice, I soon found myself walking the halls of the Veterans Administration hospital in Palo Alto, California, not far from the home in which I grew up.

Classified as a disabled veteran of World War II, my father received all of his medical care at the VA. While he underwent radiation and chemotherapy, I studied the photos of young soldiers going off to World War I, World War II, Korea, Vietnam and the Gulf War that decorated the hospital walls. The contrast between the smooth faces in the photos and the broken and bent bodies of my father and the other veterans in the VA waiting room was jarring. Most men were in wheelchairs, had limbs missing, were awaiting rounds of radiation or were connected to IVs. After a period of remission, my father's cancer had spread to all parts of his body and he was losing weight rapidly. Like the other men in the room, he looked at the floor in silence as he waited for treatment.

Having gained new insight into how my own repressed emotions had blocked my ability to absorb new experiences, I wondered at what these men still held in their bodies. I couldn't help but think that the present condition of my father's deteriorating body was the culmination of years of shallow breathing and downplaying the importance of the physical and psychic effects of serving in battle.

He was only nineteen years old when his World War II tour ended, but throughout the five decades to follow, he proudly defined himself by his veteran status. He'd opted for early graduation from high school so he could join the Navy and participate in bombing raids over the Philippines. After several months of flying in the damp South Pacific he contracted pleurisy, an inflammation of the lungs, and was so ill he was placed on a hospital ship bound for the States and given last rites.

As an adult, his common colds flared into pneumonia. Once, he came home from work with a collapsed lung. But he approached life with the grin-and-bear-it attitude he'd learned in the war. His prescription for any malaise short of nonstop bleeding was generally, "Oh, it will be all right" and a shrug, and he stoically endured his bouts of illness in silence.

I'd always been close with my father. Within a few hours of being born I was so sick that I was placed in an incubator and given the same last rites he had been given during the war, by a Catholic priest who told my mother it might be better if I died. Nonetheless, I was released from the hospital three weeks later, and it was my weak-lunged father who helped revive my breath.

"When we brought you home you were barely breathing," my father told me. "But I played with you and played with you and, finally, it was like a light going on."

The early attention he gave me and, perhaps, our both having had near-death experiences, forged a tight bond between us. While growing up, I took both his love of the natural world and his attitude toward the physical body to heart. I became the prototypical tomboy, holding my own with my brother on the playing field and shrugging off bumps and bruises. As an adult, I demonstrated my toughness by participating in competitive sports, riding bikes through blizzards and jumping out of planes, all of which thrilled my father.

As his illness progressed, the yoga studio functioned increasingly as a refuge from the aftereffects of war I was witnessing on a daily basis. The agile, well-cared-for bodies and careful attention of my fellow yoga students were a sharp contrast to the downcast eyes and bodies weakened by radiation and chemotherapy I saw in the VA.

• • •

As my father's cancer took a firm hold on his body, it became clearer to me that his attention and approval had propelled me through much of my life. He cheered on my belief in my freedom to do anything. I felt good about myself when I reported my accomplishments to him. For much of my life I had defined myself by my tangible achievements, those that bolstered my ego, and my father had been my biggest mirror. But as I wandered the halls of the VA hospital, I questioned the foundations of my father's definition of freedom and regard for the body. The photos on the wall attested to the continuity of war rather than peace.

"For you, it's about attachment," my yoga teacher said one day as I cried my way through a practice. The comment made me furious, but he was right. Simply breathing was becoming more challenging for me than assuming any given posture. Each inhalation affirmed life, each exhalation forced me to let go of both my habitual patterns and one of the most important people in my life.

I needed to learn to breathe without anyone's approval. Just as I was grieving my father's decline, Jois announced a world-wide teaching tour, which would include a month in New York. I jumped at the chance to study with someone who has such an extensive understanding of linking breath to body, and readily booked a flight.

Seven weeks before my scheduled departure for New York, my brother and I placed my father in the VA hospice care center. His last round of chemotherapy had sent his entire immune system reeling along with the cancer it aimed to kill. If the doctors gave him another blast, it would kill him faster than the disease itself. His breath was increasingly shallow.

At hospice, unadulterated oxygen from a tank by the bed flowed into his lungs. But it was not enough. Only three days after leaving his home, his health declined precipitously. When I entered his room I had to hold back a gasp at how pale and drawn he looked. When I sat down I started to cry.

"May as well accept it," he shrugged, and lifted his palms skyward. "We're all terminal."

He placed his hands back on the bedspread that covered his frame, which was as skinny now as it appeared in his war photos, and turned his head toward the window where an American flag was flying.

I was practicing yoga at home when the phone call came the next morning to tell me my father had died at five minutes past seven. He had coughed a little, the night nurse reported, and expired. In the end it had been his lungs that failed.

Oddly, it didn't upset me to see my father's dead body. He looked more at peace than he had while alive. He was lying under his bedspread just as I'd last seen him, in *savasana*, or "corpse pose," the deeply relaxing posture that concludes the Ashtanga series. His mouth was slightly open, his eyes were closed, and his palms were upturned. In that moment, I understood everything I'd been attempting to learn in yoga class about attachment, impermanence and fear. My father had died, and I'd survived it. And while he was free of the body that had pained him, I still had one, as well as a practice to help me be in it.

However, the following days were harder than that moment as the extent of my loss sunk in.

"The breath is the hardest pattern to change," I remembered my teacher telling me. "But if you're not breathing properly you're as good as dead."

The only real mirror I had now was myself. For a couple of weeks, I practiced yoga alone, breathing through my grief without anyone's prompting, willing myself to find out who *I* really was.

Though I'd felt bereft when I boarded the plane to New York, two days of practice with Pattabhi Jois and hundreds of other Ashtangis revived my spirits. In the Ashtanga yoga world, this workshop was a major event. Due to the large size of the class, the workshop was held on the basketball court of the huge modern sports complex at Chelsea Piers, a one-time port for transatlantic ships on the Hudson River. The makeshift studio vibrated with excitement despite the early hour and the jet lag and sore muscles that were the common denominators among the spectrum of yogis in the room. Among them were some of the world's best yoga teachers, as well as a handful of famous actors and models.

We all snapped to attention when Jois, a small, barrel-chested man, called out *"Samasthiti,"* the Sanskrit word for "equal standing," and began to lead practice by calling out the names of postures and counting down breaths.

During the next hour-and-a-half, Jois, whom many devoted yogis call *"Guruji"* for his wisdom, circled the large room, pausing occasionally to give a verbal instruction or adjust a student's limbs. A few people who had come to the sports center to work out stopped and watched us through the black mesh fence as our collective breath filled the huge hall.

One of the finishing postures of the Ashtanga sequence is *padmasana* (seated lotus pose). That Tuesday, when I sat with my legs crossed, my ankles at my thighs and my hands on my knees in the classic meditation posture, Jois came by and placed his hands on my shoulders, pulling them back as far as they could go to send my heart forward. When I lay down for savasana, the same corpse pose my father had been in on his death bed, I spontaneously burst into tears as a wave of grief overcame me. I missed being able to tell my father what I was seeing and doing, but I rose from my mat feeling calm, peaceful and grounded in my self. A sense of gratitude for my life trumped the urge to continue crying. For the first time during my visit, I joined the line to bow at Jois's feet and convey my appreciation for his teachings.

After class, I met up with some friends from California and walked to a nearby café. As we ate and planned the day's entertainment, I noticed a man with long blond hair and a yoga mat by his feet at the next table. It turned out Tony had also just come from the Ashtanga workshop. We asked him to join our group. In our post-practice ebullience, we were oblivious to what was going on out on the street and the subsequent rise in radio volume. Tony and I waved goodbye to my friends from home and carried on with our conversation. When one of the café employees came over to our table and asked us to quiet down, we were taken aback.

"A plane has just hit the World Trade Center," the café worker informed us. We looked at each other, stunned. Then we gathered our things and joined the hundreds of other people walking down the sidewalks attempting to piece together exactly what was happening. The exact nature of the situation had yet to sink in. We headed for a nearby vantage point from which to see the buildings for ourselves.

"The south tower has collapsed!" a passerby exclaimed. No one knew exactly what had happened. The sidewalks were filled with crying people. Those who weren't in tears were desperately punching numbers into their suddenly-useless cell phones.

With chaos surrounding us, Tony and I attempted to define our respective lives. I was grateful to be with a fellow yogi amidst such extreme circumstances. A couple of times we just looked at each other and consciously took a few deep breaths. By the time we reached Greenwich Village, we had exchanged family and relationship histories as well as the logistics of our trips. I was lodging in another yogini's apartment on the Lower East Side; he was enjoying a similar arrangement on the Upper West Side near the Cloisters.

"There's a beautiful park and an old building with tapestries of medieval maids and unicorns," he told me. "And a lot of religious iconography."

"Maybe after all of this we can go there," I said. The streets were full of fast-moving ambulances, fire trucks and police cars.

The thought of a natural setting sounded both improbable and heavenly.

A woman with curly red hair and a small terrier on a leash stopped and reached out for my arm.

"Did you hear?" she said. "It was intentional. There are more planes in the sky." The horror of what had truly happened finally sunk in. Two miles away, thousands of people had perished.

As we neared the place where we would have a clear view of what remained of the Twin Towers, I looked down on the sidewalk to see a large chalk drawing, in red and gold and blue, of a blond woman with a unicorn.

Then a collective gasp sounded and we raised our eyes from the drawing to see the second tower go down in flames. For a second everything stopped as nearly everyone on the street seemed to suspend their breath. Then we all turned away from the view of smoke, overcome with shock.

We continued walking to find out more about what had happened, repeatedly stopping to listen to strangers on the sidewalk share their stories or worries. Cars whirred past covered in ash. People lined up at phone booths attempting to contact their loved ones.

We ran into a small grocery store for water. Above the cash register was a TV set. Already there was talk of retaliation and the possibility of World War III. I thought of my father's role in the last world war and the long-term effects of war I'd witnessed in the VA hospital. What would be my role in what was perhaps my own generation's biggest crisis? I didn't want to perpetuate or add to the destruction of the past and the present moment.

Yoga practice, the practice of union and opening to life with equanimity, now seemed more necessary than ever.

After another hour of walking, we decided to head to the Jiva-mukti Yoga Center, a popular studio in SoHo. There we joined an impromptu meditation circle led by the center's founders, owners and yoga teachers, David Life and Sharon Gannon.

"The challenge at a time like this is to keep our hearts open," Gannon said to the small group of stunned people. The room was quiet and dark save a for few candles. Above Sharon's head was a small altar containing a statue of the Virgin Mother. I folded my legs back into padmasana and, recalling Jois's adjust-ment, pulled my shoulders back.

The remainder of the day would be one of bearing witness and listening as impromptu and highly diverse gatherings sprung up on the street. We spent some time talking with a group that included a man in a business suit, an elderly citizen in athletic wear, a cab driver from Pakistan and a woman who worked at a realtor's office. Eventually, we wound our way back to my friend's eighth-floor apartment on the Lower East Side. When we hung our heads out the bedroom window we could see a great plume of gray smoke streaming out of lower Manhattan. A few more friends came over and we cooked dinner and watched the news, trying to reconcile the footage of the plane slamming through the building with our general well-being. At one point in the evening, all of our cell phones started ringing at the same time and the room filled with our voices telling our loved ones, "Yes, yes, I'm okay."

We found out the next day that shortly after Jois's Tuesday class, Chelsea Piers was transformed into a triage center. The workshop was canceled on Wednesday as organizers scrambled to find a suitable venue. Nonetheless that morning Tony and I woke up and rolled our mats out on the living-room floor. We didn't know what we'd face once we left the apartment, and the only thing we were certain we could connect with was ourselves. Occasionally, we gave each other adjustments. The sound of our breathing was accompanied by the blare of sirens and what would become an omnipresent smell of burning wreckage.

Jois's class resumed the following day at a new location, a relatively small yoga studio in SoHo. My staying on the Lower East Side turned out to be a mixed blessing: I was near enough to ground zero to hear sirens and see war planes . . . and to get to practice with Jois's guidance every day. Police had blocked off lower Manhattan to everyone except those with addresses south of Houston Street. Many students couldn't get to class. As I wended my way through the police barriers filling Little Italy, Chinatown and SoHo, I held a handkerchief over my mouth and nostrils to keep out the smoke as I attempted to keep breathing.

"Samasthiti," Jois intoned to the greatly diminished group of students. Equal standing. I took my fullest breath of the day and the room filled with the sound of inhales and exhales as we practiced observing, balancing and infusing ourselves with spirit rather than reacting or attaching to the fear and panic swirling around outside.

On the last day of my stay in New York, Tony and I lingered to watch the advanced yogis go through Ashtanga's second series. A gasp went up as Jois bent one yogi so far back that he could grab his ankles, unfurling his ribs from his heart cavity and hinging his hips at an extraordinary angle. It was one of the most inspiring images of the week. To bend back and expose the heart so completely was the ultimate white flag: an act of complete trust in the teacher and in the moment, and a display of the human capacity to have faith in life even in the face of extreme circumstances. It summed up the lesson I was striving to learn: the pursuit of liberation must occur through the body, through breathing and surrendering to what is given, rather than clinging to fear and giving in to the urge to counterattack or escape.

That afternoon, we took the subway to the Cloisters. We walked through the park and into the old stone building, looking at tapestries and wood carvings, finally finding ourselves in a small courtyard garden. We leaned against the stone wall under the shade of a few fig trees, taking in a view of the park and distant rooftops. The trees were green, the sky was blue and the river below flowed gentle and lazy. For the first time in a week, the air we breathed was relatively smoke-free. Below us I knew were bruised psyches, shattered windows, ruined gardens and broken dreams. But many hearts—nearly six billion human ones on this planet—were still beating. Much work, and even more healing, still needed to be done. We were part of the equation. I took a long deep breath . . . and let it out.

God is Grape

Gail Hudson

When I was four years old I joined my family in the nightly
ritual of grace. Bowing my head, I solemnly whispered, "God is
grape. God is good. Now we thank him for our food." Having
attached to this delicious word, it was easy for me to find evidence of a grape-colored God everywhere—in the wild lavender
growing in our neighborhood, in my softest pale-purple
pajamas. When I looked at the river behind our house, I saw
God in the color of the waning Chesapeake sunset as it yielded
to indigo twilight. I even felt the texture of God in grape snow
cones at the amusement park, as crystals of violet ice slipped off
my lower lip and trickled down my warm, suntanned chin.

One Thanksgiving when I was five years old my father poured
purple-red wine into crystal goblets as he explained that wine
came from grapes. Suddenly it all made perfect sense. Wine was
what people drank during Communion at our Episcopal
church. "Take this and drinketh of me," our minister would say
to my parents.

As a young child, "grape" was an ideal container for my understanding of God. It taught me that God could actually satiate my
hunger and thirst. It taught me that what we revered, what we
gave thanks to each night at dinner, was something that resided
in the beauty of everyday life. And it taught me that God was as
reliable and constant as the deep purple crocuses that returned

each spring. Of course, I could have expanded this understanding to include all the colors and flavors that delighted me, everything that made me feel safe, all things bright and beautiful. But as a small girl, I was content to accept the confines of "grape" as the boundaries of God. Somehow, having this sense of boundaries made the whole notion of God easier to latch on to, easier to fathom.

Although I was too young to take Communion at church, every Monday morning I participated in my own grape communion. My mother would pull our station wagon up to the bank's drive-through window to deposit my pediatrician father's weekly checks. Before the teller sent back the white envelope filled with grocery money, she always leaned into her microphone and asked, "What flavor lollipop, Miss Gail?"

"Grape," I eagerly replied, cupping my hands as I saw the adults do in church. My mother reverently lifted the lollipop from the metal drawer and placed it in my open palms.

So much that went on in church, where the grown-ups took Communion and talked about God, didn't make sense to me. But here in the car I understood the reassuring flavor of God melting on my tongue. As I focused on God gradually dissolving in my mouth, everything slowed down, making me feel steady and quiet as the Annapolis scenery flickered past my window. After the communion was complete, down to the gummy white stick, we arrived at the grocery store where I could find more God—in the Kool-Aid section, in the produce department, in the jars of jelly, in the big jugs of Welch's grape juice.

That summer a frail boy around the age of four wandered

onto our property, having gotten lost in the woods between our home and the summer rental cabins on Crab Creek. When my mother found him sobbing behind our garage, she hoisted him onto her hip and carried him into our kitchen. Immediately she poured grape juice into a Flintstones glass. "Don't you worry," she said, gesturing toward me. "I'm this little girl's mommy and I know that if she were ever lost I'd *never* stop looking for her. Your parents are looking for you right now, and we're going to help them find you. Now have a drink of this grape juice and you'll feel much better."

As he sipped the deep purple potion I watched with awe as the boy's tears magically stopped flowing. By the time he swallowed the last drop of God he was looking at my mother with all the trust that something as true and reliable as grape juice engenders. Once again my mother lifted the boy to her hip—this time to carry him through the woods as she called out his parents' names amongst the lush trees of summer. Within minutes the boy's mother came crashing and stumbling through the green underbrush, arms hungrily reaching forward. "Oh, thank God," she wailed, gathering the boy to her chest and crying into his pale, thin neck. The boy smiled back at my mother with a stain of deep purple on his lips.

The following autumn, that feeling of perpetual safety was destroyed. We had just completed the dinner grace, and I was about to spoon out the cheerful, half-moon-shaped bit of grape floating in my fruit cocktail, when my brother announced, "Gail thinks God is grape." The room fell silent, as if a candle had just been snuffed out.

I immediately looked to my mother. "What are you talking about?" she asked my brother, carefully avoiding my worried eyes.

"Gail says, 'God is grape, God is good,'" Jimmy reported, his mouth looping into a grin. My father smiled and coughed into his napkin.

"Well, that's right, isn't it?" I asked my mother.

My mother looked down at her lap. She sat the closest to me and must have known for a long while that I believed God was grape. In that moment she looked guilty and sad all at once. "I know you like to say 'God is grape'," she began, "but that's not how the grace is supposed to be said."

I felt as though someone had just lifted my world, turned it upside down and shaken all the pennies out. Suddenly all that I had been certain of was a jumble of questions. My face twisted into a tight fist, trying to hold back an explosion of tears. "Then what is God?" I asked urgently. "What am I supposed to say?"

"God is great," she answered softly.

"Great?" I said, wrinkling my nose. "Great" was what my parents said when I took the training wheels off my two-wheeler. Great was just a dumb old word. It didn't have a taste, or a smell, or a color. Great was nothing.

Eventually the ridiculousness of "God is great" ebbed and I was left with my embarrassment over having made such a public mistake. The next Monday morning I quietly asked for a cherry lollipop. The bank teller looked surprised, but passed it on anyway. Of course it didn't taste as complete and perfect as the grape ones had—it simply tasted like plain cherry.

Losing my grape God was like a death. That same winter I

began Sunday school lessons in which God was introduced as an old, bearded white man with a judgmental nature. "What's so great about him?" I wondered to myself, sulking in my Sunday school chair. The more I was taught about God, the more betrayed I felt. All those years God had just sat in his throne and let me lie to myself. He probably even laughed at me.

I began taking my rage out in church, purposely saying the wrong words during prayers and hymns. "Our Father who does art in heaven, Harold be thy name," I'd say smugly. At Christmas time when the congregation began, "What child is this who laid to rest," I gleefully added, " . . .on Mary's lap is peeing?"

Finally my mother couldn't take it any longer. "Either say the right words or be quiet," she hissed. So I chose to stop speaking altogether, dramatically silencing myself in church with my arms crossed and a scowl on my face.

Though my parents weren't especially religious, they did insist that we continue to attend church each Sunday so we could worship God in uncomfortable wooden pews and sing him joyless, droning songs from hymnbooks. As time went by, I gained better control over my disappointment and boredom in church. I learned how to keep from scuffing my white patent leather shoes and how to sit still while wearing a scratchy dress. But I never could wrap my brain around the Christian "great God" belief. It just didn't compare with the grape God of my childhood, the one I could touch, smell and see. The God we learned about in Sunday school resided in a distant heaven. My grape God had been of this world, right in my backyard, right in my mouth, right inside my body. We were taught about Jesus dying for our sins and how God loved all his children, but everything seemed to focus on language and discussions. I never learned to carry God out of the church and into the sensory, experiential world of my childhood.

By the time I received my First Communion at age twelve, the wine that our minister lifted to my lips tasted sour and watery. The white wafer dissolved into a tasteless paste upon my tongue like an elusive Holy Ghost, so different from my robust grape God. It seemed such a stingy and meager offering to those of us who knelt with empty palms at the altar. Painfully, I realized that the church's version of Communion would never quench my thirst or satisfy my appetite.

It shocks me now that I allowed myself to become so indoctrinated and disillusioned that I doubted my early connection with God. Over the years I read that many indigenous and ancient religions believed that God dwells in the natural world; that God resides in the flesh and beauty of the physical. Perhaps the silliness of "God is grape," the cuteness of it all, made it easy for me to dismiss it as a mistake, rather than hold onto it as my innate connection with the divine. It was tragically easy for me to believe that the way I knew God was "all wrong"—that God could only be found within the confines of religious dogma.

Was it because I saw myself as a powerless, even foolish child that I quickly doubted my unique connection to God? Or was it because I was a girl, learning how to be compliant instead of rebellious and righteously angry? Or was it because so many religions of my culture speak to a God in the sky, a Father in Heaven, rather than to an Earth Mother embodied in the luscious bounty of the world? It is hard to know why I became so lost and self-doubting that I couldn't claim my childhood vision of God. I told myself that mature grown-ups couldn't behold God's violet and lavender hues with their open eyes, as if this affirmed that those images of God were unreal. And of course it was no longer possible to taste God upon my tongue, or inhale God's scent.

Then, when I was twenty-nine years old, I became unexpectedly pregnant. Suddenly I felt the urge to eliminate all that was false in my life. I resigned from my newspaper job, which had grown stale and confining. My husband and I sold our possessions and drove to the West Coast to find new jobs and a new home. By the time our baby daughter spilled from the depths of my body, I was ready to greet her with uncluttered arms.

I was surprised by the rapture I felt for her little body and fledgling being. Her skin was the color of a scallop shell. When she closed her eyes, I could not resist kissing the vulnerability of her lilac-veined eyelids. Her head smelled of milk and summer air. When she slipped her wet, curled fingers into my mouth they tasted like salty pears.

One morning, soon after her birth, I held my daughter in my open palms and noticed the way a sunbeam lit up the golden-brown wisps of hair on her head. It was then that I began to feel the abiding presence of God again. Of course God existed. Of course God could be found in the physical world. It seemed so obvious now. Here, right before my eyes, was all the proof I ever needed. How could anything but the divine create something so beautiful, so precious, so loved?

I could never build a bridge to the Judgment Day God or the scolding, guilt-inducing, son-sacrificing God. But I could find a relationship with a God that dwelled in a world that was at once fragile and powerful. All along my early love of the grape God was my way of grasping the vastness and meaning of God. God is greater than grape. God is as immense as an ocean, as terrible as an earthquake and as reliable as the golden grains of summer. God is everything and everywhere, with more colors and flavors than I ever imagined possible.

Holding my dimple-fleshed baby in my hands, I finally understood that this amazing physical God has a purpose. This God is our constant inspiration to connect with—and I mean really connect with, as in touch, taste, smell and nurture—what we love. My God of the physical world inspires a mother's love for her child, a woman's devotion to the wild forest behind her house, humanity's hope for this barren, lush, diseased and ever-evolving planet.

As the hazy, sleep-deprived months of infant care passed, I felt almost giddy in my ability to see, smell and taste God's presence in the world. There, in the trembling winter tree branches as I pushed the stroller along the sidewalks of Seattle. There, in the patch of blue sky against a charcoal landscape. Here, in the warmth of our morning bed where the three of us awaken each day—arms, legs and breath entwined in a trinity of love. The God of my childhood never left me. It was I who abandoned the sensory, physical connection with the divine. And now that I have recaptured that connection, I feel satiated once again.

One afternoon, when my daughter, Gabrielle, was just over a year old, she awoke from her nap with a cry that was panicky and frighteningly hollow at the same time. I quickly ran to her and lifted her warm, moist body from the crib. Pulling her against my chest, I could instantly feel her hunger—an enormous appetite that intimidated me with its urgency. Gabrielle continued to cry a scorching, chest-rattling wail. Since she was already weaned, I could not bring her to my breast. Instead, I planted her on my hip and set off for the kitchen to find some immediate food. Opening the refrigerator, my eyes settled on a freshly washed bunch of grapes. Gabrielle saw the grapes too and eagerly lunged for them. But I knew grapes need to be cut into small pieces before being fed to young children.

Quickly, I lowered Gabrielle into her highchair and turned to find a paring knife. As soon as I turned my back, Gabrielle screamed and stretched her fingers toward the bowl of grapes. This hunger could not wait.

Instinctively, I plucked one of the grapes and crushed it inside my mouth, letting its cool juice burst upon my tongue. Lifting the crushed, purple-red grape from my mouth—juice and saliva glistening like icing—I placed it into her wide-open mouth. Unexpectedly, these words came to me: "Take this and eateth of me." Perhaps my daughter, like me, was born with a fiery hunger to know God. Maybe all I can do is feed her the God that I know, hoping that someday she will learn to feed herself.

Her cheeks were red from the heat of her nap and her sweaty dark-brown hair curled into damp ringlets. As she closed her

mouth and began to chew I could almost feel the grape's cool-
ness and tangy flavor upon her bare gums and warm tongue.
Feeling a love as pure as the purple juice my mother once
poured in my childhood kitchen, I crushed another grape and
placed it in Gabrielle's eager, open mouth.

Agnostic Dyke Seeks Goddess

Jennifer M. Collins

*Acolyte seeks deity. I am: butch agnostic, freelance writer,
NS/ND, social drinker. You be: Omnipotent, with whole world
in hands, good with cars and words.*

I am, at the age of thirty, on a quest for a Greater Understanding.
I have a desire for some connection with that which is outside of
myself, outside of the materialistic, xenophobic American culture in which I find myself living.

My question, however, is this: how do I find One from whom
to Learn Greater Truths out here in the real world? I see the evidence of religion and worship around me every day. On my
drives into town, I pass billboards asking God to bless America.
At family gatherings, I bend my head at mealtime, thanking a
God I've never met for the food we are about to receive. I flip
quickly past the 700 Club's televangelists, who promise Jesus in
exchange for a contribution. I need more excitement, more challenge, than what I've come upon so far in the spirituality scene.
While I am eager to communicate with something beyond my
everyday experience, I've never found any One enticing or liberal enough to draw me in. And I'm ready to resort to desperate
measures to find my soul mate, my own private deity.

Finding a Supreme Teacher who will take you as you are,

particularly when you are a freaky leftist dyke like me, seems easier said than done. Back in the day, I went to some Sunday morning meet-and-greets at an assortment of Catholic and Protestant churches, and what I found—a home with Jesus and quiet time with Mary, as long as I was a good, quiet, heterosexual girl—didn't really do it for me. I don't see myself fitting into a traditional congregation, and I want to spend less time defending my political, sexual and gender choices, and more time communing peacefully with a Sacred Other.

I decided to check out the spirituality section of my library, see who was hanging around there, and do a little networking. The folks writing many of the spirituality books available today seemed at first to have a connection to some Others I'd want to know. However, I eventually realized that each author was convinced that his or hers was the Only Way to Enlightenment. Oh, sure, there were other options, the author might concede, but those were inferior imitations, not the Real Thing. *Uh-huh*, I'd think, closing the book. I decided to let these folks take their Real Thing somewhere else.

I saw you: Are you a Greater One who's losing her faith, frustrated with humans who expect you to take control of and responsibility for their lives, offering nothing in return? I think I saw you last week, mascara running and fishnets torn, walking down my street. You were kicking cans and seemed to be conversing with someone I couldn't see, gesturing wildly with all four of your arms. I was the sturdily built woman who passed you on her bike, paying more attention to the glow of

your third eye than to the potholes. My leg is finally healing.
Coffee sometime?

Thinking I might take a shot at finding the All-Powerful Female, I looked to some of the periodicals gracing the shelves at my local mega-bookstore. I did manage to find a couple of magazines devoted to the Feminine Spirit. However, I quickly realized that she demanded that her followers grow their hair down to their waists (and I'd been so happy to cut all mine off when I came out!), braid flowers in its lengths, clothe themselves in flowing skirts, prance barefoot through meadows and compose badly rhymed verse to the Almighty Her.

So my intact dyke haircut and I decided to spend some quality time with Buddha and then the Hindu goddess Kali. They both seemed cool, easygoing, grounded. I had high hopes for a little more chemistry, and a lot more fashion options. But I knew from the get-go that I didn't want to be just another one of those exotic-culture-dabbling Westerners, taking what felt good and leaving the rest. I wanted to respect Buddha and Kali for all of who they are, not just try to make them into who I want them to be.

For me, in this case, there was just too much of a cultural divide: it seemed too hard to know which parts of such an unfamiliar spiritual path were important, which could be challenged and which could be abandoned altogether. To be true to the teachings, to find true connection, I would need to spend a great deal of time learning not only about the particular tradition I chose to follow, but also about the culture and the history from whence it originated. I was dubious about my abilities to do justice to this task. Sometimes, if you have to try too hard to make it work, you've got to wonder if it's meant to be. I parted amicably with Buddha and Kali. I'd learned a lot from them, but I was still searching.

I was becoming despondent. Where does a girl go these days to find a Great Spirit? Someone intriguing, open-minded and fun enough to date for a while. Someone who might be LTR (long-term religion) material but doesn't expect you to bring your U-Haul to the first date. Like so much else in this universe, it sometimes seems as though all the good Ones are taken, or unsuitable, or already corrupted by the white supremacist capitalist system.

Not that I was about to give up. I still believed in Love. But I was tired of hoping the right deity would just happen to cross my path. I didn't think I'd find One in my usual hangouts. So I finally resorted to desperate measures: I sat right down and wrote my plea, my own woman-seeking-deity personals ad.

How often had I heard my friends (the alt-spirituality folks, anyway) talking about "puttin' it out to the universe" when they want some change in their lives? That's just what I was going to do. But instead of engaging in mindful prayer, surrounded by incense, candles and the tones of tape-recorded Tibetan pipes, I'd be sending five dollars to my local alternative weekly to print my desires in their personals section. Seriously—is five bucks too much to pay for a shot at Greater Understanding? And God/desses are omniscient, are they not? All-seeing and all-knowing? Even if I placed the ad in just a handful of papers, doesn't it seem like there would be a better-than-average chance that it would catch the third eye of my Goddess-to-be while she was taking a break from more reverent reading?

Really, placing a personals ad in search of a deity is not so strange, if you think about it. Personals ads are where countless people turn when they are tired of waiting for fate to hand them the perfect sexual/romantic partner, and the sexual aspect of religious worship has been around forever, no matter that many modern-day (Western) religions would like to obscure its importance. In the past I've often looked to the otherworldly to explain my ecstatic experiences, in addition to my unanswerable questions. Maybe I'll find the One willing to introduce me to *all* the heavens, including the seventh.

> *Butch dyke seeking deity. Would prefer an obdurate optimist, able to take hard knocks in stride. Must be inspirational and ready to kick some ass (mine included) at a moment's notice. Am interested in giving myself over to someone more powerful than myself and exploring this "ecstasy" thing: what happens when sex isn't just sex anymore? Are you Hothead Paisan, Mary Magdalene and Annie Sprinkle all rolled into one? Call me.*

What is this desire to revere some special One? I believe there is more to this world than I can perceive with my naked senses, and I conceive of that elusive something as some form of God or Goddess. For me, it's comforting to imagine a human face on this incomprehensible energy or intelligence. I like the idea of being able to talk with whatever it is that sometimes seems to be with me in my backyard, at the edge of a pine forest, while I plant seeds in a late-May garden. Fantasies of slow walks through the park while my One points out the spark of spring in a maple bud and long conversations (over candlelit dinners) about the meaning of life fuel my desires to get in touch with this member of the Universal Beyond.

> *Militant agnostic seeks Muse for mutually confusing and challenging intellectual and spiritual investigation. Friends first, with possibility of LTR if the connection is right. Serious replies only. Light drugs okay.*

I had never written a personals ad before and was cautious about the wording. How would I make myself sound exciting yet sane, and worth a Supreme Being's time and attention, in one hundred words or less? There was also the issue of whether to run the ad as a straight-up personal (if only there were a women-seeking-deities section!) or place it in the "alternative" section, between the heterosexual couples looking for a well-endowed third party and the diaper-wearing men seeking a ruler-wielding disciplinarian. Of course, next came the waiting, and the nail-biting calls to check the mailbox, hoping for responses. How would I do the screening? How would I be able to tell whether that voice on the other end of the phone was an actual deity and not just some dyke with a God complex?

What I'd like to have is a face-to-face with a Representative of the Great Beyond. Have some tea, get to know each other's likes and dislikes, see if there's a spark. I already have my questions lined up: how does one get into the deity business anyway? Is it a family thing, or is there an apprentice period? Are there any other acolytes with whom I might speak? And what sorts of requirements do you have for followers: do I have to believe everything you say without question? Would I have to commit to a monogamous, 24/7 sort of relationship? How have your past relationships worked out? Are you still friends with your ex's?

All this time, a little part of me can't help but wonder whether I really want to worship a Supreme Being who is so hard-up for acolytes S/He has lowered Her/Himself to slumming through the personals ads? But maybe it's just as hard to find believers as it is to find someone to believe in. Should I let my skepticism get in the way of what could be the start of a beautiful relationship?

Here is a frightening thought: what if I do find a Holy Other who meets my criteria, and whose criteria I meet as well? Could I then take the next step of becoming reverent? If I were a deity who had gone through all the trouble of contacting a potential worshipper, setting up an earth-based meet, consuming some poorly brewed caffeinated beverage and spending several hours discussing history and boundaries and philosophies, I might be the slightest bit frustrated if said worshipper tucked tail and ran when I turned out to be all that she was hoping for.

But then, we all have to take risks. If it did work out, this would not be a one-way relationship. From me, the lucky Sacred One could expect belief, trust and faith. In addition, given my big mouth, there's a very good chance that I would talk up this new relationship in my community ("Hey, I can't make it for dinner . . . It's a full moon and I promised to meet The One in my back-yard with my homework . . . Yes, I actually did it this time, and tonight's lesson has to do with some connection between the stars and women's sexuality . . . "), thus giving my new deity the chance to acquire additional followers without having to continue pawing through those pesky personals.

The truth is, I would love any responses at all to this ad, even if I only end up talking with a delusional store clerk who believes that she's seen an image of the Buddha on an eggplant. Each time I talk with someone else about faith, spirituality and the Great Beyond, I have the opportunity to clarify what I do (or definitely do not) believe. And, as I am often reminded, it never hurts to ask. Why not put out to the universe the message that I am not happy with the selection of deities with which I have become familiar, and am hoping that there is one more appropriate for my needs waiting in the wings somewhere? Why shouldn't I have the same chance so many others have to learn some Greater Lessons about myself, about the earth, about the universe?

> *Faith-challenged dyke ISO spiritually centered Universal Other. I have some questions about this world I'm living in that I need to have answered (or at least addressed), and would appreciate some guidance. I am willing to travel, enjoy new experiences and appreciate out-of-body spiritual moments. You have patience, a love of challenge, hope for humanity, an aptitude for delivering difficult information in creative and enigmatic ways and a fondness for coffee. Am looking forward to your call.*

After Christ

Teena Apeles

THIS CHILD: Christina Lardizabal Apeles

DATE OF BIRTH: 12-26-72

HOUR: 12:10 A.M.

PLACE OF BIRTH: Hollywood Presbyterian Hospital

COLOR OR RACE OF MOTHER/FATHER OF CHILD: Brown

BIRTHPLACE OF MOTHER/FATHER OF CHILD: Philippines

My mom spent her Christmas evening giving birth to me, bringing me into this world just ten minutes after Christianity's most celebrated holiday. And if there had been a Catholic hospital in the area, my birth certificate would really tell the story of my origins: a brown, Catholic baby girl born in Hollywood and given a name that reflects her Filipino parents' love of Christ and her delivery in the wake of His birthday. But the heart of my story is not the birth certificate. It is the roller coaster ride of faith I have experienced as a first-generation American girl of Filipino-Catholic parents. And my brand of Catholicism is unlike any others—especially my parents'.

I was born Catholic, just like the rest of my family. I say "born" and not "raised" since Catholicism always seemed an inherent thing, not a matter of choice. But it wasn't just that my parents foisted the religion on me (even though that was part of it). The choice of Catholicism was not my parents' either. My family's faith was determined hundreds of years ago when Spanish explorers and missionaries brought the religion to the Philippines and forced it on the island peoples. Today, although the Spanish are gone, more than 85 percent of the country is still fervently Catholic. So, really, my faith was decided by people who lived more than 500 years ago. My parents only think they were the ones calling the shots.

When I was young, my parents would say to me, "Don't forget where you came from!" At the time, I traced my cultural and religious roots only as far as my grandparents. My father's parents were very active at St. Columban (also known as *the* Filipino church in L.A.). My *lolo* (grandfather), president of the church's Holy Name Society, read at Masses and helped organize community events. When he died suddenly when I was seven, the priests of St. Columban visited our family. The church held a funeral mass and the place was overflowing with people—just for Lolo. They loved him like family and the sense of community I felt then has never left me. For me, Catholicism was this feeling of love and community.

I spent most of my childhood as an obedient Catholic girl. I went to a parochial school, attended Mass every Sunday, honored the proper holidays, fasted when I was supposed to and even said my prayers in the evening. In grade school, all of my classmates (a mix of white, Latino and Asian kids) were baptized and received Communion. These rituals were perfectly normal to me. In fact, I celebrated them happily, loving my First Communion ceremony, when I got to dress up in a little white dress like a miniature bride, walk down the center aisle with my girlfriends and receive Jesus. It was a rite of passage, which was rewarded with gifts and attention. I felt blessed. I had no reason to believe that I wasn't on my way to Heaven or that God wasn't out there somewhere, taking care of me and my loved ones.

But that sentiment inevitably changed over the years. It wasn't just one shattering moment or epiphany that put me on my unexpected roller coaster ride of understanding and resisting my Catholic faith. A number of events and bits of knowledge gained initiated the sea change. First there were the historical elements. It seemed everything I began to learn of my family's—and Filipinos'—history was marked by colonial rule. The words my parents spoke and the God they worshipped—two of the most personal things I can imagine—were not *really* their own.

One night my grandmother and aunt were reviewing the family will. I was amazed to see it had been drafted in the 1800s, and moreover, was in Spanish. Then, a couple of years later, in an emotional gesture to demonstrate the great love affair that my grandparents had had, my mom turned over the love letters her parents had exchanged in the early 1900s. But it wasn't the wooing words or heartfelt notes that caught my attention—all the letters were written in English! And then, just this past year, I saw my *lola*'s 1904 baptism certificate and 1927 wedding certificate—again, in English. My parents and grandparents were bilingual, but it was strange to see that official and even intimate documents were not in the Filipino language of

Tagalog. It was obvious the Spanish and American occupations of the Philippines had had a greater impact on the cultural landscape—religion included—of my parents' country than I had known, and the documents only scratched the surface.

When my family moved to the suburbs for my junior high and high school years, my sisters and I started to rebel in typical teenage fashion. One of the first things that came under attack was our family's beloved religion, and my mom and dad certainly weren't prepared.

Let's just say communities in the suburban sprawl of Ventura County were unlike those I was accustomed to in Los Angeles. On one hand, there were very few Filipinos or other "brown" kids at my all-girl high school. My previous schools had been more diverse ethnically (not to mention coed). I was a minority as a first-generation American, especially a Filipino American. On the other hand, although I was attending an all-girl Catholic school, there were many girls of different faiths: Baptist, Baha'i, Muslim, Buddhist and even atheist. This too was surprising and new to my sisters and me, since we'd spent most of our childhood with people of the same religion.

The questions "What are you?" and "Where are you from?" came up often. As the new girl at school in the midst of adolescence, I had enough to deal with that I certainly didn't appreciate my identity being called into question almost daily. My confusion only increased as I encountered girls (potential friends) whose home lives didn't include the Catholic practices and beliefs that played a major role in my family's day-to-day life. "I believe in God, the Father Almighty, Creator of Heaven and Earth . . ." Blah, blah, blah. I knew it by heart, I even believed in those words, but was I the only one in my social circle who did?

"You don't go to church?" I asked some of my new girlfriends. A few responded with, "Hell no, my parents sent me here as punishment." Others said, "We don't practice, I just came here for the education," or "I'm not Catholic, I'm . . ."

This was a difficult time for my parents, who had never given much thought to other faiths or lifestyles. Now their three American-born daughters were hitting their teens and encountering all sorts of other practices, belief systems and values. For my part, I wanted to make friends. My "uniqueness"—devout Catholic, first-generation American girl of Filipino parents—was less a source of pride than an obstacle to building relationships. My girlfriends and their public-school friends obviously weren't interested in the Word of God or virtues; they indulged in the basic teenage vices of drinking, smoking, sneaking out and, of course, premarital sex. Unconsciously I began to trivialize my differences in exchange for a feeling of camaraderie. I assimilated. Going to church wasn't cool, I was "American," not "Filipino" and I began to share the belief that parents sucked.

I believe my mom and dad thought that by sending us to Catholic schools, they had ensured that religion would remain an undeniable part of our identity. We'd continue to honor all the major holidays, pray the rosary, meet nice Catholic boys, get married in church, have baptized kids and continue the cycle. That was their life, it would be ours.

"Do you want to go to the mall on Sunday?" asked my new

best friends, Julie and Jenny. "We're going to meet up with Sonny and Jody for lunch."

"Mom, can I go out with Julie and Jenny today?"

"No. You know we have to go to Mass."

"Just because I miss one Mass doesn't mean I'm going to Hell . . ."

That's when the slap would land on my face.

And so I'd have to call my friends and say, "I can't. It's church and family day."

Every event counts when you're in your teens, and if you can't make that one day of goofing off with boys or picking out a new outfit in the department store, your whole social life is at stake. You feel left out and out of the loop. And whom and what did I have to blame? My parents and Catholicism.

So I started to make my case against what I now saw as a stifling regimen of going to church, praying the rosary and honoring Jesus, Mary and God (whom my friends couldn't care less about, except to the extent that they affected my going out or talking on the phone). With a little help from my friends, whom I felt raised interesting questions about my faith (a lot of these friends had no faith at all), I began posing questions my parents had never even considered: if Jesus and Mary are white, does that mean God is too? If God is everywhere and in me, why can't I talk to him whenever I want? Why do women only get to sing in the choir, do the Bible readings at Mass and serve Communion? Why couldn't I be a priest?

To my dismay, these questions about Catholicism were answered with punishment. After not-so-obedient behavior at church, my sisters and I would be lined up, slapped on the face and then ordered to pick weeds in the yard for a whole afternoon.

"Don't you think it's odd that we pray to a white family, Mom?"

She could never respond. I'd receive a dirty look or be threatened with being grounded. But generally the response was silence. What could they say? My parents wouldn't face the fact that the religious statues and pictures we worshipped depicted people who looked different than we did. In many ways, this conflict I had with my parents was an extension of the historical conflict of Filipinos, who have long been immersed in religions and cultures that are not their own. Those who questioned the foundation of these beliefs and practices also faced difficult consequences, likely more painful than anything I had to confront. It was a vicious cycle that I wanted to end.

I did not realize then that my parents and extended family did incorporate certain Filipino traditions into their Catholicism: the extended mourning period, which involved praying the rosary after the death of a loved one for what seems like weeks; the inclusion during wedding ceremonies of a cord, representing unity, and coins, symbolizing prosperity; and the singing of Filipino songs at Mass. But as an adolescent all I could see was that the Church itself was not indigenous to our culture.

But I wasn't ready to abandon Catholicism altogether. I still wanted to respect my parents and hold on to some basic practices I felt were right and comforting, like treating people well and not lying or stealing. I still wanted to be "good." I did, on occasion, defend my faith. When friends asked why I went to confession, celebrated a particular holiday or took Communion,

I could have said, "That's what I've always been taught," "Because the Bible says so," "It's cheaper than a therapist" or, better yet, "I like the taste of Jesus in my mouth on Sundays and besides, it's the only time I can drink wine legally." But instead, sometimes I would just say, "It's family time and it happens to be spent at church." I was young, I was still searching, I was working toward understanding why I thought as I did, versus simply rebelling against my parents' faith.

I'll never know how different those high school years could've been had my mom or dad said to me, "Don't forget Spain ruled the Philippines, and much later the Americans occupied the country, and that's why we ended up in Hollywood as Catholics." I doubt that answer would've been enough to prevent my roller coaster ride of faith, especially with my friends adding bumps and revolutions along the way. Yet, knowing these facts would have been worth more than anything I was taught in school. Only now do I realize history's relevance to my life and faith.

But those weren't the sort of history lessons my immigrant parents taught me. As I felt myself drifting away from Filipino culture and getting more and more into my American-bred identity during my teenage years, I could hear my parents saying, "Remember where you came from." I was a brown, Catholic baby girl born in Hollywood. Unfortunately, I was proud of only one piece of that description—"born in Hollywood." Why? Was it the move from a multicultural urban community with strong church ties to a primarily Caucasian suburb with little religious cohesion that put my ethnic and religious identity in peril? My older sister Tricia and I always wondered what might have happened if we had stayed in Los Angeles—would we be devout Catholics married to Filipino boys, speaking Tagalog and active in the Mother of Good Counsel parish?

We will never know, but my little sister Linda and I have since returned to our old neighborhood and certainly feel more at home there than we ever felt in the suburbs. Los Angeles is our home. Every day I walk by my old grade school and the church where I received my First Communion, I feel proud to know where I came from.

At my mom's request, Linda and I recently attended a Mother's Day Mass in my old parish. The priest called all the mothers up to the altar and half of the congregation left the pews. My mom walked up to the priest with what seemed like a hundred other women. Each shook the priest's hand as he handed her a carnation. Then all the mothers lined up on the steps in front of the altar, holding their red and pink flowers, as the priest celebrated them publicly and the congregation gave them a round of applause. *This is what I love about this place*, I thought. I was proud to be part of it. In that moment, Catholicism wasn't just about saying "I believe in God the Father" or receiving the body of Christ. It was about community, about celebrating the women who have made community possible—throughout history.

Everything I hold dear—family, rituals, holidays, heirlooms—is so intertwined with Catholicism that to break away from that faith completely means trivializing, or worse, forgetting these precious relationships. On a recent visit to the Philippines, where my parents renewed their vows at a special Mass led by the priest who originally married them, I felt that same sense of community and love for the Church. I loved every part of it. Surrounded by family in an open-air church, the prayers came freely, without resistance. These experiences bring me moments of clarity and belonging that transcend everyday life. They are important reminders of the spirituality that exists in spite of historical context.

Every moment my family has come together for a baptism, a holiday dinner, a funeral, Mass; artifacts like my mom's wedding suit, my Communion dress; the blessing of my car and our family home . . . all these are celebrated, and all are related to our faith, no matter what language is used or how much less "brown" my family becomes with each generation. How can I deny the importance of these things?

I can't. You will only catch me attending Mass a few times a year these days, and I don't know any of the prayers by heart anymore. It is no longer Catholicism that brings me back. Rather, it's my own spirituality, which stems from the personalized faith my parents and extended family have created to fit our way of life. I don't think of the Bible, the Pope, Jesus, Mary or Joseph when I think of Catholicism or faith. I think family, community and celebration. My spirituality is about believing in and sustaining the love that is demonstrated in different Catholic ceremonies; it is about how my family and I add our own special touches to such occasions.

Though the Spanish brought Catholicism to the Philippines, Filipinos have incorporated their own customs to make it more meaningful to their culture. This means wedding masses last almost two hours, so that big Filipino families can involve everyone in a ceremony led by a Filipino priest. There are Black Rosary groups that bring together families who emigrated from the same province in the Philippines. And Filipino couples don't limit their kids to just one set of godparents: my goddaughter has five.

I am a first-generation American girl born to Filipino-Catholic parents in Los Angeles. And my brand of Catholicism is unlike any others, but my sense of spirituality is not unique.

There are a lot of customs and rituals that have become second nature to me, and it's still difficult to discern whether these originate with Catholicism, Spanish tradition, Filipino culture or merely quirky practices my family has come up with. My aunt says never to cut my toenails at night because one of my parents will die. My mom puts dollar coins over every doorway during Christmas. Regarding such superstitions, I remember what my dad said at dinner one evening, "Y'know those things probably came about because some person wanted to prevent another person from doing things he didn't want them to do."

"Sounds like our religion," I said.

He smiled at me and replied, "Respect your father and mother."

Touché.

That's a commandment I'll never forget. Just as my parents have done with Catholicism, I have done with my Jesus-inspired name and faith: I've tailored it. I never go by "Christina" anymore (except on legal documents). But "Teena" is not devoid of Christ: I see him as an example of a person who loves and honors his family and people—kind of like me. Being blessed with a mixed bag of cultures and religious traditions, I have managed to take bits of each to create my own belief system. And I will encourage my kids to do the same.

I still fall asleep at Mass (when I go at all), make the sign of the cross during airplane take-offs and build altars of all kinds. These days, my altars contain mementos and pictures of friends and family (rather than crosses or images of Jesus and Mary) amidst candles and incense. These are the people and artifacts I treasure in my life. My friends and family often look like or reflect me; they share similar life experiences and maybe, just maybe, they seem closer to Heaven because of their place in my life. When I build and look upon these shrines or think about the special individuals they honor, I feel better about the world and the future. These people and the precious moments they've shared with me make up my faith, I pray *to* them and *for* them and sometimes, God (the mysterious being my parents told me about) even gets kudos for bringing them to me. Amen.

Pilgrimage
Pramila Jayapal

A ten-day trek in the Garwhal Himalayas took Alan and me up and down mountain ranges, over lush high meadows, among shepherds and their hundreds of grazing sheep and finally to the amphitheater of majestic Kuari Pass, where the rising sun threw a circle of red and pink across the top of dozens of Himalayan peaks.

We walked on broad paths made of inset rocks, paths similar to those in the garden of a landscape architect, perfectly sculpted but created by natural hands. Our feet crunched on pine needles, releasing nature's pure fresh fragrance.

Rhododendrons and kharsu trees lined the sides of the paths. The kharsu tree is a gnarled tree with sturdy branches that curl outward in unnatural twists. Its leaves are spiky, clumped and dark green, with roots like long talons, pushed apart by wind, rain and erosion. The roots clung to the hillsides, and even though the tree trunks bent permanently over the plunging valley below, they stayed attached to the hillsides because of their roots. Without them, the kharsus would have fallen, headfirst, and all their branches and spiky clumpy leaves would have splintered into countless shards on the green fertile ground below.

The Hindu pilgrimage town of Badrinath is set in the middle of giant fissures of rain-stained granite slabs and below the blinding snowy summit of Neelkanth Peak. Badrinath, one of the four centers of God established by Shankaracharaya, the great South Indian monist philosopher, is the destination of hundreds of thousands of pilgrims from all over India. According to the Hindu texts, no pilgrimage is complete without a visit to Badrinath, the place where Lord Krishna, an incarnation of Vishnu, commanded his disciple Uddhava to go and meditate on him.

The road to the temple from Badrinath town leads down a small hill through a narrow alley lined with prasad shops, stalls selling devotional videos, books and other trinkets. Jostled between all the holy men and women clad in faded orange clutching their alms canisters, I would make my way to the bridge that crossed the Alaknanda River to the temple. From the far bank of the bridge, just below the temple, were the hot springs where pilgrims bathed before entering the temple.

I would walk across the bridge, sandwiched between the hundreds of young, old, decrepit cane-leaning bodies. Halfway across the bridge, I would slip to the side, standing among a few squatting, alms-seeking sadhus and turning back to watch people set foot on the bridge with the first unfettered view of the temple. "*Jai Badri Vishal!*" The cry went up and was echoed by hundreds, as they touched their hands to the bridge's cold, stony surface and to their foreheads, then raised their hands in a high namaste.

Unlike the other pilgrims, who went immediately to enter the temple, it took me three days to set foot inside. I stood outside and watched the thousands of people make their way eagerly to the temple. Despite the religious importance of Badrinath, I found myself reluctant to enter because it was inside temples that I often felt like a kharsu tree whose roots had let go. Inside temples, I felt as if I had fallen and splintered into a thousand pieces because I could not feel the same devotion as do the millions of people who come to Badrinath, the devotion that I thought every "true" Hindu Indian should feel.

I was raised as a Hindu, whatever that means. I say that because it seemed to me that Hinduism was a loose, fluid religion—more a way of life than a religion.

There were a few rules but not many, and even those, it seemed, were simply guidelines that one could choose to follow or not. I knew, for example, that Hindus were not supposed to eat beef, yet my parents did. There were no temples that we visited weekly or even monthly. We celebrated our special holidays, like Onam, at home with no priests. At my wedding our simple South Indian ceremony had no officiant; our consecrator was the fire, around which we walked seven times, one round for each of the seven principles of married life: ideals, strength and power, wealth and fortune, happiness, progeny, love life and spiritual comradeship. We worshipped the goddess Devi, while other Hindus worshipped Shiva or Rama. Basically, Hindus were left to decide how, who and when to worship.

As children, the one ritual my sister and I observed without fail was the lighting of the lamps, once in the morning and once at night. In the mornings, when our eyes were still blurry with sleep, my mother would lead my sister and me to a small room at the corner of our veranda. Inside, we would stand in darkness as she lit the twisted, oil-soaked cotton wicks on two

Kerala-style lamps. The lamps were of a brass-colored alloy, each about a foot tall, like fully bloomed lotus flowers emerging out of their round bases.

After lighting the lamps, my mother would set aflame one or two small camphor squares in the middle of a brass tray. In that flickering light, we stood in front of the lamps and a picture of our goddess Devi, and recited the prayers we had been taught by my grandmother: "*Namo Shivaya, Naraya aya nama, Achutha aya nama, Anand aya nama, Govind aya nama, Gopal aya nama . . .*"

We did not know much about these gods and goddesses whose names we recited, but we knew these prayers were important. At the end of the prayers, my mother would take the brass tray and circle the picture of Devi with it three times. Then she would hold it in front of us, and we would cup our hands over the flame and bring them up to our face, spreading the aura over ourselves like rain water. We dipped our middle finger in the camphor ash and marked our throats with it. My mother would then wave her hands in front of the lamps to put out the fire—"never blow it out"—and we would leave, putting the ritual and its meaning behind us as we went about our day.

Nostalgia says those morning and evening rituals grounded me. At the time, though, I did not particularly want to be marked by ash or by rituals. In fact, I probably did not even feel the need to be protected. Religion was just a hand-me-down, perfected by the ages, honed by the wise and passed down through prayers; but it was not *mine*, not a personal part of my life or belief system.

It was not that I did not enjoy the rituals as an observer. When we visited my grandparents in India, for example, I loved watching my grandmother Ammamma pray. Early in the morning, I would go out onto the cool veranda before the sun began baking the earth. My grandmother would be in a curved wicker easy chair, a basket of jasmines in her lap. She showed me how to thread together the jasmines into a thick garland, head of one to the stem of the other so that there would be no holes in the garland. "Never smell the flowers before giving them to Devi," she would admonish me kindly. "They must be fresh for the goddess, no smell taken out."

After making the garland, Ammamma would take her bath. She would emerge from the bathroom in a petticoat and blouse, her long hair wrapped into a cheesecloth towel. Inhaling the smell of sandalwood soap, coconut hair oil and sweet talcum powder, I would lie on the bed and watch her dress. After donning a crisply ironed sari, she would open the wood doors on one side of the bed to reveal a small cupboard that housed framed pictures of various gods and goddesses and a shelf with a set of Kerala lamps and trays like we had in our puja room. She would string the garlands around the frames and then settle into a surprisingly nimble cross-legged stance to recite her prayers. As Ammamma sat chanting on the ground, she would toss loose jasmines at the gods and goddesses. I believed she had a hotline to God, because anything she prayed for seemed to come true.

Only at the very end, when she would motion me to sit next to her, would I quickly recite my prayers. Just like in Badrinath, where I watched others rejoice over reaching the temple I was so hesitant to enter, I much preferred to observe others

275

practicing their religion than to practice it myself. Perhaps that is because I simply had no idea what I believed.

I began questioning the existence of God years ago, in my mid-twenties. For the first time I stopped saying my prayers before I went to sleep. Who were these gods whose names I was chanting? I saw no logic, no reason for praying. Every once in a while, however, I found myself secretly saying my prayers, usually when I was scared or lonely. I would pull my bedcovers over my head and start reciting. The prayers slid off my tongue, an invisible ferris wheel spinning effortlessly. With the prayers I recreated the smells of safety and companionship, of my grandmother, of jasmine and of Devi's protective aura. This felt right while praying, but afterward I felt only guilt, as if I had done something I knew I should not do.

Hinduism has no founder nor prophet; its creeds are many; its forms of practice varied. Although the philosophies of Hinduism are explained in such books as the Upanishads, they are themselves esoteric. *Tat Tvam Asi,* say the Upanishads. *I am That.* How does a young mind capture that? The written texts hold concepts that are simple yet so broad that they become lofty, which makes it easy for people to forget the concepts themselves and instead become attached to the rituals.

The most popular texts quoted by the average Hindu are not the scriptures but rather the popular epics, the *Ramayana* and the *Mahabharata* thought to have been completed by the fourth century AD. When discussing appropriate moral and ethical behavior, Hindus will often refer to the *Bhagavad Gita* (literally

"Song of the Lord"), the sixth book of the *Mahabharata* in which Lord Krishna and Arjuna (one of the five Pandava brothers in the epic) engage in a philosophical discussion about Arjuna's duty, dharma, as a warrior. Krishna explains to Arjuna that to uphold his duty, even if it means killing his cousins in battle, will both display his devotion to God and guarantee him salvation. The *Ramayana* has been turned into a television series that has swept India with its popularity. Every Sunday morning, millions across India in villages and cities gather around television sets to watch the young handsome Rama as he undertakes new trials and battles, conveying in each episode a new moral platform.

For me, the Hinduism I was seeing in today's world had too many priests who were more interested in power and money than in salvation, too much exclusivity and divisiveness, too much fighting over who had the right to be religious and which was the true religion. Not understanding Hinduism (in a rational, logical sense) gradually progressed into a distancing from it, a disdain for religion itself. Moving from the private sector to the nonprofit world years ago had opened another channel of thought for me. The shift itself was not about spirituality per se but rather about fulfillment (which, at the time, seemed quite separate). This understanding that I needed to work at something that was in line with my own personal values and beliefs about the world was the beginning of looking at the accepted goals of life differently. If making money was not the end goal of life, what was? These thoughts were jumbled, as vague to me in some ways as Hinduism. But they were the beginning of a small spark of spiritual awareness that eventually would take me, many years later, back to India. I had begun some sort of profound shift.

And yet, now, back in India after so long, not having religion occupy an irreplaceable space in my being, as it does for many Indians, made me feel incomplete, unsteady and insufficient.

An unpretentious building next to the main temple held the residence of the Honorable N. Vishnu Namboodiri, the thirty-third Rawal (head priest) of Badrinath Temple. All the Rawals of Badrinath were the same sect of Namboodiri Kerala Brahmins from which the famous sage Shankaracharaya hailed.

I had heard that he met with pilgrims, and when we entered the main room where he saw people, we found ourselves miraculously alone with him. He was probably in his late thirties. Immediately, I sensed that, unlike some other so-called religious teachers I had met in Varanasi, the Rawal was uninterested in power or in emphasizing his own enlightened status. He wanted us close to him, where he could watch us intently as we spoke. He forbade us to take notes, wanting us simply to concentrate on our words. The Rawal alternated between being intimidating and humorous, childlike and sagelike. He displayed his humility in various ways, often leaning forward to bow before those who touched his feet in respect, once even touching the feet of a child who folded his hands in namaste. He downplayed his own knowledge and talked about his weaknesses. He was approachable and human, something I had never expected from someone of his stature.

Over the next few days, the Rawal spent many hours each day with my husband and me, letting us sit with him as he received people who had come to pay their respects. He periodically left us to conduct pujas at the temple next door, instructing us when to come back. At the following session, he remembered exactly where he had left off and began by asking us to summarize our understanding of the past session. He often clicked his tongue impatiently if we did not give the answer he was looking for, once even cutting me off midstream when I was getting long-winded. But always, regardless of how long it took, the Rawal made sure that we understood his concepts.

Nothing I said went unquestioned, and for the first time I found myself trying (rather unsuccessfully) to define such words as *man, service, religion* and *Hinduism*. Though it might sound like a philosophic discussion, it was not. The Rawal was interested in placing people on the practical path of the ancient Indian belief of *sanatan dharma*, or "right living."

The Rawal spoke limited English, and I could not always grasp in Hindi the complex ideas being discussed. For some of these discussions, a visitor named Krishnan would sit in and translate. When Krishnan was not there, and the Rawal sensed that we did not fully understand his words, he would look around, his eyes scanning the room for something he could use to illustrate his ideas. One of our first lessons was devoted to the idea of the essence of humankind. He had brushed away my simplistic explanations of the physical being of humankind. Humankind is *nash*, he said, except for the service one renders to others. We could not understand the meaning of nash and *anash* (its opposite), so he gave us several examples. You eat food, and it is nash. Ah, we said: gone, finished. Not quite. A few more examples and then he thought of something, leaping up excitedly and pulling out from a cupboard near the puja platform a box of incense sticks. He lit them and told us to ponder the burning incense. Then he dipped his finger in the fallen ash and smeared it on his forehead and waved his hands to indicate the sweet fragrance of incense floating through the room. Incense is anash, he explained, after taking us as far as we could go ourselves. It gives pleasure through its sweet smell and service through its fallen ash used to bless those who come to do puja. This is its significance in the puja rituals. It is eternal. Nash and anash: transient and eternal. Humankind, the physical being, is transient, but the service one does is eternal.

The Rawal refused to comment on Hinduism, saying it was just a name. Instead, he distinguished religion as the path of *sanatan dharma*, the eternal law of nature that guides the universe. "This is the way of our ancestors, of this country, what is written about in the Puranas (the mythical histories of gods and coped mostly in the first millennium of our era). The essential elements of right dharma are truth, good intention and nonviolence. If we carry out all our actions based on these three principles, we will be on the path of true dharma."

We spoke for hours about this true religion, an ancient, all-inclusive, tolerant practice, one that allowed me to begin to retract my own rejection of religion. Sanatan dharma was not the radical, exclusive, phobia-ridden fanaticism ravaging the world in the name of religion. It was simply a kind of selfless focus, of interdependence among all individuals and beings that are a part of Nature, of a belief that we are simply part of a larger cosmic universe.

The Rawal liked to emphasize the similarities between different religions, often referring to Christianity (probably for my husband's benefit, although Alan had probably read far less of the Bible than the Rawal had). In these comparisons the Rawal wanted simply to show that all religions seek oneness with a universal power, and the path toward that oneness is essentially the same.

The Rawal's conviction about the similarity between religions helped take away some of the sour taste left in my mouth by the discrimination and fanaticism propagated by so-called religious people. I was also reminded of how my own nondenominational views of religion were formed, how my distaste for religious singlemindedness was born through a series of experiences early in my life.

The school I attended as a child in Jakarta had a large contingent of Southern Baptist missionary kids—Baptist MKs, we called them. Their parents had been stationed by the Baptist Church in various remote parts of Indonesia to actively convert Indonesians to Christianity. The children were schooled at home by their parents until the seventh grade, after which they were sent to Jakarta to live in a Baptist missionary hostel near the school.

They were a talented group of children, accomplished in sports, music and academics. Most of all, though, they had each other. Their large, close-knit community seemed to have a tremendous amount of fun at Baptist parties and dances, movies and dinners, competitions and contests. The Baptist MKs took their meals together in a big, noisy dining room at the hostel. After dinner and homework they would linger in the common room talking.

To them I was a perfect target for conversion. Hinduism, as a religion, remained abstract to me. Nor did it hold out any special offerings of community as did Christianity. Because I was not particularly attached to my own religion at the time, converting religions did not seem too high a price to pay for a ready-made set of friends. I was serious enough about converting that (around the same time I was chosen to play Jesus in a church choir musical) I announced my intention to my mother. She was horrified—perhaps equally by my announcement as by watching her little brown Indian child wrapped in a white sheet, crown on head, singing "kill the fatted calf!"

Needless to say, my conversion did not come to pass. Even then, I recognized that I was attracted to the community aspect but not necessarily to the form of religion and worship. Christianity, as it was practiced by the Baptists I knew, was terribly structured compared with Hinduism. One had to go to church on Sunday mornings and youth group on Sunday evenings. One had to sing, kneel and pray along with the hundred other people in the church. And, if a convert, one had to declare in front of everyone exactly when and how Jesus came into one's life. It felt too confining. And besides, Jesus had not appeared to me as yet, and I had no confidence that he would any time soon.

Ultimately, the turning point came with Eric's betrayal. Eric was a Baptist MK, a few years older but in the same grade. One day, he righteously told me that if I did not convert to Christianity, I would burn in hell. I was twelve years old. Eric's words conjured up pictures of red demons with horns and pitchforks, of flames that would devour me limb by limb, hair by hair. I have never responded well to pressure and even then, scared as I was, I could not believe that my Devi would not have mentioned this small necessity of conversion to me. Nevertheless, Eric had succeeded in hurting and confusing me, singling me out and making me wonder what religion and God were all about if, in the end, one would be condemned simply for praying to a different form. Could it be that arbitrary?

It was another friend's father (a pastor, ironically, although of different faith) who finally consoled me. The pastor viewed religion, he said, as a big mountain with God at the top. Depending on where you stood at the base, the mountain top and the paths leading to it looked different. "Different religions take different paths," he said, "but ultimately they all lead to the same place." Since then, I have substituted God with the idea of a universal power or spirit, but the analogy of the mountain has stayed with me.

Before I left Badrinath, there was one question I knew I had to ask of Rawal: Is full acceptance of the path of sanatan dharma contingent on some form of worship and prayer? I could not rid myself of the pictures in my mind of men and women blindly praying, the idea that rituals were simply meaningless acts repeated over and over again.

Rawal clearly did not expect the question. He looked down and thought for a minute. His answer, when it came, was distinctly distant. "Yes. Definitely. They are important disciplines that must be maintained." There was silence. I do not know what I had expected him to say, but somehow I felt deflated. Once again, it seemed, religion had been equated to ritual.

The Rawal did not say much more. He excused himself to go to the temple for his nightly service. Krishnan (our translator friend who had been sitting with us), Alan and I sat quietly. Krishnan, sensing that the conversation was far from over, gave us his own interpretation: that the Rawal knew we were not at a stage where he could just tell us to drop puja, that there were certain techniques of worship, like mantras, that were known to invoke the sense of oneness, of respect for that universal power within one's soul.

"It may not be for you to go to the temple and pray," Krishnan said to me later. "I go, but only with appreciation for its history, its significance in the lives of so many of our enlightened sages. You may find your own way, your own acts that create meaning for you, your own methods of discipline. Go to the temple, take what you can and then create something for you."

After that last conversation with the Rawal, I finally did go to the temple. It was drizzling, so the line that normally stretches up to half a kilometer long was relatively short. I wound my way up the steps of the temple entranceway, past the two silver painted lions on either side, and slowly into the inner sanctum where the sacred image of Shri Badri Vishal was kept. There, around the iron bars that surrounded the tiny covered rectangle where people peered in to get a glimpse of the black stone image, I was pushed with the crowd to the front. The Rawal was inside, conducting the puja, plucking and throwing flower petals on the idol. It flashed through my mind that by questioning the need for rituals, I was in essence challenging what he did, what he stood for.

The temple and the pilgrims looked different to me that day. Had I missed, all this time, the kind of from-the-bottom-of-the-soul emotion, tears, overwhelming happiness that these devotees felt in front of their gods? How could any process that produced that kind of feeling be wrong? With more than a little envy, perhaps I wished that I too could feel that way. Seeing this emotion for what it was broke through my academic limitations, my endless negative analysis of rituals, of one-dimensional definitions of Hinduism.

Rituals are rituals only when they become habits, actions that are not accompanied by meaning or understanding. To me, all that I saw—pouring milk on a Shiva lingam, giving offerings to an idol, saying prayers—were rituals because I did not understand them, because they had no meaning to me. I had forgotten that the key person in this picture who needed to understand the rituals was not I—it was the person who was performing the actions. To that individual, those actions that I called rituals might have produced the kind of joy that the Rawal had been talking about; it might have been accompanied, at least for some, by the actual practice of sanatan dharma.

I did not see the Rawal again. We left suddenly, without even thanking him. I was as reluctant to see him again as I had been to go into the temple, but for completely different reasons. I did not know how I would thank him, what I would say. He had given me a new way to look at what religion means to me; an insight into the kind of effusive joy that can fill a devotee who comes in the presence of something that reminds him of that universal power. He showed me that the essence of Hinduism—indeed, of religion—is the path of sanatan dharma, a dharma that embodies concepts I believe in, concepts that I can feel proud to have passed on from my heritage, my ancestors, those wise men and women who spoke not of Hinduism but of what were the seeds of Indian spirituality.

In many senses the Rawal gave me back my roots, the beginnings of a sense of connection to Indian spiritual traditions. His words challenged me to look differently at the actions of those who worship and to understand that the role of religion in people's lives is intensely personal. He opened a pathway for me to create actions for myself that complement my own belief in spirituality, actions that are a genuine part of acknowledgment, respect and self-expression.

I no longer felt like a kharsu tree about to fall. My roots had dug themselves in and were holding me—however tenuously—to the hillside.

Sex and Catholic Girls

Caurie Miner Putnam

For the first sixteen years of my life I was the quintessential "good Catholic girl." Then, I went on my first date, and the schism between my faith and my feelings officially began. His name was Aaron and he took me to see *Robin Hood: Prince of Thieves*. The saying "Sweet sixteen and never been kissed," was not cliché in this situation. Until Aaron, I had never been permitted to date, something that some of my peers found shocking (though not quite as shocking as the time my mom yanked *Dirty Dancing* out of the VCR during a slumber party because of the abortion scene).

For the most part, however, not being allowed to do such seemingly normal teenage things as swoon over Patrick Swayze, watch MTV or date seemed normal to me and the other "good girls" I hung out with. Having a boy hold my hand was abnormal, and that was what Aaron did the moment he had me alone. Then, in the movie theater, out of my parents' reach, I felt Aaron's cool hand slide away from my sweaty one and into my shorts. Of course, I automatically pushed him away. Was this the same Aaron who attended an all-boy Catholic school and called my parents "Sir" and "Ma'am"? I had felt safe accepting a date with Aaron, naively believing that all Catholic teens were as stringent about their religion as I was. Obviously I was mistaken.

I don't know what made me finally give in to Aaron's advances—if it was the dark anonymity of the theater, years of repressed raging hormones or Kevin Costner riding a horse—but when I finally stopped brushing his hand away I fell into a pit of ecstasy. I had never felt so good in my life—the tingling, the ringing in my ears, the floating, the wave. . . . As my body shook from what I would later learn is called an orgasm, I thought to myself, *God, if you killed me now I would be the happiest girl in the world*. Then, when it was over, I thought to myself, *Omigod, what have I done?*

As a practicing Roman Catholic (of the parentally induced kind), I had been raised to believe sex of any kind before marriage was a sin. I equated premarital sex with pregnancy and pregnancy with marriage, neither of which I wanted at age sixteen. My parents had become pregnant with me when they were young, and I had always vowed that would never happen to me. Although I knew they loved each other greatly, I often wondered if their lives would have been better if they had not become pregnant when they did. They were immediately forced to choose between marriage and abortion—an act their Catholic faith strictly prohibited. Although they always assured me that marriage was an easy choice for them, I sometimes wondered if they just said that so I would not feel unwanted. I never wanted to have to make such a choice and never thought I would be in a position where making such a choice was remotely possible—until I met Aaron.

My blissful movie-theater encounter with Aaron marked the first friction between my own sexuality and the sexuality prescribed by my religion. Due to years of a staunch Catholic upbringing and education, I believed that my experience with Aaron would send me to hell, or purgatory if I was lucky.

I told Aaron we could never do "that thing with the fingers" again and we could certainly *never* have sex. But, whenever I was with him, his hands exploring my body felt too good to resist. During my years with Aaron I let him touch me only in the way he had on our first date. My rationale: If I had already committed the sin, I was allowed to commit it again. We dated for two years, until Aaron dumped me the summer before college. Apparently my good-girl endeavors finally became more of a turnoff than an exciting challenge, and he found a girl who was not so whipped by her faith. Looking back now, I can't blame him.

During my first two years of college I committed "the finger sin" quite a bit, and added even more body parts into the mix, but I always stopped before intercourse. I was terrified of becoming pregnant, because I knew I would never choose to have an abortion and I wasn't ready to be a mother.

But, when I turned twenty-one, the pressure to have sex became overbearing. I was the only twenty-one-year-old I knew who was still a virgin and it was embarrassing. All my college friends were having sex and none of them were getting pregnant. Even my best friend from high school, my former fellow good girl, was having sex. "You don't know what you're missing," she would wag at me. "It's great." On top of all this, I had a boyfriend who, like Aaron before him, was getting bored waiting for me to come around.

So, I decided that since I was technically an adult by the government's standards, I had the authority to override some of the teachings of the Catholic Church. To avoid pregnancy, I went on the birth control pill *and* made my boyfriend wear a condom and made sure he pulled out before ejaculating every time we had sex. I tracked my menstrual cycle obsessively and would not have sex during certain times of the month, although I knew the pill prevented ovulation. There was no way in hell I was going to get pregnant.

I did, though, think I was *going* to hell. All throughout college I was still a practicing Catholic, even while I said yes to two big no-no's of the church: premarital sex and artificial birth control. Despite feeling sacrilegious, the rules of Catholicism were so ingrained in me that I continued to attend Mass every Sunday. I even continued to go to confession every few weeks. But I would never tell the priest about my sexual activity with others or (gasp) myself, or that I was on the pill. I was too afraid of what he might say; too afraid I was going to hell.

In an attempt to atone for my own sexual guilt, I became an even stronger opponent of abortion. Some part of me desperately hoped and believed that if I vehemently opposed a sex-related sin bigger than my own, perhaps I could still be considered a good Catholic. I didn't join any pro-life groups or march in any rallies, but I did join the Republican Party (based strictly upon their reputation as being anti-abortion), put a pro-life sticker on my date book and told anyone who asked for my views on abortion that it was immoral. I also considered those who had abortions or performed abortions bad people, with whom I wanted no association. Rumors spread around campus that a fellow sorority girl had had an abortion, and I felt disgusted every time I saw her. At the time I didn't see myself as self-righteous, I saw myself as resourceful. I was creatively saving myself from the embers of hell.

The sex I had during this time was pretty awful—it's hard to enjoy pleasure when you're more concerned about your soul than your clitoris, and less focused on an orgasm than on the question "If I got pregnant right now, could I really *not* have an abortion?" Once my boyfriend and I split and I started graduate school, I decided abstinence was the only way to keep myself out of hell. So I swore off intercourse and serious dating, instead falling back on casual hook-ups and skilled "I can make you happy in other ways" techniques.

My second virginity ended when I met Art, the man who is now my husband. From the first time we met, I knew I would marry him, so I believed we could have premarital sex based on a technicality. If Catholics could only have sex with their spouses, and he would be mine one day, I figured I was in the clear. Although I finally felt safe in the respect that if I did accidentally become pregnant I would not have to consider abortion, we still practiced my quadruple birth control method. I did not want to be forced into marriage and parenthood like my parents had been.

Of course Art thought I was nuts when it came to protection, but he didn't make a big deal about it. "It's a Catholic thing," I would tell him, and he had no real basis upon which to argue. Art was not a religious person. He had been raised in an agnostic household. His mom had been Catholic and his father Jewish until they got married, had kids and decided religion would not be part of their world. There was still a menorah on the bookcase and a set of rosary beads on his mom's bureau, but words like "baptism" and "bar mitzvah" were foreign to Art.

Yet, while he was not a religious person, Art considered himself a spiritual person—a concept that made absolutely no sense to me no matter how hard he tried to explain it. How could you be spiritual without going to a church, synagogue, mosque, dog house, whatever? At that point in my life, I could not fathom spirituality taking place in any realm other than within a tangible and concrete institution. Art, however, said he could see God everywhere—in the blue of my eyes, the sound of my laughter and the beauty of a sunset.

Despite Art's contention that he did not need a religion to be close to God, I pleaded with him to go to church with me. Once he saw how important it was to me, he went through the official process of becoming Catholic so we could get married within the Church. This was extremely important to me because the Church does not acknowledge a marriage as legit unless it is performed within its walls. And, in order for a marriage to be performed as a blessed sacrament (in other words, a "big deal"), both parties must be baptized Catholics. After five years of premarital sin, I wanted to make good and sure my marriage was real.

However, my true spiritual journey did not happen during our marriage-preparation classes or the year of intense classes Art and I had to take in order for him to become baptized. Both were interesting experiences that taught me more about my religion, but my true *spiritual* journey happened while I held the hand of a so-called sinner.

Art's mom Anne was an obstetrician/gynecologist from Buffalo, New York. In October of 1998—about a year after Art and I began dating—her friend and colleague Dr. Barnett Slepian was murdered in his suburban Buffalo home in front of his children by a pro-life fanatic. The crime committed against Dr. Slepian was deplorable, and I in no way condoned it—in fact, it made me feel pretty uncomfortable about my previously staunch views on abortion, so I decided to keep my mouth closed. But his murder brought the issue of abortion to my world's water cooler. In the wake of this crime, everyone, it seemed, was talking about abortion. It was inevitable that my views on abortion would surface too.

When I told Anne I was pro-life, she told me something I was shocked to hear: she had performed abortions. I suppose the thought of Anne performing abortions never crossed my mind because, as she had been raised Catholic herself, I had assumed she would not perform this procedure. Anne asked me why I was against abortion. For once in my life, "Because I am Catholic" did not seem like a good enough answer. "I really don't know," I said, as the chilling thought entered my mind that she herself could be in danger of attacks by pro-life extremists, "I just think it's bad." Anne did not chastise or lecture me, but asked me to truly think about my views objectively. She also did not ask me the question I dreaded was on the tip of her tongue: "Do you think *I* am a bad person?" It was a question I was not ready to answer yet, because it was a question that I believed totally challenged my allegiance to the Church.

Exactly one year after Dr. Slepian was assassinated, Anne received her own death sentence: lung cancer. She had struggled with a bad cough for about a year, but had always brushed it off as the result of not getting enough sleep. When she finally went to see her own doctor at Art's urging, the cancer was very far along. I suspect those pro-lifers who were zealous enough to rejoice over Dr. Slepian's murder would see my mother-in-law's lung cancer as a punishment for performing abortions. Actually, Anne saw her cancer as a gift of life.

She was diagnosed with the cancer at the pinnacle of her career: she had just opened two clinics for women in the Buffalo area. She was sixty years old and intended to practice medicine for at least another decade. Art and his siblings rarely saw her—she was always on the go, answering pages, delivering babies and popping m&m's to stay awake. But when she was diagnosed with cancer and forced to retire, she found a whole new love: living.

When Anne retired from practicing medicine those closest to her thought she would be devastated, but instead she embraced her newfound time to spend with her family and herself. Hundreds of cards poured into her home from patients thanking her for giving them the gift of life and praising her as a doctor, and she blushed with humility and gratitude for being a part of their lives. Any questions I had about Anne's being a good person were further eradicated when I read the messages in these cards, in which patients thanked her in great detail for helping them get through some of the most difficult and most wonderful times of their lives.

I was with my Annemom the starry winter night that she passed away in a hospice room in Buffalo. Art and his brother were out getting a bite to eat, but I had stayed behind so she would not be alone. Nobody had expected her to die that night, but as soon as her boys left her breathing began to taper. The nurses told me she had only hours—if not minutes—left. She had signed a "do not resuscitate" order and had always made it perfectly clear to everyone that when it was time for her to die they should not interfere medically. Although she was unconscious I told her I loved her and talked to her about each of her children. I thanked her for being such a wonderful mom and an outstanding doctor. I stroked her soft cheeks and made sure she was as comfortable as possible. I tucked the blanket she had recently finished knitting for her future grandchildren tightly around her. I prayed out loud. I held her in my arms. I tried not to cry. I tried to be strong for her. "You can go now, Annemom," I reassured her as her breathing got slower and slower, "We'll be okay."

Watching my beloved Annemom die was like watching her be reborn. Never had the cycle of life been so apparent to me. As she took her last breath it was like she was taking the collective first breath of the thousands of babies who entered the world with the help of her skilled hands and kind heart. And as her hands turned lifeless I felt a tingling sensation run through my body, as if her spirit was leaving her body, passing through mine and traveling upward. When her pulse ceased a single tear came from her eye. It was not a tear of pain, I believe, but of great joy.

I knew my Annemom was seeing something beautiful, something the Church calls heaven.

Yes, heaven. And while Anne entered heaven I entered a new place in my spiritual journey: a place of knowing that one's "final judgment" is based not on one's "sins" but on the cumulative way one lives one's life. As Art tried to teach me years ago, you do not need to practice formal religion to get to heaven, but you do need spirituality. Spirituality comes from being happy and living life in a way that adds more goodness than heartache to the world. That is what my Annemom did. She was my definition of the perfect "good Catholic girl."

According to the tenets of my Church, my Annemom should have gone to hell for her sin of committing abortion and never repenting to a priest for it, but she did not. As a witness to her death—which was blanketed in such peace and tranquility—I know damn well my mother-in-law went to the best place you can go when you are gone from here, whatever and wherever that may be.

I did not honor her passing in a church funeral. In keeping with her unassuming personality, she chose not to have a memorial service of any kind. Instead, she donated her body to a medical school for research—another act the Church condemns. I don't see that as a sin either, but as Annemom's final act of charity. Anne was a giver of life, not a taker. Until the very end she gave to others, including me. What she taught me about religion and spirituality in the four short years I knew her was more than I had learned in two decades as a practicing Catholic.

Anne stirred in me a desire for change—both in the way I live my life and in the way the Church operates. I recently changed my political party to Democratic—based in large part on their more open attitude towards abortion—and I have begun volunteering as a rape-crisis counselor with one of the biggest abortion providers in this nation, Planned Parenthood. The organization—which does far more than just offer abortions—knows about my newfound support of abortion rights, but they also know I was once pro-life. They have accepted me into their fold regardless. I do not know if my church will be so forgiving.

There is a part of me that fears someone in my church's hierarchy may read this book and find my words blasphemous enough to initiate the process of excommunication. I considered using a pen name for this piece, but decided against it. If the Church decides to throw me out, I truly believe it will be their loss. Numbers don't lie, and membership in the U.S. Catholic Church is on the decline, especially among my generation of twenty- and thirty-somethings. Not surprisingly, when I discuss my new views on abortion and politics with my Catholic girlfriends I learn they often agree with me, even if they would not necessarily announce their views to the world.

Announcing my new feelings and political positions is difficult, but I need to do it. And it gets easier with each step I take. I liken it to my experience as a volunteer at Planned Parenthood. The first time I walked past a herd of pro-life demonstrators outside the Planned Parenthood building and was called "one of the devil's little helpers," it made me cry. The second time I was verbally harassed walking by the demonstrators, it still stung a bit. The third time I walked by them I felt this incredible inner conviction that what I was doing was right. I knew just then, in that Planned Parenthood parking lot, that my Annemom was looking down from heaven and giving me the encouragement I needed to keep walking.

If I can walk past hissing anti-abortion protestors with my head held high, I can certainly walk into a Catholic church believing that my ideals are right for me and that God thinks no less of me for possessing them. I continue to walk into church because I do not believe I am a sinner. I believe God still loves me and that I have always been a "good girl." I am a "good girl" because I am a loving girl, a caring girl, a giving girl, a thinking girl and a considerate girl. I am not a "bad girl" because I had an orgasm before I got married or because I believe that women should have the power to control their own bodies. Walking into a Catholic church aware that I am breaking rules and holding firm to beliefs the Church frowns upon is empowering—it makes me feel good; it makes me feel like I am getting the last laugh. But I am not laughing. I am completely serious when I say the Church must change.

The only leverage I have to help change the Catholic Church is my presence. I continue to walk into church because I believe that it—like me—has the capacity to change. It is time for the Church to reexamine many of its tenets, primarily its identification of anything related to sex as sinful. That reexamination and the change I hope comes with it can only be initiated from within the Church's walls, and I want to be part of the process. I cannot be part of the process if I am not there.

The Catholic Church is at a pivotal point in its modern history.

As I write this, debate has begun amongst the highest leaders of the Church itself—the bishops and the Pope—on whether Church laws relating to its leaders' own sexuality should be changed. In the midst of sickening sexual abuse scandals worldwide, leaders of the Church have finally begun talking about reform on many levels. I find it both tragic and grossly poetic that it has taken sexual crimes and sins committed by Church leaders to initiate discussion of changes.

While I still consider myself Catholic, I definitely have undergone a partial-faith abortion over the past several years. I obviously do not believe in or observe many rules of the Catholic Church, and I want to see these changed. I would love to see more women like myself—who were raised Catholic but strayed from the Church during young adulthood for political and sexual reasons—come back to the Church. Not as silent enablers, but as crusaders. The Church will only change if its members speak out like I am doing now and initiate reform on a local level.

I now attend Mass at a Catholic church on a college campus. I find the parishioners more open-minded and the community leaders more liberal and open to suggestions than those at the more traditional Catholic church in my town. In fact, at a recent Mass on campus, one of the priests insinuated that the Church's policy of denying the sacrament of communion to homosexuals was wrong. To hear a priest openly question a Church rule was amazing and exhilarating to me. It fed my hope that sweeping changes within the Church are a definite possibility.

As I reflect upon everything I have written, I do find it somewhat mysterious that I still want anything to do with my religion. I suppose my desire to stay in the Church—despite my qualms with it—is partly due to the fact that it is all I know. Being Catholic is a common bond I share with my parents, grandparents, great grandparents and beyond. There was a time when my ancestors in Ireland could not practice their Catholic faith because it was forbidden by a foreign government. I have grown up knowing that the ability to practice Catholicism freely is not something to be taken for granted—people have died for this faith of mine. History runs deep in the Catholic Church and part of me is just not ready to abandon my roots quite yet. I also stay in the Church because, although I do think many aspects of Catholicism are archaic, there are some very good things I have learned as a Catholic, primarily about giving back to others and the value of faith.

As a Catholic, I have been taught to have faith in that which cannot be explained, that which is presently intangible. I cannot see God, but I have been taught to have faith in his existence. I do not know if saints really exist, but I have been taught to believe they do. Thus, although I have been taught to deprive my body of sex, contraception, abortion and masturbation, I have faith that these and other repressive rules can be changed. If the Church wants to survive in the twenty-first century and keep young, intelligent members like myself in its pews, change is a necessity, not a sin. I am living proof.

A Call to Service

Trudi M. H. Frazel

In my twenty-nine years, I have not met a more dedicated servant of God than my late grandmother, Mary. A salt-of-the-earth woman with whom I happen to share a birthday, my father's mother taught me the practice—the importance—of selfless service. She was more of a mother than a grandmother to me: she looked after my brother and me every afternoon and every summer. As a child, I began attending First Baptist Church (FBC) because that's where Granny always was. She taught me from an early age that "God loves a cheerful giver," and "If you can't do it with joy in your heart, you'd better just not do it at all." When I was feeling particularly bratty, I'd say, "Okay, then I guess I just won't do it."

"Guess again," she'd say.

In junior high and high school, I was involved in the whole smorgasbord of extracurricular activities at FBC. I attended Bible study, was in the youth group and sang in the choir. I taught Sunday School for the younger kids and even directed a handbell choir for the junior-high kids. I dished out and cleaned up after Wednesday night dinners in the gym. I volunteered during the summers to help with vacation Bible school for the little ones. If there was something to be done, I did it. It was as natural to me as breathing. Granny had set the example.

It never occurred to me then, but for a woman born in 1919,

a lifetime of service to others was a given. My grandmother was a florist by trade, but she was really everyone's Mama and Granny. She'd wanted a big family, but in her late twenties, after giving birth to only two children, she'd had to have a hysterectomy. This shaped the woman I knew, the woman who would bake dozens upon dozens of cookies for the church bazaar, tend the roses in the church garden and care for the aged, for babies, for the sick and disabled. I wanted to emulate her. It never occurred to me that her habit of serving others was expected of her—by her family, by society. Her religion, her faith in Jesus and the Bible, made her role in life, in an America where women were the servants of the family, not just palatable, but joyful.

At seventeen, after spending a summer away from home, I became disenchanted with Christianity and my religious community. I wanted to experiment, to try new things, to feel like a worldly woman instead of the sheltered girl I had been. Moving away from Christianity was connected to moving away from an attitude of service.

Fast forward ten years, through my dropping out of college after my freshman year, completing cosmetology school and passing the state board exam, beginning my career as a hairdresser and meeting and marrying my husband. When Tom and I met, I was serving my *other* grandmother—with whom I was not nearly as close—attending to her needs as she endured chemotherapy and battled lymphoma. Though I lived with her while she faced death, I thought very little about the state of my spirit, or God, or what I might possibly believe in now. I discovered that it is indeed possible to serve without being "spiritual."

In my late twenties, after I'd built up a steady clientele and opened my own business, I cut down my work schedule to three days a week, and started doing the volunteer thing in my local school district. Working with high-school students on their writing assignments was a spark of reconnection with my spiritual self, and yet, something was missing. I knew I was doing good work with these kids, but it wasn't for any reason other than wanting to feel good about myself. The desire to give something back is a powerful motivation to be of service. But at that point in my life, I was looking for something more, something bigger than my own ego, something to replace my daily pot habit and the growing suspicion that I was sleepwalking through my own life.

Then I picked up a copy of *The Teachings of the Compassionate Buddha*. I'm sure some people feel a thunderbolt when they first read the Bible. Maybe someone's even become a Krishna devotee in response to a simple flower handed over at the airport. All I know is, compassion became my mantra, and I signed up for introductory meditation classes. The Four Noble Truths seemed to make a lot more sense than John 3:16. The first time I heard that suffering comes from wanting things to be different than they are, I realized that it was possible to change my notions of what service really is; that, rather than trying to help someone out of a desire to change her circumstances, I could simply awaken my compassion and be present with her. I began to see that simple awareness is an act of service.

Service is not mere generosity, though a generous heart is a portion of it. It is possible to be generous and still not *serve*.

There's a small family-owned meat market, near my little business in Berkeley, whose owners give, every week, enough roasted chickens to feed seventy-five people at the Center for AIDS Services in the East Bay. Seventy-five people. Every week. For years. The Center has tried to honor them for their ongoing contribution, but the family consistently refuses. Now, many business owners would use their generosity to keep their business name in the community consciousness, which is the accepted tit for tat, quid pro quo of company donations, from small businesses to international corporations. They may as well call their budget for charitable donations "advertising." This exchange of service for gain lessens the spiritual aspect of the transaction in my mind. Granny taught me at a young age that people who strut around, calling attention to themselves because of their good deeds, are serving themselves and their own egos—and perhaps the bottom line of their businesses—more than they are serving God.

I was maybe twelve or thirteen when the First Baptist community held a large dinner and honored Granny with a plaque for her many years of service. In the days leading up to the event, she rather grumbled about it. She was very uncomfortable with the notion of being recognized for something so ingrained it was a source of comfort and joy for her. During the dinner, she hung out in the kitchen, serving food and washing up. When she was finally called up on stage, she hugged the pastor, took the plaque and smiled at everybody. I don't think she said anything at all, just stood there while Pastor Walton reminded the congregation of all her faithful service. I have no doubt she hated it. I stood against the wall near the kitchen and glowed inside, because the church loved her just as much as I did.

And yet, selfless service transcends ego. By design, the very act of serving becomes the reward. Granny didn't want a plaque; she wanted to go about her business quietly, because she understood that the most gratifying aspect of service is the communion of spirit that occurs between the one serving and the one being served. When I truly want to serve, authentically, it's not from a place of wanting approval, or a desire to store up treasures in heaven. When I really want to be of service, it is from a place of gratitude for all I have, for all I've been given. I mean, I *want* to wash the mirrors at my yoga studio because it feels like church, like home.

I can tell when my spiritual practice of service is off-base; the ego lets me know. I find it's time to reevaluate my motivation when I offer a lot of unsolicited information about my volunteer activities. That's a sure sign that I'm looking for praise, acknowledgment, validation. The paradox about servitude is that it can seem to be a real position of power (I have something they need and only I can give it to them), and can lead to a lot of strutting and preening. The truth is that if I didn't get some satisfaction out of making myself a servant, I wouldn't do it. I'm no selfless saint. It feels good to think of myself as "good." Which is okay, because my meditation practice keeps my ego in check.

Vipassana meditation, also called insight meditation, is a practice of simply paying attention. Using the basic technique of following the breath, I sit on my cushion and I watch my thoughts, feel the sensations in my body, hear the sounds in the room and outside my window. From the outside, meditation appears quiet and serene. But there's a lot going on inside. When I first started sitting and paying attention, I was shocked at how loud it was inside my head.

All of this silence and sitting is, for me, directly related to the idea of service. Before I began a regular practice of meditation, I thought it was an awfully self-absorbed thing to do. I mean, if someone's meditating, they're by definition *not* running around, putting out fires and saving the planet. Of what use is sitting with your eyes closed and your hands in your lap? While I haven't fully answered that question for myself yet, I do have a clear sense that it is of use, that it is deeply connected to action and service.

The first point of connection is that my perspective on pain, suffering and unpleasantness has changed fundamentally. The first few weeks of my practice, I experienced a good deal of physical discomfort: I had pain in my shoulder blades, my feet kept falling asleep and I got headaches on the right side of my forehead. And I just sat with it. I didn't jump up. I didn't run away. And it didn't last forever. I'm learning to breathe through the pain, through the unpleasantness, and I see a beautiful shift happening. Buddhism appeals to me because it is based on compassion, a desire for all beings to be free from suffering, and it begins with learning to find compassion for my own faults, my own pain.

Serving others reminds everyone involved in the transaction of the possibilities of humanity. Every day, I am reminded of how far I have yet to go, as I serve my clients in the salon. Though I've not consciously made career choices based on this ideal of selfless service, it's no accident that I've been in the service industry the whole of my working life. Just the other day, after reading a chapter on gratitude toward everyone—especially those who push our buttons—I came smack up against a client I find particularly difficult, with very little cause. She's a perfectly nice woman who, perhaps because she repeats herself, I happen to find rather batty.

"Trudi, how long do you think it will take for my bangs to grow out?" she wants to know for the seventh time.

"Oh, maybe four to six more months."

"Yeah, they're really growing, aren't they?"

"They sure are."

"I used to wear them really short, for a long time, my husband didn't like them at all . . ."

She tells me this every time I see her.

For no good reason, she's incredibly difficult for me to serve. What can I do? I can be humble, and I can breathe. Some days, though, it's difficult to even breathe. But I continue to try, and every time I do it's an opportunity to learn patience and compassion for others, as well as for myself.

A shadow side of servitude is the danger of feeling uncomfortable with being served. I've been thinking about Granny a lot lately; we just had our birthday. She was the kind of woman who, after cooking all day for her family, wouldn't sit down at the table with us until she'd loaded up everyone's plate herself. It's taken me a long time to combat the sense that if I'm being served by someone, or if I have to ask for help, I'm not as "good." I'm grateful that I've had other women in my life—friends, colleagues, mentors—with a more balanced sensibility about service work, who've taught me that I'm best able to serve when my spirit's been replenished. Granny had Jesus and hymns. I have meditation, yoga, bodywork, writing, intimacy with my husband and friends . . . endless ways to recharge and remember why I do what I do. Choosing service as a spiritual practice, rather than having it imposed on me by society because I happen to be a woman, allows for more spiritual freedom than Granny had in her life. Though as a young Christian I felt uncomfortable asking others for help, I'm much better now at recognizing that the delineation between the server and the served is fuzzy at best.

When I was in high school, still active in my youth group, we had an evening of foot-washing. It was a powerful and profound experience for me. The church was quiet and dimly lit. The group split up into pairs and each pair found a semiprivate space in which to wash each other's feet. I don't remember having my feet washed, but I remember doing the washing: the small, soft feet of the youth pastor's wife, the clean scent of Ivory soap, the warm water, the stiff towel. Not long after, I decided to wash Granny's feet. At first she wouldn't let me. But I opened the Bible and read her John 13:14-15: "If I then, your Lord and Master, have washed your feet; ye also ought to wash one another's feet. For I have given you an example, that ye should do as I have done to you." Granny could never argue with Jesus.

It was a warm day, and she'd been working in the kitchen. She put me off as long as she could, even putting on the stove a completely unnecessary pot of beans. Finally, she sat down on a simple, straight-backed chair, in the back bedroom next to the ironing board. I filled a plastic dishtub with hot water while she rolled up the bottoms of her sweatpants, exposing the calves I knew so well, thick with varicose veins from years of standing on her feet. The whole procedure couldn't have lasted more than fifteen minutes, from soak to towel-dry, but in that short time, I felt a shift. As I rubbed the soap into her tough, callused soles, it felt as though I was actually relieving her of a burden, as though she was able to shed more than just old skin cells through my symbolic act. When it was over, she dried her eyes and thanked me, and then headed back to the stove to stir her beans.

On Ki

Eleanor Martineau

Three or four times a week I train in aikido, which is as close as I've come to a spiritual practice. In this I feel lucky because aikido is mostly fun and physical instead of boring and liturgical. It won't get you in great shape but it will improve your balance and flexibility, unlike church.

The spiritual aspect of aikido comes with the territory, so to speak. "Ai" is love or harmony, "ki" is spirit and "do" is way. So it's the way of harmonizing with spirit, or the way of loving ki. Does this mean that three or four times a week I train to love ki? As a beginner, I'm just figuring out the techniques. You run into Buddhism and Taoism pretty quickly when talking about aikido, but I'm not a Buddhist or Taoist. I'm a student and massage therapist. I feel reverence, and I want to do right. So far, aikido.

I've heard people say ki is good, the opposite being an absence of ki. At my dojo, when we perform a technique smoothly, with little effort, and our partner (whom we're throwing) remains relatively comfortable, we say we performed with ki. Smooth and flowing = ki. Stumbling and poking = no ki.

You're either with ki or against it. A joke is to say of someone that they have no ki. It's not a huge insult, but it's kind of funny. It's also kind of funny to be moving around in the oxygen of all this ki everywhere and just keep blowing it. As a beginner, I'm always stumbling all over the ki and everything else. Oddly, this feels good.

What is ki? Attempting to answer this question feels taboo. Sure, it's energy and life force and universal spirit. Aristotle might have called it the Unseen Mover, although one of my aikido teachers claims to see ki all the time, and says it's light gray. It's definitely the Japanese word for what the Chinese call *chi*, which is definitely energy and life force and universal spirit. Probably *prana* in most of India, and many cultures across the globe would nod or indicate assent if we identified an animating spirit in the physical world. How about that Holy Ghost?

But I still want to be very careful. Poking into ki pokes at the Tao, at Zen, at nothingness. About which I know very little.

I want to say ki is everywhere, but I don't know.

When I go to see the acupuncturist she puts needles in me to adjust my chi-ki. I can't make a distinction between what she's poking into and what I stumble across on the aikido mat. And mostly I just lie there thinking and trying not to think, and sometimes I get the spins a little (which she tells me is wind) and sometimes the needles prick a little but usually not. So far my health complaints are somewhat relieved. I have no idea what points she's pricking into with the needles, I just give myself over. Is this faith? Is this belief? Is this spirit?

You could ask these questions of any art: precision and timing; how to tell a joke.

Is ki good? There are destructive and creative uses of ki. Apparently in Japan death is profoundly anti-ki, but there is ki in compost. Entropy. Science. Is physics good or bad? Is that question answerable? There was a science show on TV the other night with physicists describing the essential matter (animating spirit?) of the universe as "quantum foam." Sexy.

My boyfriend tells a story that I totally love about training in aikido with a friend of his and breaking the friend's foot. He never touched the foot, but while they were sparring (intensely!) with wooden swords my boyfriend summoned up all his ki and made himself into a tsunami, bringing the sword up, over and down on his friend's sword. And the story goes that when they struck swords the ki traveled through the friend's body and broke through his foot on the mat, like a grounding rod. What a great story! Especially since the friend wasn't mad.

For both of them, and for me, this was simply a demonstration of being powerfully aligned with ki—for good or bad. This is where ethics comes in. What responsibility comes with knowledge? With power? I practice because I respect that power. I'm humbled by it. Stumbled by it. And because practice and belief are two different things, we have choices. In the rush of every present moment we have choices. But practice—of most kinds— is based on belief, on an awareness of the animating spirit. If you don't feel awe, there's no reason to practice—to respect.

We are awestruck by hurricanes. The H-bomb. Hatred.

And awe is, simply, when I see a flock of barn swallows over a highway and they catch my breath—my chest swells as they rise and I am moved—and they move me. Experiencing presence and distance as one. Reverence. A grateful smallness. I love this feeling.

Does this make me a spiritual person? This question always makes me think of a hippie girl in high school giving me a very earnest look and saying of her pot-smoking, nature-loving, philandering boyfriend, "He's a very spiritual person."

Okay, but am I? Here's what happens. In my massage practice I often "feel ki," usually in my nose, like I have to sneeze. I am training myself to "send ki" down through my body and into the earth, so it's no longer stuck in my client's body or in my nose. One of my massage teachers would, upon experiencing a release of energy in her client, burp. She's a very good massage therapist, so the burping takes the form of a frequent gurgling in the back of her throat, and she accepts this situation with dignity and good humor. Is she a spiritual person? Is there gas behind it all?

In a way, I don't have to know. What a relief. In aikido we train to stay centered, calm and grounded amid a rush of sensation, in the presence of an attack. Of whatever.

Here's what whatever feels like. One of my favorite books is *The Divine Comedy*, which is a comedy because it has a happy ending. For me the heart of the poem is in Purgatory, when Dante finally meets his beloved, Beatrice. She asks him why, if he loves her so much, he is so often unfaithful, untrue, impious. She asks him what could possibly be more compelling than divine love. The poem reads, "Weeping I said, 'The present things.'" The attack of the present. Distance.

Often when I'm training in aikido I end up laughing, not just because it's sort of slapstick-funny, or because I'm laughably incompetent, but mostly because when my ki collides with my partner's ki (arm, nose, foot) the collision has a punchy funny tickle. It's jangly and sudden. The rush of an amusement park ride, or a first kiss.

This is what it feels like. During rush hour on the subway each sane person maintains a precise distance from every other person. They maintain these precise distances while the train joggles and swerves along, while other people get on and off the train, while un-sane people misjudge these distances. Everybody participates, continuously and silently.

In aikido you always practice with a partner, whom you are attacking or who is attacking you. You train each other, and yourself, to throw the attacker away from your body and away from harm. To protect them. To respect them. In a way, to love them, just as you love ki. We are taught to breathe in the attacker, take their balance, and breathe them out.

On a beautiful day you walk outside and notice what a beautiful day it is, especially if the sun is shining, especially if the air is clear. Then you might very well close your eyes and take in a deep breath through your nose. Then you breathe out. This feels great.

Contributor Biographies

Teena Apeles loves writing about subcultures. Her work has appeared in the pop culture magazines *Giant Robot* and *BUST*, and the journalzine *disOrient*. She has also contributed to the popular L.A. guidebooks *Hungry?* and *Thirsty?* (Really Great Books), as well as RGB's anthology on the L.A. Riots of 1992, *Geography of Rage*. Her book on historical female fighters, *Cool Women: Warriors*, is being published by Girl Press. When she's not writing she serves as literary programs coordinator for PEN Center USA.

Diane Biray Gregorio is a Ph.D. student in Sociology and Organizational Behavior at Harvard University. She is inspired by Thai Forest Tradition of Theravada Buddhism, especially the lineage of Ajahn Chah and Ajajn Sumedho, and the Tibetan Buddhist teachings of His Holiness the Dalai Lama. She lives with her partner, Robin, in Somerville, Massachusetts.

Jennifer Collins is a freelance writer whose work can be found in *Set in Stone: Butch on Butch Erotica, Young Wives' Tales: New Adventures in Love and Partnership, Best Bisexual Women's Erotica* and *Tough Girls*. She lives in southern Maine with her partner, Anna, and is currently working on her Master's degree at Goddard College.

Deborah Crooks writes for magazines, papers and web publications including *Northern Lights, AOL's Digital City* and *Velo*. She is the editor of PracticeAshtanga.com. In the wake of September 11, she cofounded Art Not Arms, an organization dedicated to promoting peace by providing showcases for thriving, cross-cultural collaborations between visual artists, writers and musicians. She lives and creates in the San Francisco Bay Area, where she studies yoga with the guidance of John Berlinsky.

Bernadette Adams Davis is a native South Carolinian who now lives in-between alligators and strip malls in Florida. She is coauthor of *The Whirlwind Passeth*, a historical drama about the Ocoee, Florida massacre of 1920, which was sparked by African-American residents' attempt to vote. Her other writing credits include articles in *Black Enterprise*, *Family Digest* and *Modern Fiction Studies*, as well as a few struggling years as a newspaper reporter. Bernadette's other passions, in no particular order, are Caribbean and African-American culture, France, her marriage and Internet technology (well, it pays the bills).

Tanessa Dillard has written essays for numerous small press publications. She hopes to someday publish non-fiction books for teens. Her AmeriCorps experience inspired her to pursue a graduate degree in teaching. She now looks forward to her first year in a middle-school classroom in Seattle.

Trudi M. H. Frazel is a writer, hairdresser, mentor and yogi, and is still trying to decide what she wants to be when she grows up. She and her husband live in Oakland with their menagerie of small animals.

Twilight Greenaway is a writer and editor based in the San

Francisco Bay Area. She has spent the last several years editing *WireTap*, an online magazine for socially conscious youth, and is currently a student of the creative writing MFA program at Warren Wilson College. She has also contributed to *Alternet*, *HUES* and *Curve* magazine. She likes giraffes, street art, good conversation and the color orange and, if pressed, she will tell you that she believes in the higher power of static electricity.

Stephanie Groll is a freelance writer and editor living in San Francisco. Her writing has appeared in a number of local, online and national publications, including the *San Francisco Bay Guardian*, *The Industry Standard*, *Business 2.0*, *Fabula*, *ChickClick* and *Alternet*. She is the politics editor of *Kitchen Sink* magazine.

Shoshana Hebshi is a newspaper copyeditor and independent fiction writer who continues to search for the words she needs, to say what she has to say. She is currently working on a group of short stories about young people who are lost. She hopes her parents won't disown her after they read this essay. She lives in San Francisco with her husband and inspiration, Kurt. They plan to raise their children in an environment of rich spirituality without dogma and hate.

Claire Hochachka is an editor and writer based in New York City. She snowboards in the winter, surfs in the summer and in-line skates all year round. But despite feasting abundantly on the freedoms of a Western lifestyle, Claire has always been drawn east. She maintains a dedicated practice of Ashtanga yoga and spent last summer studying with her teacher in Mysore, India. For the last ten years, she has traveled on and off throughout the

Muslim world, including Egypt, Syria and Bangladesh. During her time in Muslim countries, Claire became drawn to Islam. She can be reached at clairehochachka@hotmail.com.

Juleigh Howard-Hobson lives in northern California with her husband, three children and numerous figures of the Goddess. She has written one novel, one novella and numerous essays that are scattered in various zines and e-zines across the globe. Every April she walks a labyrinth. Every night she looks for Baba.

Sonya Huber is a writer and activist based in the great state of Ohio. She has published journalism and creative writing in many magazines, including *In These Times, Labor Notes, Fourth Genre, America* and *Psychology Today.* Her work has also appeared in anthologies published by University of Arizona Press, Prometheus Books and Seal Press. She teaches and studies at Ohio State University, and spends her spare time drinking coffee and organizing with Columbus Jobs with Justice.

Gail Hudson is Amazon.com's spirituality editor and is currently writing a memoir about mothering. Her personal essays about parenting, marriage and miscellaneous forms of angst and confusion have appeared in *Utne Reader, Self, Parents, Child* and *New Age Journal.* She resides in Seattle with her husband, two children, two cats and a scrappy vine of Concord grapes in the backyard.

Pramila Jayapal is the author of the travel memoir *Pilgrimage to India: A Woman Revisits Her Homeland.* She is currently at work on a book of short fiction. She lives in Seattle, Washington.

Eleanor Martineau was born in 1968. She lives in Berkeley, California, with the cutest dog in the world.

Maliha Masood grew up in Seattle. She is currently residing near Cambridge, Massachusetts, where she is attending graduate school. She has been writing a book about her travel adventures in the Middle East, and has worked in Cairo as a freelance journalist. Her mission is to continue increasing understanding between the Islamic world and the West. She has also written and coproduced a documentary film on the lives of Muslim women in the Pacific Northwest, entitled *Nazrah: A Muslim Woman's Perspective*, which premiered in Seattle in September 2002.

L. A. Miller is an editor and writer living in Seattle. Her nonfiction has been published in *Sex and Single Girls: Straight and Queer Women on Sexuality, Young Wives' Tales: New Adventures in Love and Partnership* and *The Unsavvy Traveler: Women's Comic Tales of Catastrophe*. She is currently working on a book about young women and food called *Women Who Eat*.

Caurie Miner Putnam is the quintessential Gemini—never sure about anything, except her passion. She is twenty-seven and lives in Brockport, New York, where she pursues her love of writing as a freelancer. A graduate of the University of Rochester, Caurie is a newlywed and mom to an African Grey parrot. She can be reached at caurieanne@hotmail.com.

Andrea Richards is the author of *Girl Director: A How-To Guide for the First-Time, Flat-Broke Film and Video Maker* (Girl Press) and a contributor to various magazines, including *BUST, FringeGolf* and the arts journal *Documents*. She currently lives in Los Angeles, where she is still searching for a decent bowl of grits.

Lisa Schiffman, the author of *Generation J*, earned a master's degree in social anthropology from Oxford University. She was formerly the associate editor of the *San Francisco Review of Books* and has published her prose in *Zyzzyva*, where it was nominated for a Pushcart Prize. She currently does Internet brand marketing for USWeb/CKS.

Kara Spencer is a mama, doula and massage therapist living in Seattle. Her written work has previously appeared in *MamaZine* and *SageWoman*.

Griselda Suárez is a Xicana from East Los Angeles. She has degrees in Spanish and studio art from Pitzer College. Her most recent publication, "La Reina del Norte," appears in *Through the Eye of the Deer: An Anthology of Native American Women Writers*. She is the associate director of AACE Talent Search-TRIO, an educational equity program in San Francisco. Griselda believes that art and writing are indispensible tools for the empowerment of communities of color.

Liesl Schwabe lives in Brooklyn. She has a BA from Antioch College. Her writing has been previously published in *Breeder: Real-Life Stories from the New Generation of Mothers*, also from Seal Press.

About the Editor

Angela Watrous is the coauthor of *After the Breakup: Women Sort through the Rubble and Rebuild Lives of New Possibilities*, and the recently published *Love Tune-Ups: 52 Ways to Open Your Heart and Make Sparks Fly*. Her work has appeared in a variety of magazines and websites, including Women.com, PlanetOut.com, AOL.com, *Moxie* and *The Urbanite*. Angela has been featured on television, iVillage.com and radio programs nationwide, including NPR. Before becoming a freelance writer, she worked as an editor in the book publishing industry for five years. She lives in Oakland, California, and she can be reached at www.AngelaWatrous.com.

Selected Titles from Seal Press

Shameless: Women's Intimate Erotica edited by Hanne Blank. $14.95, 1-58005-060-3. Diverse and delicious memoir-style erotica by today's hottest fiction writers.

Sex and Single Girls: Straight and Queer Women on Sexuality edited by Lee Damsky. $16.95, 1-58005-038-7. In this potent and entertaining collection of personal essays, women lay bare pleasure, fear, desire, risk—all that comes with exploring their sexuality. Contributors write their own rules and tell their own stories with empowering and often humorous results.

Chelsea Whistle by Michelle Tea. $14.95, 1-58005-073-5. In this gritty, confessional memoir, Michelle Tea takes the reader back to the city of her childhood: Chelsea, Massachusetts—Boston's ugly, scrappy little sister and a place where time and hope are spent on things not getting any worse.

Listen Up: Voices from the Next Feminist Generation edited by Barbara Findlen. $16.95, 1-58005-054-9. A revised and expanded edition of the Seal Press classic, featuring the voices of a new generation of women expressing the vibrancy and vitality of today's feminist movement.

Young Wives' Tales: New Adventures in Love and Partnership edited by Jill Corral and Lisa Miya-Jervis, foreword by Bell Hooks. $16.95, 1-58005-050-6. *Wife.* The term inspires ambivalence in many young women, for a multitude of good reasons. So what's a young, independent girl in love to do? In a bold and provocative anthology, 20 and 30 somethings attempt to answer that question, addressing who the wedding is really for, how to maintain one's individuality and the diversity of queer unions.

Breeder: Real-Life Stories from the New Generation of Mothers edited by Ariel Gore and Bee Lavender, foreword by Dan Savage. $16.00, 1-58005-051-4. From the editors of *Hip Mama*, this hilarious and heartrending compilation creates a space where Gen-X moms can dish, cry, scream and laugh. With its strength, humor and wisdom, *Breeder* will speak to every young mother, and anyone who wants a peek into the mind and spirit behind those bleary eyes.

Body Outlaws: Young Women Write About Body Image and Identity edited by Ophira Edut, foreword by Rebecca Walker. $14.95, 1-58005-043-3. Filled with honesty and humor, this groundbreaking anthology offers stories by women who have chosen to ignore, subvert or redefine the dominant beauty standard in order to feel at home in their bodies.

Seal Press publishes many books of fiction and nonfiction by women writers. Please visit our Web site at **www.sealpress.com**.

www.ingramcontent.com/pod-product-compliance
Ingram Content Group UK Ltd.
Pitfield, Milton Keynes, MK11 3LW, UK
UKHW022304280225
455674UK00001B/159